River of Song

Sunset over the Mississippi River, Davenport, Iowa

River of Song

A Musical Journey Down the Mississippi

Elijah Wald and John Junkerman
Photographs by Theo Pelletier

Smithsonian Institution
and Filmmakers Collaborative, Inc.
in association with

St. Martin's Press, New York

Production funding for the River of Song Project was provided by Hitachi, Ltd., Kajima Corporation,
the Corporation for Public Broadcasting, the Public Broadcasting Service,
the National Endowment for the Arts, and the Southern Humanities Media Fund.
Additional funding was provided by the Missouri Division of Tourism, the Tennessee Department of Tourism,
the Louisiana Office of Tourism, Mississippi River Country, and the Adler Foundation.

The Mississippi: River of Song is a coproduction of the Smithsonian Institution, the Filmmakers Collaborative,
and KajimaVision Productions.

Designed by Martine Bruel, Cambridge, Massachusetts.
Printed in the United States of America.

For information, address St. Martin's Press, 175 Fifth Avenue, New York, N.Y. 10010.

LIBRARY OF CONGRESS CATALOGING-IN-PUBLICATION DATA

Wald, Elijah.

River of song: a musical journey down the Mississippi / by Elijah Wald and John Junkerman; photographs by Theo Pelletier.—1st U.S. ed.

p. cm.

Companion to the PBS television series The Mississippi: river of song

Discography: p.

ISBN 0-312-20059-5

1. Music—Mississippi River Valley—History and criticism. 2. Musicians—Mississippi River Valley—Interviews. I. Junkerman, John. II. Pelletier, Theo. III. Mississippi: river of song. IV. Title.

ML200.7.M73W35 1998

780'.977—dc21 98-45508

CIP

MN

First U.S. Edition: December 1998

All photographs are by **Theo Pelletier,** except the following:
John Junkerman: page 22 (top and bottom),
25 (bottom), 26, 28–29, 32, 34–35, 106, 107, 118, 120, 121, 139, and 168;
Chuck Butler, page 36 (top and bottom), 39 (top and bottom); **Duncan Schiedt Collection,** page 99;
Joe Frisch, page 167; **Center for Southern Folklore,** page 201;
Foundation of Arts, Music & Entertainment of Shreveport-Bossier, page 263;
Maia Harris, page 331 (bottom), 334, 341;
River of Song, page 160 (top, bottom, inset), 163, 202 (top, middle, and bottom).

Table of Contents

◆◆◆

Preface

It seems to me that in any country, in any culture, there are two basic kinds of popular music. First, there is commercially generated music, which flows forth on radio waves and is transmitted into people's lives through screens, magazines, and other two-dimensional things. It is the most easily recognizable face of music in a society, a face that winks at us all with the eyes of pop divas, and sneers at us with the lips of rock stars.

However, beneath the surface of mainstream popular culture, there is the ever-present undercurrent of organically generated music. This other branch finds its sources much further back than its mass-marketed contemporaries, and is comprised (in America anyway) of a seemingly endless system of interconnected musical tributaries and little regional inlets.

While these two basic forms are not mutually exclusive, and often overlap, the latter is generally born of a particular and specific community or individual expression, and manifests itself not as a commodity, but as a social activity.

I'm talking about the indigenous, unhomogenized, uncalculated sound of a culture becoming itself in the streets, bars, gyms, churches, and back porches of the real world. It ain't always glamorous, but hell, it's a lot more dynamic and interesting than most of what ends up in stadiums, on top-forty charts, and pay-per-view.

What first attracted me to this *river of song* business was the project's focus: showing music as it's happening, where it's happening, along a great murky trajectory through America. And doing so without paying particular attention to who and what has previously been canonized by the culture of commercially oriented critics and the self-appointed arbiters of cultural history.

I like the idea of tapping someone on his or her shoulder, and pointing a finger and saying, "Hey man, check out this crazy scene!" I am enamored by the idea of uniting musicians (and the noise they make) by a river, instead of dividing them by genre like bins in a record store. I cherish the idea of witnessing music as an event, and recognizing it as an integral part of life.

'Cuz music is not just something you buy, it's something you do.

—ani difranco, August 1998

River of Song
A Musical Journey down the Mississippi
Americans, Old and New
I. Lake Itasca to Davenport
Midwestern Crossroads
II. Iowa City to La Center
The Southern Fusion
III. Swifton to Jackson
Louisiana, Where Music Is King
IV. Natchez to Delacroix Island
Lake Itasca
Inger
Mississippi R.
Brainerd
Lake Superior
CANADA
Lake Huron
Wisconsin
St.Paul
Minneapolis
Minnesota
Fountain City
La Crosse
Lake Michigan
Michigan
Mississippi River
Lake Erie
Iowa
Missouri River
Davenport
Moline
Iowa City
Douds
Wabash River
Illinois
Indiana
Ohio
Missouri
Missouri River
Hillsboro
Kansas River
Ohio River
St. Louis
Festus
Ste. Genevieve
Kansas
Kentucky
La Center
Tennessee
Swifton
Memphis
Helena
Arkansas River
Clarksdale
Georgia
Red River
Arkansas
Greenville
Mississippi
Alabama
Louisiana
Vicksburg
Jackson
Red River
Natchez
Texas
Eunice
Opelousas
Baton Rouge
Florida
Erath
Mississippi R.
New Orleans
Gulf of Mexico
Delacroix Island

Introduction
TRAVELING ALONG A RIVER OF SONG

There's a story that's told about Henry Schoolcraft, the Indian agent and explorer who was the first Caucasian to reach the headwaters of the Mississippi River.

Schoolcraft and his party trekked upriver with a small team of Ojibwe guides in the summer of 1832, following the river by canoe as it flowed through lakes named Winnibogishish and Bemidji, through the dense forest of what is now northern Minnesota. When he finally came upon a deep, spring-fed lake that had no feeder streams, he knew he had come to the end of a journey that began nearly three hundred years before, when De Soto crossed the Mississippi in the fall of 1541. The origin of the Mississippi had remained on the misty edges of maps all those years, as Europeans traveled and then settled the rest of the river valley.

Satisfied that he had reached the headwaters, Schoolcraft christened the lake "Itasca," from the middle syllables of the Latin *veritas caput,* or "true head" (the name sounded enough like an Indian word that it later sent scholars searching for etymological roots in Algonquian and Siouan dictionaries).

The Ojibwe guides watched Schoolcraft erect a makeshift flagpole on an island in the lake to stake his claim to the discovery. Later, so the story goes, they told him,

"We've always known where the great river came from."

"Why didn't you tell anyone?" Schoolcraft wondered.

"No one ever asked."

Twenty-five miles from Itasca on the east shore of Lake Bemidji, we wait at five o'clock on a morning in March 1996, in ten-degree cold. We're here to film the early spring sunrise, and the snow that melts drop by drop into rivulets that feed the river. Mist has silvered the reeds along the river's banks, and grass bends into a blanket of snow. Our boots crack through the crust of ice that covers the drifts, and we're careful not to leave tracks in front of the camera.

Before us, the river cuts a black swath through the glimmering snow. The dim predawn light is outside of the camera's range, so we wait. Steam rises from the water and billows from our mouths in the frigid air. We stomp to push the cold from our toes, our parkas stiffen in the wind. When the sun pushes out from the horizon, mist dances on the surface of the river, the ice glistens like a dusting of stars, and we roll.

We rolled, then, on down the river—to the lake country around Brainerd, where we filmed a snowbound Scandinavian fiddle group in the cozy living room of a log house, then on to the Twin Cities for a flurry of performances—riot grrrls Babes in Toyland at First Avenue, the rock band Soul Asylum in their warehouse loft, "Spider" John Koerner with a band we dubbed the Minneapolis Folk All-Stars at a bar on the river's West Bank.

We flew on to Memphis, to catch the Kappa Alpha Psi steppers during spring rush at the university, and a teenage drill team filling playing fields with rhythm at the Katie Sexton Community Center. We ate barbecue on Beale Street, then dropped down into Mississippi, to film Big Jack Johnson and the Jelly Roll Kings playing steamy Delta blues at a grocery-store juke joint in Bobo.

The night air in Bobo was eighty degrees hotter than Brainerd. The two locations were worlds apart, united only by their proximity to the river, and by the pleasure and meaning the artists found in their music. The pace of the production was exhausting, but in these first two weeks of shooting we'd begun what we set out to do—to explore the remarkable depth of talent and the rich mosaic of human stories that lie in the music played along the Mississippi River.

We returned to the river eight times during a two-year stretch, to film and record music for *The Mississippi: River of Song* series. We hopscotched north and south to cover the array of music that's played in the communities along the river. We returned to the Minnesota headwaters for a powwow in August, to Arkansas for a fall blues festival, to Missouri for an old French revel on New Year's Eve.

We spent three months on the road with camera and sound crews, traveled a total of 12,000 miles, and shot seventy locations in thirty towns and cities in all ten states that line the Mississippi. We recorded live performances of more than five hundred musicians, interviewed more than a hundred.

Wherever possible, we visited musicians on their home turf: John Hartford piloting the riverboat *Twilight* in Iowa, the Mississippi Mass Choir at their home church in Jackson, Geno Delafose playing at Slim's Y-Ki-Ki, a historic zydeco club in Opelousas, Louisiana.

We set out to find lively scenes, to get close to the home base and the grassroots of music in America, and we followed that path where it took us, into a small church in Kentucky and a jam-packed Mexican club in East Moline, a veterans hall in Ste. Genevieve, piano bars in the New Orleans French Quarter. The path brought us to musicians we'd never heard before, whose songs moved us, and back to musicians we knew, whose songs moved us in new ways.

When we started this project six years ago, we were, like the explorer Schoolcraft, not certain where it would lead us. We were vague about the geography, about which states and cities the Mississippi flows through. Given the undeniable dominance of the mass media and all we had heard about the disappearance of regional culture, we weren't sure we would find enough music in the mid-country that was actually worth listening to.

But remembering Schoolcraft, we made sure to ask, and ask again. We were lucky to stumble onto people along the way who knew how to get where we wanted to go, and were generous enough to tell us. Many were pleased that we were asking, and surprised at our pleasure in what we found, as if to say, "We've always known there's great music being played around here..."

The story we wanted to tell is the story of a living legacy—the blues as they're still sung in the Delta, the powwow songs still sung at the headwaters. We narrowed our search to music that's being played live, for appreciative audiences, by people who still live near the river. We decided we'd travel from the north, with the flow of the river but against the flow of history—the jazz and blues and rock that traveled upriver from the south. This was intentional. By starting in the north, we knew we would discover deepening musical roots the further we traveled, and we'd hear history interpreted in the songs and stories of living musicians.

We followed this path because we believed it would capture something that is often lost in histories and documentaries about music—the liveness of it, for lack of a better word. Something crucial is missed when music is boxed and frozen into eras and races, genres and styles. In reality, music jumps out of these boxes: People hear each other's music, sometimes decades later and musical spectrums away, on the radio, around the campfire, in a foreign language. The music business is dominated by pop radio and record labels, but there are no rules when people get together to play on their own. There's a rare democracy in the making of music, and we wanted to find out how it works.

The musicians understood this idea from the get-go. Babes in Toyland were proud to share the stage with r&b legend Fontella Bass, and drummer Lori Barbero wanted to go along on the powwow shoot. The Memphis Horns knew, much more than we did, what it meant to talk about "Southern fusion."

Some musicians were nonplussed that we wanted to include them in the project, others were simply glad that we were paying attention to something so close to their hearts. A few begged off: the ever mercurial Jerry Lee Lewis dropped out a week before the Memphis shoot. But Ike Turner and Merle Haggard signed our releases gratis, and every musician we visited was generous, accommodating, and tolerant of our invasive cameras, mikes, and hot lights.

These musicians populate this book, their stories make up its narrative. They range from Lil' Bob Lewis, a sixteen-year-old fiddler from Missouri, to ninety-eight-year-old country legend Governor Jimmie "You Are My Sunshine" Davis of Louisiana. The saga of music is told in their words and lyrics: how they came to play, where they find inspiration, how they make their lives around music, the heritage they interpret, and the new territories they explore.

To travel down the Mississippi is to journey through a wonderfully varied American community. The journey begins, as it should, with the first Americans, the bands of Ojibwe who live at the headwaters of the river. Along the way, we encounter descendants of the first French settlers in Missouri, African-American ancestors of the slaves who turned the soil of the South into fertile plantations, Germans, and Swedes and English who built the factories, cities, and farms of the heartland. Some sought refuge along the river centuries ago—the Cajuns migrated to Southern Louisiana from French Acadia in Canada during the 1760s. Others came more recently—Mexicans to the railyards of Moline in the 1930s, Laotian Hmong to the Twin Cities after the Vietnam War.

Much of our story centers on sharing—learning music from mentors, siblings, and buddies, passing it along to others, who in turn hear something different in the music and make it new again. There is Robert "Junior" Lockwood, who learned guitar from his stepfather, the blues great Robert Johnson. And there is drummer Levon Helm, who sat at Lockwood's knee during live radio broadcasts in the forties, and later gave The Band and Bob Dylan a living connection to the roots of the blues.

The river of song is carried by Randy Kingbird, who learned how to drum by banging on metal buckets with an Ojibwe elder in Red Lake, Minnesota; by D. L. Menard, whose idol Hank Williams told him to be proud of his native Cajun songs; and by Karl Hartwich, whose first lessons on the concertina came from Syl Liebl, the star of the sixties polka circuit in Wisconsin.

It is carried by girls in gospel choirs who grow up to be soul stars, and by boys who play trumpet in the high school band and sneak into after-hours clubs to play jazz or r&b. By retired bankers and farmers, who spend their summers swapping bluegrass tunes around the fire, by zydeco dancers dressed to the nines, Ojibwe girls in jingle dresses, Mexican factory workers swirling through ballads of borderland bravura.

In the end, there's something about music that is very much like a river: It takes in whatever comes its way, and what comes with a strong current makes waves. There are tributaries and there are dams, rapids and backwaters, and of course there's the mainstream... well, you get the idea.

It is October 13, 1997. We're standing outside the Flowin' Fountain on Nelson Street, the historic blues strip of Greenville, Mississippi. A storm is rolling in, one of the few times on the road we've seen rain, and the setting sun is streaking the undersides of the black clouds that fill the sky. The sky turns a surreal salmon, and the street fills with a luminescence that warms its tired face.

We're here to shoot a homecoming for Little Milton, a get-together with some old friends at their old hangout, the original "Annie Mae's Cafe." Scrap Iron, Milton's road manager, drinks a soda at the bar, and Peaches cooks up a heaping tray of chicken and rice, as the crew wipes tables and hangs lights from the rafters. When the rains come, the back roof leaks. We drag sound cables through two inches of puddled water and hope for a respectable turnout.

Milton puts on a show for a small but buoyant crowd of friends. He shares the stage with blues showman Bobby Rush, and the floor fills with dancers. The evening peaks with a spine-tingling song by Little Bill Wallace, Milton's mentor and boyhood idol. He croons with a practiced, unforced tone, Milton answers him on guitar, and we are transported back to the forties, when Milton first heard Bill on the radio, promoting snuff and his weekend gigs.

After the show, we sit down with Milton and his friends, while the sound crew strikes the mikes. He is in high spirits, nursing a shot of whiskey, and there's so much ribbing going on that we wonder how we'll ever edit the repartee into a coherent interview. Then Bobby Rush offers a thought: "I call this man the daddy of my career, because of what he's shared with me—how to do it, when to do it, and when to shut up. I watched and I saw him survive with nothing. I watched and I said, 'Milton, if you can do this with nothing, you're a bad man.' "

Milton returns a gracious nod, but demurs. "My chest ain't sticking up because of it," he says, "but I believe the blessings that have been bestowed upon me are what the greats of the past era taught me. Old Sonny Boy told me, he said, 'Man, if you can't share what you got with somebody, then that means nobody is gonna have anything to share with you.' I didn't quite understand what he was talking about, but he was saying, 'in order to receive something you should give.' " Bobby and Milton say the last words in unison. "And once you give it," Milton finishes, "even if that person don't give it back, don't stop there. Share it with somebody else."

We've neared the end of our travels and we're ready to pack it in, but our ears perk up when we hear these words, because we've never heard it said so well. By a circuitous road and often by chance, we've come to what might be the heart of the matter, the place where connections are made and all paths taken seem predestined. There are many eloquent words spoken in this book, but Milton's are the ones to remember:

"Share it with somebody else."

Acknowledgments

The Mississippi: River of Song would never have left the dock without the early support of two major partners: Paul Johnson of Smithsonian Productions and Mitsuo Kojima of Kajima Vision Productions. They later became the executive producers of the TV and radio series, but they began as the midwives of what started out as a loosely framed question: What would we find if we made a journey along the Mississippi, looking for the best contemporary music we could find?

We turned first to music writers for answers, Elijah Wald foremost among them. Elijah is deeply versed in the music of the world, American music in particular. He steered us to stories that illuminated the lives of American musicians, then he helped us find the way there. He conducted most of the interviews, and he has written this book out of a mountain of raw material. Other writers helped guide us: Peter Guralnick wrote an early treatment for music along the Lower Mississippi; Ben Sandmel, Robert Gordon, Harper Barnes, and John Sinclair all shared the insight gained from years of searching in similar waters.

Key guidance came from a network of folklorists who have studied, preserved, and promoted indigenous American music for decades. The Smithsonian Center for Folklife Programs and Cultural Studies was, for us, the hub of that network: thanks to Richard Kurin, center director; Diana Parker, director of the annual Festival of American Folklife; senior ethnomusicologist Tom Vennum, an expert on the Ojibwe drum; and Tony Seeger, director of Folkways Recordings and head of our advisory board.

Their contacts ran the length of the river, a small army of field researchers who have fanned out across the country in recent decades to document and record music in the backroad towns, farmhouses, churches, juke joints, and bandstands of America. All proved knowledgeable, and generous with their time and support: Phil Nusbaum in Minnesota; Wisconsin polka expert Richard March; Iowa state folklorist Rachelle Saltzman; Ray Brassieur in Missouri; Judy Peiser and David Evans in Memphis; Jim O'Neal, Worth Long, and Bill Ferris in Mississippi; Scott Billington, Nick Spitzer, Barry Ancelet, Bruce Boyd Raeburn, and Mike Luster in Louisiana. Many others stepped up during the years to help us shoot performances and interviews in the best possible venues—the clubs and schools and churches and music festivals whose names appear throughout the text.

Most of all, we were welcomed into the homes and studios and hearts of the musicians, who taught everyone involved in the project so much about the spirit and soul of music.

Production was coordinated by Cathleen O'Connell, preproduction was handled by Jana Odette and Cynthia Johnson. Theo Pelletier served as associate producer and staff photographer. Additional production credits appear at the end of the book. Thanks for advice and support to editor Bill Anderson, Michal Goldman and the members of the Filmmakers Collaborative, Charles Camp, and Marc Patcher, Karen Loveland, and many other colleagues at the Smithsonian.

Leah Mahan coordinated production of this book, with assistance from Samantha Head. Thanks to designer Martine Bruel, for turning stories and images into this book; to Richard P. McDonough for hooking us up with Martine and with a supportive, music-loving editor in Cal Morgan; and to the production team at St. Martin's, for getting the book out on the streets.

John would like to thank his family: my wife Kaoru, who helped hatch this idea in New Orleans ten years ago; Maya, who was not born when we started and begins kindergarden in the fall; Kai, who will be three when this book comes out. Thanks also to my parents and siblings and friends, who bucked me up over the years.

Elijah would like to thank John for the phone call that brought me on board; my editors at the *Boston Globe,* who never complained when I headed off to the river; Preacher Jack, who kept my energy up during a couple of hard years; and Cathleen and Theo, who stayed up drinking when sensible people were in bed.

– John Junkerman, director of *The Mississippi: River of Song*

PART ONE

Americans,

Outside Itasca State Park, in northern Minnesota, the Mississippi is still so narrow that one can almost step across it. As the winter ice melts, the river begins its journey south.

Old & New

Music is often cited as a universal language that can bring people together across linguistic, cultural, and geographical borders, but it can also be the opposite: a private, personal language that holds a group together and separates it from outsiders. Immigrants, traveling with few possessions other than the clothes on their backs, carry their songs with them to their new homes, and those songs may remain long after other reminders of past lives and surroundings have disappeared. Music is the glue that keeps communities from disintegrating and, with its ability to adapt and absorb new influences, can be many different things: a nostalgic family heirloom, a proud statement of identity, or simply what brings people together to dance and have a party.

One of the central American metaphors is that of the melting pot, but, in the northern Midwest, winters are long and melting does not happen easily. The long months of icy weather keep families and friends huddled in their homes and, in these intimate gatherings, old traditions have stayed alive. Along the banks of the northern Mississippi, one still finds the music of wave after wave of immigrants, people who came thousands, hundreds, or just a few years ago. Each group has been affected by its surroundings and its neighbors, but has also retained a cultural cohesiveness that is much rarer as one moves south.

The musicians in this first part of the journey down the river come from widely varied backgrounds, and arrived over several centuries. The Ojibwe are the oldest settlers, having come to the region about three hundred years ago. They largely displaced the Dakota people, who had arrived somewhat earlier, displacing still earlier groups in a pattern reaching back at least 2,000 years. Northern Europeans—Swedes, Norwegians, and Germans—were the next to settle the area, in the 1800s, setting up solid farming communities. In the cities, there was a growing African-American population, coming north to find freedom and a better life. The turn of the century brought a wave of Mexican immigrants, seeking jobs in the factories. And so it continues, with new immigrants drawn by the Midwest's reputation for friendliness and relatively high living standards. Even people from warmer climates, like the recently arrived Cambodians and Laotian Hmong, have chosen to brave the snow and wind to build a life in the Twin Cities.

The northern Mississippi has not received the musical kudos commonly given to the lower river regions, but its contribution has been impressive. Wintry isolation has produced quirky individualists like Bob Dylan, a Jewish kid in Hibbing, Minnesota, who built a new life out of the sounds that came in over the radio. Dylan passed only briefly through the Minneapolis scene, before heading east to New York and folk stardom, but other players, like his friend "Spider" John Koerner, chose to stay in the relaxed atmosphere of the local bars, clubs, and coffeehouses. In the mid-seventies, when Garrison Keillor started broadcasting *A Prairie Home Companion* from St. Paul's World Theatre, the show was able to tap into a wealth of local talent, and introduced the country to an unsuspected new generation of players, singers, and songwriters.

At roughly the same time, Prince opened the eyes of the rock world to a Minneapolis band scene that was arguably the most varied for its size in the country. The Replacements, the Jayhawks, Hüsker Dü, and a few others broke nationally, but were only the tip of the iceberg. Less cliquey than New York or

Los Angeles, Minneapolis musicians range from punk to heavy metal to r&b, from the abrasive underground sound of Babes in Toyland to pop successes like Soul Asylum, but all seem to know and support one another, partying together and showing up at each other's gigs. Prince also appeared as the tip of an iceberg of black culture. He had grown up on the Minneapolis jazz scene, named for his father's Prince Roger Trio. When he opened his own studio, Paisley Park, he proved that one did not have to go to the coasts to make hot records, and soon stars like Janet Jackson were flying into town to record at Jimmy Jam and Terry Lewis's Flyte Tyme studio. Longtime local figures, Jam and Lewis used their prestige to record old friends like Sounds of Blackness, among the most innovative ensembles in modern gospel.

Outside the cities, kids grow up listening to the same pop radio that covers the rest of the country, but also holding on to older sounds that assert and preserve their cultural roots. Some of the current crop of rural ethnic musicians, like the members of the Skål Club Spelmanslag, are self-consciously preservationist, seeking out old-country traditions in an attempt to find and explore their familial past. Others, like Karl Hartwich, play local styles that developed among immigrant communities in Minnesota or Wisconsin, and are quite different from the music played by their European forebears.

Moving down the river, we arrive in the factory and farming area centered in the Quad Cities: Davenport and Bettendorf, Iowa, on the Mississippi's west bank, and Moline and Rock Island, Illinois, on the east. There, a strong Mexican-American community has flourished for many years, interacting with other immigrant groups while keeping up with developments south of the Rio Grande. La Otra Mitad plays everything from *corridos* of the Mexican Revolution to Columbian *cumbias* and inner-city Hispanic rap, while trumpeter Manny Lopez has emerged from a mariachi background to become heir to the jazz tradition of the area's most famous musical product, the cornetist Bix Beiderbecke.

These performers emerge from an amazing range of disparate styles and traditions, but all share a deep affection for the region, and an appreciation of the variety and richness of the music available here. More than any other group down the river, they seemed interested in what was happening in other communities, often speaking with pleasure of the cultural interaction. All were proud both of where they came from and where they are going, of their roots and their ability to create a new, American, identity. Their music reflects all of that, with deep roots and broad, flowering branches.

◆◆◆

The Grand Entry begins the powwow on the Earl Robinson Grounds at Inger, Minnesota.

1
The Powwow Lives On: CHIPPEWA NATION

The drum is the heartbeat of our nation. When the Indians first got the drum it was the means of talking with the Creator, that's the way we were taught about it. 'Cause when he hears the drum, he's looking down on us and he's watching us dance. This is the center of our people, and when our people dance around this drum, when they get this heartbeat within themselves, or when they're at this powwow and they hear the drum, it gives them strength. It brings wellness to their heart and their mind, and they're having fun, and that's what we're here for. We're here to have a good time and respect what is given to us. 'Cause everything on this land is given to the Indian people—to the Anishinaabe, to the Ojibwe.

Pete White is one of the eight singers who make up Chippewa Nation, a drum from the Leech Lake and Red Lake reservations. Among the Ojibwe, a "drum" is both the instrument and the group of men that plays it. The members sit in a circle and beat out a steady, unison rhythm, while singing in strong, keening voices. Chippewa Nation travels to powwows all over northern Minnesota, but today they are playing on their home turf, the powwow grounds of the tiny town of Inger, on the Bowstring River between Sand and Bowstring lakes.

The members of Chippewa Nation are in their twenties and thirties. For them, the powwow is a way of preserving their heritage, and of rediscovering ways that were once in danger of disappearing.

This powwow here only started up again about seventeen years ago. When I was young, we didn't really go to a lot of powwows; just once in a while we'd go up to Red Lake. But the way we learned how to sing was pretty much the way Ojibwe people have been doing it for years and years. They would have three or four people out around here that are always singing, just about every week, and that's how we learned: just being around a drum, and getting out there and trying to dance. We never really went to powwows until maybe we were about fifteen, sixteen years old, but yet when we were about seven years, eight years old we were already learning, sitting here watching these guys sing songs around a drum all the time. Then we'd go ahead and take anything that sounded like a drum and just start trying to bellow out some song, and pretty soon we started learning these songs.

This is part of our tradition, Randy Kingbird chimes in. *When I first started out, I got taught by an old man named Chester Murrell from around Lake Wisconsin. He was in his seventies and he'd get a bunch of us kids and say, "Come on boys. I'm gonna teach you some songs." He'd do it on his own time. He said that's the way he wanted to pass it down, so people can have that kind of music. And I'm pretty glad he did. You know, I been singing now for—it'll be twenty-five years this year.*

Chippewa Nation, which also includes Randy's brother Doug and Pete and Bruce White, has been singing together for some four years. Randy is the leader and principal songwriter. Pete is a few years younger, and grew up listening to Randy's previous group, the Little Earth Singers.

I had a lot of respect for Randy when I was a young guy; he was singing way before we even got started, and they were at the tops, the tip-tops of of singing, and they were right on. We used to admire them and tape their music, and me and my brother we used to sit back and say, "You know, some day we're gonna sing with these guys."

Originally, we were in different groups, Randy says. *We had the Little Earth Singers, and usually we wouldn't have too many guys, 'cause most of our singers settled down; and they had Leech Lake Intertribal, and they had a hard time getting their singers together all the time. So, we were talking there one time, and we said "Let's go check out the powwow in the [Twin] Cities." You know, we'd sung together before and we liked the way we sounded. So, we were driving down there and Pete said, "What should we call ourselves?" He said, "It wouldn't be right to call ourselves Little Earth Singers; wouldn't be right to say Leech Lake Intertribal; 'cause we're gonna make one drum." So, you know, we had people from Red Lake Reservation, Leech Lake Reservation and a couple of singers from White Earth, so I said, "Why not just call ourselves Chippewa Nation? Three of the biggest reservations in Minnesota are getting together. It would be a good name."*

The powwows are designed to bring people together and preserve old traditions, but they are also a new and growing symbol of Indian (or Native American, a term rarely used here) pride. Some powwows try to stay as close as possible to the old ways, discouraging tourists, concession stands, and electric sound systems. Others have become almost an Indian equivalent of the rodeo, "competition powwows" with a grand entry parade and prizes given out for the best singers, drummers, and dancers. In either case, they are proof that, although they may wear cowboy boots and jeans and work in factories or casinos, the first Americans remain a people apart, with their own history and heritage.

Back in the thirties and forties, where they had that segregation or whatever you call it, they tried to depress our identity, Randy says. *A lot of people went into hiding to practice their religion; it wasn't out in the open like it is now. But the*

Above: River scene near Inger, Minnesota. (inset) Chippewa Nation performs. Pete White (second from left) and Randy Kingbird lead the singing.

sixties and seventies, that's when the power start coming back, and coming back strong.

The Leech Lake Ojibwe have been able to retain more of their customs than many Indian groups. They are still in the area they settled some three to five hundred years ago, after years of war with the previous inhabitants, a branch of the Dakota people (who are often called "Sioux" in a mispronounciation of their Ojibwe name). They were traveling, as legend has it, from the shores of the Atlantic Ocean, following the chain of Great Lakes to the wild rice country, called "the land where food grows on the water" in some old Ojibwe stories. Now, at the end of August, they still go out in their canoes to harvest the rice crop. The landing is only a mile or so from the powwow grounds, and the young men are there at dawn, backing their pickups down to the edge of the lake, then paddling out into the waving reeds. One man stands in the stern and poles the canoe through the water, while the other kneels just in front of him and bends the tops of the plants, heavy with the ripe crop, over the thwarts, then beats them with a wooden stick, sending a shower of green grains to pile up and fill the boat bottom. Later, these will be parched, and their husks sifted off, leaving the brown wild rice that is a staple of the local diet.

This is naturally rich country, with rice in the fall, maple sugar in the spring, lakes full of fish, and forests full of game. Now, there are also the new casinos, which are paying for schools and civic centers and providing service jobs in an area where there is all too little work. To a newcomer, the contrast is unnerving: It is hard to imagine two worlds more different—the glitter and clang of the slot machines, the bright lights and rhinestone cowboy band singing the latest country hits, and the tribal gathering a few miles away by the rice-rich lake.

Dave Morgan, Ojibwe elder and storyteller

Standing outside a log house on Lake Winnibigoshish, Dave Morgan is reminiscing about the old days. Morgan, a medium-size, solidly built man in his early sixties, grew up speaking Ojibwe, and his English still has the careful hesitancy of a non-native speaker. When he shifts into his native tongue, his voice takes on a poetic lilt, as if he was speaking not only for himself, but for his parents and grandparents. Now, he is talking about the powwow: ***As far back as I can remember, I heard it called powwow, but the Ojibwe people call it niimi' idiwago. Powwow, that comes from somewhere else. Like in the movies, when they wanted to talk to the Indians, they said, "We want to powwow with them."***

They used to have different kind of powwows. They had a traditional powwow, and then they used to have a "friendly gathering." It was the Sioux who had the powwow, after they quit battling with each other; then they got together and that's when they'd dance the friendship dance and celebrate that everything is over with.

I heard this story, I think it was from one of those people from Sugar Point. They said that the powwow drum—you know that sometimes you see it painted half red and half blue? Like I say, the Sioux is the one who had the powwow, and this man said the Sioux gave half of that drum to the Ojibwe people, because of this get-together of friends. That's what this old man was saying.

The powwow in Inger is a local event, drawing people mostly from the surrounding towns. It is small, with some half-dozen drums clustered together under a round central shelter, and maybe a hundred dancers circling around them. Off to the side, people sit in their folding chairs, watching the dance and joining in as the spirit moves them. Many of the adults wear ornate regalia, with brightly colored cloth and great spreads of feathers, but the kids are likely to be in T-shirts and jeans. There are a few concession stands, selling soft drinks and "Indian tacos," made like the Mexican variety, but with fried bread instead of tortillas. As the day wears on some of the dancers drift off to the parking lot and pitch horseshoes. Clearly, this powwow is not completely traditional, but it carries on the feel of the friendly gatherings, a blend of good-time, interfamily get-together and ceremonial event. There are offerings of tobacco to honor and placate the spirits, and memorial songs for those who have died in the last year. When a film crew comes in, it is advised about what may and may not be photographed, and there are watchful elders making sure that the rules are followed.

For the Ojibwe, the sacred and secular exist on a continuum, and it is virtually impossible for an outsider to understand where one finishes and the other begins. At first, as one asks for guidance from tribal elders, native Ojibwe speakers, school teachers, and assimilated city dwellers, it seems as if people's willingness to talk about the ancient songs and traditions is in an inverse ratio to their knowledge. A storyteller who is Christian and speaks no Ojibwe is happy to tell old tales, but the so-called "Traditionals" say that her stories are all mixed up. An elder, Rueben Goggleye, is introduced as deeply knowledgeable but, after politely receiving a gift of tobacco, he replies to inquiries about local lore with a short parable, drawn from his days working for a tourist camp on the banks of one of the many lakes:

One day, a tourist came up and began asking about Ojibwe beliefs. Goggleye pointed out into the lake. "Do you see that rock out there?" he asked.

Overleaf: Powwow dancers at Inger.

The tourist nodded.
"Do you know what that rock means?"
The tourist shook his head.
"Well," said Goggleye, "I do."

It is the same with the powwow songs. Some can be filmed, others are too sacred. Some songs are so private that they are not even sung in public. *I got some songs I made, but they're meant for my use and I don't sing 'em out at the powwows,* Randy says. *I don't know what they mean yet. You know, they come to me in a dream, and one of these days I'll find out what they mean, what they're for. See, right now I'm still learning, learning about the drum. Even though I've been singing twenty-five years, I'm still learning.*

The drum songs come from many sources, and have many purposes. Some have words, whereas others are simply wordless chants, preserving older melodies. Many are not even Ojibwe, reflecting a musical interchange that apparently has gone on for millennia, and has picked up with the current renaissance of Indian culture.

Some of the songs we got are intertribal songs, Randy says. *That means they're passed in different tribes, like we sing some songs from the Hidatsa tribe, Sioux tribe, the Cree. Most of the singers nowadays sing just about the same, really. A lot of the time, you can't tell which tribe it's from, unless they have the word-songs. Like if they have words in 'em, you can hear Sioux words and Cree words and all that. But most of the songs that we use at the more traditional powwows, like where we are today, they're from the Chippewas.*

Some of these songs are sacred and they're part of our ceremonies. We've been brought up to respect them, and we don't just sing them any time. Like when they asked us earlier today, we had to sing a memorial song, and that's the only time we sing that kind of song, is if some people come and give you tobacco and want you to sing for their loved one that departed. Then there's certain songs, like if you're gonna honor someone really hard, really good, like if I was gonna take a person as my brother, I would make a song for him and I would sing it for him, and that would be his song. And the only time I was going to sing that was if I was going to honor him, and I would explain it to people, why I was singing it.

Seems like most of the time when they do have word-songs, they're songs that have a special meaning for a certain person or thing that's happening, Pete says. *When people need a special song, they always come to our drum, and we always give that responsibility to Randy. He's our lead, actually, and his responsibility is to think of the song.*

According to Chippewa Nation, there is little divide between the word-songs and those that are simply chants. Every song has its place. Some are old, handed down orally from generation to generation; others are Randy's own compositions.

They could be dream songs, you know, sometimes you could just have one come to you in a dream. That's the only way you're supposed to make a song, really. But then sometimes people come to you and tell you what the song is for. Like if they give you tobacco and stuff and say, "I want you to do a song for me," it might not come to you right away, but you know, if you can dream it, then it will come. And sometimes it comes with words, sometimes it comes without words.

To an outsider, the subtleties are often rather baffling, and even the distinction between word-songs and wordless chants is lost in the drawn-out syllables and unfamiliar tonalities of the Ojibwe language. As the powwow goes on through the day and well into the evening, one pulsing, hypnotically repetitive song follows the next, while the circle of dancers moves slowly around the drum arbor, and each hour seems much like the last. For the dancers, though, there are obviously differences. When a less experienced drum is playing, the dance ground will be almost empty, and the dancers will sit with their families and friends, drinking sodas and exchanging news. When a group like Chippewa Nation takes over, everyone is on their feet. The adults dance in careful, measured steps, while the kids are bouncy and energetic. Sometimes a special "jingle-dress dance" is played, and the space is filled with women in bright dresses strung with hundreds of metal cones, gleaming and jingling as the dancers twirl and stamp.

This is not the sort of dancing performed for tourists, the elaborately choreographed pantomimes that have long been a staple of Hollywood westerns. It is dancing for the dancers, a chance to meet old friends, to show off new dance attire, and to assert and come into harmony with a tradition that is less and less part of the everyday world in which most of them live. It reminds both dancers and observers of a time when life was more slowly paced, moving with the seasons rather than flashing by on the highways or the evening news.

◆

THE VISION OF TAILFEATHER WOMAN

Here is the story of the beginning of the ceremonial powwow drum. It was the first time when the white soldiers massacred the Indians when this Sioux woman gave four sons of hers to fight for her people. But she lost her four sons in this massacre and ran away after she knew her people were losing the war. The soldiers were after her but she ran into a lake. She went in the water and hid under the lily pads. While there, the Great Spirit came and spoke to her and told her, "There is only one thing for you to do."

It took four days to tell her. It was windy and the wind flipped the lily pads so she could breathe and look to see if anyone was around. No—the sound is all that she made out, but from it she remembered all the Great Spirit told her. On the fourth day at noon she came out and went to her people to see what was left from the war. The Great Spirit told her what to do: "Tell your people... to make a drum and tell them what I told you." The Great Spirit taught her also the songs she knew and she told the men folks how to sing the songs. "It will be the only way you are going to stop the soldiers from killing your people."

Her people did what [the woman] said, and when the soldiers who were massacring the Indians heard the sound of the drum, they put down their arms, stood still and stopped the killing, and to this day white people always want to see a powwow. This powwow drum is called in English "Sioux drum" and in Ojibwe bwaanidewe'igan. It was put here on earth before peace terms were made with the whites. After the whites saw what the Indians were doing and having a good time—the Indians had no time to fight—the white man didn't fight. After

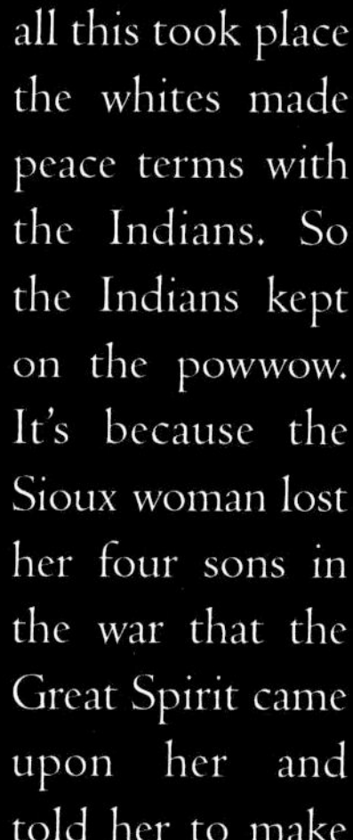

all this took place the whites made peace terms with the Indians. So the Indians kept on the powwow. It's because the Sioux woman lost her four sons in the war that the Great Spirit came upon her and told her to make

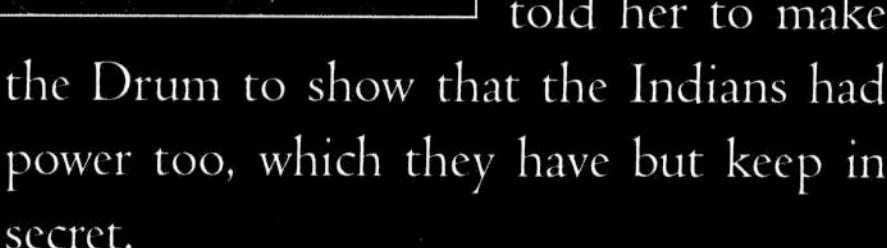

the Drum to show that the Indians had power too, which they have but keep in secret.

—William Bineshi Baker, Sr., Ojibwe drum maker (from Thomas Vennum, Jr., *The Ojibwa Dance Drum: Its History and Construction.*)

On the afternoon of the powwow's second day, Randy brings over his cousin, Mark Kingbird. Mark is a quiet man, but he has a reputation as one of the region's best singers. Mark is a member of a powwow drum, and also a master of the softer, more intimate Ojibwe music, the courting songs that a lover would sing to serenade his sweetheart. Away from the noise of the powwow, he sings a light, lilting melody, keeping time on a round hand-drum decorated with a traditional bear-paw motif.

Ni wii jii wagan
Nizaagi'aa, I love her, hy ya ah
way ya hey, way ya

Those words, "ni wii jii wagan," that's your partner, or your loved one, and "nizaagi'aa," that says you love her. It says it in Ojibwe, then says it in English.

I just make my own words in the song, from the different round-dance songs that we come across. When you make a song, it don't come just like that. It takes a lot of practice to make a song. You've got to have the right melody and the right tune, and the words that go in the songs have got to sound like they fit the melody.

Mark picks up his drum again, and starts beating a quiet, steady rhythm. As he sings, Randy joins in, and the two voices form a cousinly counterpoint, sometimes together, sometimes just slightly out of synch, as if Randy was commenting musically on Mark's lead.

Come on over, later tonight
I need some company
Come on over and we'll have
Cookies and tea
Hey yah hey, hey yah

The words seem oddly out of place in this locale, and because of that seem all the more personal. In the distance, the big drums of the powwow are faintly echoing, but Mark sings with a gentle, almost lullaby-like cadence. Randy is nodding his appreciation.

Come on over, later tonight
I need some company
Come on over and we'll have
Cookies and tea
Hey yah hey, hey yah

Randy Kingbird (at left) joins the dancing.

In the winter months, the old people would tell us stories, Dave Morgan remembers. *And those old legends did make sense, what they were telling us. You learned a lot, to respect Mother Earth and all that is put here for us. They told us what your life is about. They just didn't throw you here and there. They gave us things, they taught us things that we need, and about everything that goes on with this life.*

They said that when the time started, they don't know where we come from, but God put us here on this world. He knew what he was going to do. And then he put all these things here for us. Everything that you see here that the Indian uses, even these trees, they got medicine. These leaves, these plants, everything. And all these things that he put here, they told us to have a lot of respect, take care of them, don't raise Cain with them. That's God's gift. And if you just throw it around, you're disrespecting the things that he gave you.

I remember when I was a little boy, I was down to the lake one time with these children older than I am, and they were going swimming. And I told them, "I'm going to go swimming." Then [this older woman] says, "Come here, sit down here." So we sat at the table, and she started explaining to me, she says, "Don't say you can swim across the lake or swim across this little body of water, little river. Don't ever say anything like that on that water. Even if you can swim a long ways, don't say you can swim across or swim against the waves and stuff like that. Don't say anything about that you're better than that water."

That's what she told me, and then she says, "Have a lot of respect for that water. If you're on that water, remember where that comes from. Even when we go out here to pump that water and bring it in a pail, take a cup and drink it, you remember where that comes from. The creator put that there for us to use." And then she said, "It can do anything to you it wants to, whenever it wants to."

They told us so many things. And now we have to tell this to the young people, to pass it on. Because that's the way you learn.

◆◆◆

The powwow provides a chance to meet friends and exchange news.

Paul Wilson (left) and Arnie Anderson on the front porch of Arnie's house. (inset) Paul's front door

2
North Country Fiddles: THE SKÅL CLUB SPELMANSLAG

It is late March, but the snowdrifts are still piled high around Arnie Anderson's house.

When I got married, we moved up into the North Woods here. My grandfather came from Sweden, and he homesteaded just a quarter of a mile through the woods over there. So I was given a chunk of land here, and decided with all the timber and logs on the land I would build a log home.

The house is an ambitious structure. The lower floor is walled with stones, and the main floor boasts a wide, gabled porch, with a staircase leading up to the front door. The central room is large and comfortable, with a high ceiling, solid beams and rounded log walls. Off to one side is a big, neatly organized kitchen. To the other is the room where Anderson works, building violins and other stringed instruments. Today he is scraping out the back of a cello, working with a tiny, finger-size plane. He will scrape for a minute or so, then pull out a measuring tool and check how wide the wood is in the spots he has been working, then scrape some more. On the next workbench, Brendan, his teenage son, is doing the same to a piece of wood that will form the back of a violin. The room is small and warm, and along one wall hang a dozen violins in various states of completion.

I've been making violins for twenty-two years now. I grew up in Brainerd, about twenty miles from here, and then went away and taught the string instruments in southern Minnesota. Then, while traveling in Italy, I got interested in the violin-making part of it and gave up the teaching. I studied violin-making in the north of Italy, in Cremona. Cremona's the town where Stradivari lived and worked, and there's a school there now for violin-making and I attended that school for three years.

I started playing the violin when I was about twenty years old. My first instrument was actually the accordion, when I was eight years old. Everybody in the family played an instrument. My father was Scandinavian, so Swedish music was big with him. He played the violin, Mom played the piano, one of my brothers played cello, another clarinet, another string bass, another piano, and myself the accordion. In the evening, after the supper meal, we would sit down and have a half hour's music, and that's how I got started. Most of the music we played was old Scandinavian tunes, and then a lot of hymns and church music as well. We used to play in the Sunday evening service.

In those days, playing in the family, it was more American Swedish music. The music that we're playing now is more authentic, older Swedish and Norwegian music.

As the afternoon wears on, musicians start to arrive. They park down below the house, then walk up, carrying their instruments, shake the snow off their boots, and peel off the layers of sweaters and parkas. By five o'clock the whole gang is here: ten fiddlers, an accordion player, a guitarist, and an older man with a string bass. Together, they form the Skål Club Spelmanslag, one of Minnesota's foremost traditional Scandinavian ensembles.

The musicians sit in a large circle, the violins spread around the room and the rhythm section stationed near the kitchen. To Arnie's right sits Paul Wilson, the group's founder and director. He is an energetic man with a big, bushy beard and a mischievous gleam in his eye.

The idea of having a group like this started in my head quite a long time before we actually got formed. I was thinking of a Scandinavian organization that would involve not only music, but possibly dance and other cultural activities, and would cross Scandinavian lines. Like, we had Sons of Norway, which is a Norwegian group, and then there's a Swedish group in the Cities, and I was thinking, as the generations get farther removed from their immigrant past, it might be better if we try to band together all the people who are interested in our Scandinavian heritage. I was thinking we could call it Skål Club because "skål" is a Swedish word that means "to your health." You usually have a little drink after saying it, but it could just be coffee or whatever.

Then, "spelmanslag" is a Swedish and a Norwegian word that has come to mean "fiddler's group." Actually, it just means "player's group." A spelman is somebody who plays an instrument, it could be a bottle or anything. But for some reason it has come to mean "fiddler's group." Our group started at this concert that a friend of ours, the accordion player, organized about four years ago. He got together some friends that played Scandinavian music and called it "Scandinavian Afternoon." Four of us got together and started playing, and then it turned out that those four people knew four more people, you know, and it just grew like that. Besides the music, we all liked getting together to have what they call "a little lunch," so that's always a big part of our rehearsals too—we've got to have our coffee and some treats.

We mostly meet in our various homes, though the Spelmanslag is getting kind of large, so we've been spilling out into a few church basements. But everybody really prefers to be in homes, because that's the feeling of the group. All of us live in the countryside; there isn't one person in the group who lives in town, in Brainerd. So it's

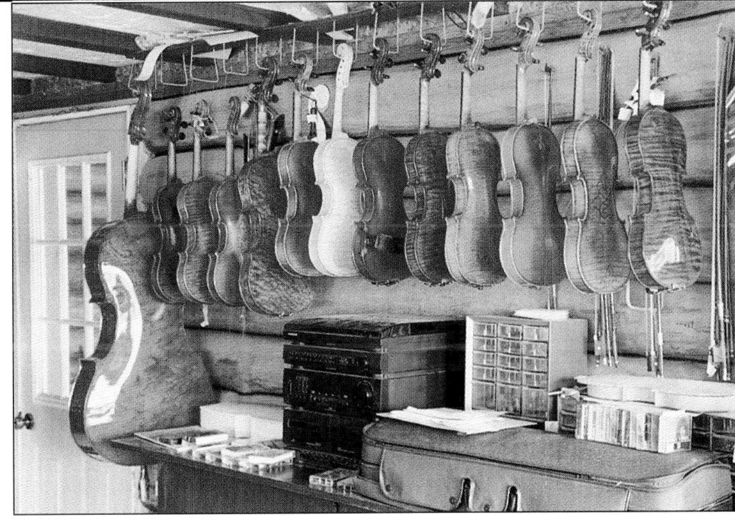

Paul Wilson (left) and Arnie Anderson in Arnie's workshop; (bottom), the workshop wall.

a little bit of a task to get everybody together, but because of the community feeling in this group people will make the extra effort and drive to different people's homes to play. In a way, I think, it's an older tradition, from when communities used to be small enough that people could get on a sleigh or something and go down to Jan Janson's place, you know, and get together. People in general are kind of hungry for some kind of a community feeling, and music is a way for them to share something with each other.

Wilson counts off the beat, and the Skål Club swings into a Norwegian polka. The fiddles play in unison, while the rhythm section keeps a steady, chugging beat. The players are a varied bunch, ranging in age from young couples to white-haired elders. Paul says that many of them first heard Scandinavian traditional music when they joined the group.

Some members have some Scandinavian background, but probably half of them don't have any, so it's been starting from scratch for a lot of them. Then, there are people like Arnie, he's pretty much grounded in his Swedishness and several other people in the group also have some feeling for their roots. For me, my mother's grandparents came from Sweden. My dad, half of his family is Norwegian and the other half is German. That's a pretty typical mix in Minnesota.

Musically, I'm a product of the sixties folk movement. I was interested in Bob Dylan, Peter, Paul and Mary. I didn't grow up hearing much Scandinavian music at all, because my parents mostly liked big band music. At one time I also played electric guitar in some rock 'n' roll bands, but I could tell even when I was doing it that it wasn't my thing; it was too loud. Then, after college, I got interested in international folk dancing, and that started me thinking about my roots and my heritage. We did a few Scandinavian dances, and I just started to explore at that point. I picked up that fiddle and the accordion, I hadn't ever played either one of them before that. There's a base of musicians down in Minneapolis that I learned from, and we'd get together and jam, and it just kind of went from there.

To me, this music helps me to understand my place, where I am a fairly recent American as things go and it helps me make more sense of being an American, and helps give meaning to my life. I don't know, it just makes sense to me. Also, I've got a thing just about live music in general. I think there's way too little music going on now that

The *River of Song* crew (from left, second cameraman Brett Wiley, cinematographer Foster Wiley, and director John Junkerman) films the Skål Club Spelmanslag. (right) Arnie Anderson's living room

people are making themselves—they're just turning on switches and buttons and listening to it, and they're not doing it. So I try to get people to make things happen rather than being passive and having everything happen to them.

Paul announces the next tune, a Swedish waltz that he says was a favorite of Al Capone's. On his count, the musicians strike up the melody, the fiddle bows dodging and swaying in rough synchrony. The music has a gentle lilt and, despite the number of players, does not sound busy or overcrowded. It is flowing and comfortable, the perfect music to play inside a warm house with a group of friends on a cold winter night. In the kitchen, a woman waltzes slowly with a baby asleep in her arms. Other kids sit on the stairs up to the second floor, listening and talking quietly among themselves.

It seems a timeless scene, but in fact represents something rather new for northern Minnesota. Much of the Skål Club's music was unknown in the area when Wilson and the other players were growing up. The Scandinavian community, having largely arrived in the nineteenth century, had Americanized its music, developing a different repertoire and styles from those in the old countries. The Skål Club is part of a revivalist movement, growing out of the folk music and dance world and looking across the Atlantic to the root traditions. The group has toured in Scandinavia, and plays a large repertoire of tunes learned from traditionally oriented players over there

Basically, we play two kinds of music. There's what they call "gammaldans" music—waltz, polka, and schottisch—which is actually the newer dance music. Then there's an older layer of tunes from Scandinavia, the polskas and springdans. Those are very much rooted in violin, fiddles, and for some reason that music didn't make it across

the ocean very well. There were just a few players and they didn't keep the tradition going, so really what was left was the gammaldans, which came up from Europe to Scandinavia. Around Minnesota, people call it "old time" music. That's what they know it as. The Scandinavians have their own style of playing; the waltzes are faster than, say, the German style, and not as heavy. The dancing is the same way; the Scandinavian style is real light.

The Skål Club, in keeping with its mass of fiddlers, specializes in dance music. Paul, however, has looked farther afield in his efforts to keep alive the regional tradition.

There's another style that is kind of typical of the upper Midwest, and those are the songs that originated in what they call the vaudeville period of Scandinavian music. That was in the twenties, and there was a guy that lived down in Minneapolis, in a place they called "Snoose Boulevard," which is on the West Bank, University of Minnesota area. His name was Olle i Skratthult, Olle from Laughtersville, and he had a whole vaudeville show. He'd travel around and set up the show and they'd have music and jokes, skits, and then they'd usually have some kind of a meal and afterward they'd have a big, open dance. So there are a lot of comic songs from that period.

We have a dialect around here that they call Swenglish, kind of a mix of Swedish and English, and it was real common in this vaudeville circuit to steal a popular tune and put Swenglish words to it. Like this one song, "Redheaded Swede," a man named Stan Boreson, he stole the tune from an old song called "The Band Played On"—"Casey would waltz with a strawberry blond..." and he changed it around. It's sort of a funny courting song about Hilda—several of these dialect songs deal with Hilda for some reason—who meets this redheaded Swede.

Paul sets down his fiddle, and gets a harmonica out of his bag. His wife meanwhile picks up a guitar, and Arnie goes into the workroom and fetches a saw. The other members of the group lean back in their chairs, and settle in for what is clearly a favorite show piece. Arnie fixes the saw handle between his legs, bends the blade back with his left hand, and starts to bow it as if it were a violin. The sound that emerges is eerie, an ethereal wail that changes pitch as he bows wider and thinner sections of the metal, and shimmers as his left hand keeps the saw-end vibrating. The saw and harmonica play the melody through and then, with a grin, Paul starts to sing in a broad, vaudeville-Swedish dialect:

Hilda would dance with a redheaded Swede, at the smorgasbord
The others would plead, but she paid them no heed, at the smorgasbord
Now, Hilda was daring, she ate pickled herring

And drank all the beer that was poured
His heart it did melt as she sliced him some smelt, at the smorgasbord

Hilda she married that redheaded Swede, at the smorgasbord
She had eighteen kids, now they all flip their lids, at the smorgasbord
But I am not kicking, though I took quite a licking
For now I feel fully restored
For I am that Swede, yah, that redheaded Swede from that smorgasbord

Paul lovingly extends the final word, and it seems like a cue. The club members put their instruments aside and head out to the kitchen to partake of the potluck collection of cookies, coffee, and Swedish meatballs that have been spread out by the nonmusical family members. A few remain a while to chat with the camera crew, one man showing off his new guitar and another a hardanger fiddle, an old Norwegian instrument with elaborate inlay work and a set of extra strings under the bridge to provide sympathetic vibrations.

The food is eaten, then a brief business meeting is held to outline upcoming ventures. There are festivals ahead this summer, and plans to raise money for another visit to Scandinavia. New tunes must be learned, and everyone needs to know where the next rehearsal will be held. Finally, in small groups, the club members drift out into the night. Arnie straightens up the chairs and sends the kids off to bed. Tomorrow, there is maple syrup to get in, and more work to be done on the cello he is building. And then, next month, another meeting with his fellow musicians.

For me, the Skål Club started out just as a fun thing, to get together in a home and play this Scandinavian music, and of course have lots of cookies and coffee on the side. But then it's grown. And now I hope the music that I'm playing will carry on. I think it will. All three of my children have interest in it, and we all get together and play as a family too: Mom on the piano and myself on violin, Brendan on violin, Sarah on the cello and string bass, and Mindy is just starting the violin. So I'm sure that it will go on.

◆◆◆

"We Are Family." Babes in Toyland have made the old r&b hit into an anthem of Minneapolis youth culture. At a gig at their home club, First Avenue, the audience crowds on stage, dancing and singing along.

3
Rockin' the World: BABES IN TOYLAND

Lori: *One time at practice these two birds got into the basement, remember?*

Kat: *We killed them.*

Lori: *We had these two birds flying around, and by the end of practice they were both dead.*

Kat: *Like in a coal mine or something.*

Lori: *We really didn't mean to, but it just kind of, you know...*

Kat: *It was kind of sad. They were songbirds.*

Lori Barbero is laughing. Kat Bjelland is pensive and laughing, alternately. Maureen Herman is smoking a cigarette and enjoying the story.

Babes in Toyland are sitting at a side table in Blues Alley, around the corner from First Avenue, the rock club where they headline tonight. Despite the cameras, microphones, and lights, they seem relaxed, and even amused by all the fuss. As they talk, they often sound like sisters, finishing one another's sentences and supporting each other's opinions. Like siblings, they have each fallen into a role, though they sometimes switch around: Kat is the serious, introspective one; Maureen is low-key and friendly; Lori is the loud one and the clown, breaking up the interview to show her prowess at turning a drinking straw into a whistle or, with Kat urging her on, demonstrating her ability to stuff her entire fist into her mouth.

Together, they are one of the loudest, hardest-rocking bands to come out of the Minneapolis scene.

Lori: *The band got together back in 1986, at a yard party. A garden party, Ricky Nelson, everyone was there. I was managing a band called Run Westy Run, and the drummer was selling his drums and this guy, Jim Harry, talked me into buying them, 'cause I jammed one night with them when the drummer was passed out at one of their practices. He kept saying, "You gotta get drums, you gotta get drums," so then when Bobby was selling his drums, Jim called and said "You've gotta buy them." And I've always wanted to drum, but like, jeez, I was twenty-six by then. But I bought them and they sat up in my attic for a little while. Then I met Kat and she said, "Do you know any drummers?" and I said, "Well, I have drums, but I've never really drummed before at all."*

Kat: *And I was like "Aahhhh. Perfect." Plus, I'd seen her dance and I knew she had really good rhythm by how she danced. I was like "You have drums; you have rhythm."*

Lori: *So then we started playing in my basement. That was really fun. I mean we were just jamming, and we would play a song and as soon as we were done we'd start laughing hysterically.*

It just kind of snowballed, from practicing in my basement to doing a few shows here and with this other band on the road, and kept going until I started booking tours for us. I had known so many thousands of band people that came through town—every band that came through town stayed at my house, from Nirvana to Mission of Burma, until they were big enough to get a hotel—so they helped me out because I'd helped them out, the way it should be.

In the eighties, Minneapolis had become a hot spot for alternative music. Prince had focused attention on the scene, and new bands were appearing almost daily. In fact, Kat had moved to Minneapolis simply because of its musical reputation.

I'd started playing when I was nineteen, in Portland, and I played in like three or four bands before I came here. I was pretty adamant about doing music for my life—I mean, I moved to two different states for it, from Oregon to California, then from California to Minnesota. I moved here specifically to do music, that was my whole thing. I'd worked at this club in Portland, Satyricon, and I'd see all these good bands coming through and they'd always be from here, or around the Midwest. I thought, "Well, there must be an abundance of musicians there."

It seemed like not pretentious, you know, like people who wear crazy clothes or whatever. It seemed down to earth. I'd played music in Oregon and California, and it was really competitive and they don't want you to do well. Then I came here, and it was really nice and friendly. I didn't know anybody when I came here, but I said I wanted to start a band and everybody was like, "Yeah, yeah." They pointed me in the right direction.

Lori: *Minneapolis is the kind of city that, when people move away, it has the yo-yo effect. You always come back here, because it's a real nice place to live. It's an intimate little city, a lot of people know each other, and the music scene, for the size of the city, has been very successful. I was born here, then went to high school in New York, and I came back in '79, '80, and at that point it was Hüsker Dü, the Replacements, the Suburbs, the Suicide Commandos. There's been so many bands, and not all the music has a certain sound. You know how you go from city to city, New York is real guitar-crazy-oriented, then L.A. is more g-g-g-g-g, metal, 'core, then Seattle has whatever that sound is. Minneapolis doesn't have any really specific sound, I don't think. Like Babes*

Top: Babes in Toyland onstage: (left to right) Maureen Herman, bass; Lori Barbero, drums; Kat Bjelland, guitar.
Bottom: Kat and a fan hang out backstage at First Avenue.
Inset: The Babes go bowling; Lori laughs with Kat.

in Toyland doesn't sound like Soul Asylum, Soul Asylum doesn't sound like Hüsker Dü, Hüsker Dü doesn't sound like the Replacements.

But we have like a million and one bands, 'cause in the wintertime there's really not much else to do. And we have basements here. Like in California they don't have basements and stuff like that, so it's really hard to find practice spaces. But, you know, I've got a house and there's a lot of warehouses with empty space, and it gets cold and about the only thing you can do is either be a couch potato or start a band.

Kat: You get cabin fever, so you need some kind of outlet. 'Cause when it gets all snowy you get the angst coming out. Angsta rock.

At First Avenue, the club where Lori used to work as a waitress and Kat first saw her dance, the amps are turned up high and the room is packed with jumping, shaking bodies. For a moment, the snow and ice that have paralyzed Minneapolis for the last two days are forgotten, and all is heat and motion. The fans, crowded at the foot of the stage, come from every corner of the rock world: there are studded dog collars and lumberjack shirts, wool hats and baseball caps, down jackets and T-shirts, and motorcycle leathers.

On stage, the Babes form a hypnotic triangle. On the left, Maureen rocks back and forth like a metronome, keeping time to her throbbing bass rhythm. On the right, Kat attacks her guitar, fretting the strings with a drumstick and sending out screaming high notes that bounce off the ceiling, then moving into the mike to sing a harsh, pained solo. In the back, Lori holds it all together on the drums, arms and legs flailing in impeccable, powerhouse rhythm, laughing and shouting and driving the dancers into a frenzy.

How y'all doin'? she yells at the crowd. They shout back at her, and she throws back her head and laughs. Y'all, y'all, y'all—I just spent two weeks in Texas. Y'all.

With a crashing rim-shot, she kicks off another song, shouting two lines over and over, with Kat adding a second voice:

Where were you? I thought that I knew
What could I do but think about you?
Where were you? I thought that I knew
What could I do but think about you?

Most of the time, the words are lost in an abrasive wall of noise, a huge, pulsing mass of bass and guitar, broken up by the click and bang of the drums. The drums are the most melodic instrument onstage, rocketing around the lyric while the guitar casts out wailing sheets of sound and the bass drones underneath. This is live rock 'n' roll, a wild animal that no recording will ever capture. After a decade on the scene, the Babes rule. They have a tight, unified sound, but it is the energy that makes them special. Once they start playing, it is impossible to keep still, and the local fans swear that they had that excitement and power from the first time they played in public. Maureen, who joined the band four years ago replacing original bass player Michelle Leon, still remembers what it was like.

I was at the first couple of shows they did and, being in the audience, it was just like oohh!—the cool thing was they just played, and there was so much energy, and nobody else was doing what they were doing. And especially women. It was really great.

The Babes' early audience was largely male, college boys drawn by the novelty of three chicks rocking out, but soon they spawned a host of young, female fans who would come to be dubbed riot-grrrls. The riot-grrrl movement, a loose network of fans, bands and homemade 'zines, was briefly a media sensation, with cover stories and photo spreads (many featuring Courtney Love, who was at one time Kat's best friend and briefly played with her and Lori before leaving to start her own group, Hole). The press attention largely missed the point, though. The Babes' success, and that of bands from L7 to Shonen Knife, was less a trend than a new reality, a recognition that the world had changed and women could rock as hard as men—maybe harder.

It was not exactly a new idea. Fanny had played some pretty straight-ahead rock in the 1970s, and in the 1980s the Runaways' punk onslaught moved things into high gear. Lori will even go back to the 1960s, tracing her musical aspirations to the girl-band cartoon "Josie and the Pussycats." Still, the press thrives on trends, and "women in rock" was first a flavor of the month, then of the year. By now, it has become the flavor of the decade, without ever being accepted as totally normal. As a result, the Babes have regularly been damned with faint praise, and Maureen expresses their shared impatience at being cheered more for their gender than their music.

After nine years, people still are surprised that women are all in a band together. Which is weird, 'cause all the guys are in bands together, so—there's something totally off about it, because a new band will come out with women in it and they'll focus on the gender issue instead of what they sound like, and lump people together.

Lori: *Yeah, it's always, "They sound like so-and-so," another female band. It's never "They sound like themselves."*

Kat: *They keep you in a corner. But it's always been the same. They've been*

surprised by that stuff since Billie Holiday. They're just so shocked we can do music. Especially rock 'n' roll music, I guess, but just that we can play instruments.

Lori: *Like it was a novelty thing. But well, the world is male-dominated, that's all there is to it; they always have the upper hand. But it is changing, even as far as audience goes. I mean, I've been going to rock shows for umfmfm years, and when I started there just used to be a few token women, but little by little now it's gotten a lot, lot more cool. They always used to be in the back, and now women will be right up in front, right up against the stage all night long.*

Kat: *They get mad sometimes when the guys try to push them away. Remember the woman that beat that guy with that umbrella?*

Lori: *Oh yeah. This woman kept going on stage, to stage dive, and he kept like pushing her away and she just took this umbrella, and by about the fifth time he had jumped up there it was completely bent and broken in like five pieces. She was dressed in a nurse's uniform.*

Maureen: *That's one of the really great things of being in a band, seeing how excited these girls get, like "Wow! I can do this!" and the next day they want to start bands.*

Lori: *It's pretty neat, because everyone's not like, "Oh, I can't do it, I can't do it"—too afraid. Everyone's getting bolder. We get a lot of mail from all over the world, and we get so many women writing to us saying that they've started playing an instrument because of us or they've started doing writing or just doing something artistic. It's really neat. We have probably the best fans ever. They are really intelligent, young, and write us*

Lori Barbero plays drums; Kat Bjelland rocks out (Maureen Herman in background).

Babes
In Toyland

letters like, "Hi I'm fifteen, and I don't care if my parents don't think I should play drums because of my gender." At fifteen and fourteen and stuff like that—you just read it and go "Maaan. There are some really cool people out there."

The Babes are natural role models, because they are totally true to the music's homemade, do-it-yourself ideal. Aside from a friend or relative showing them how to hold their instruments, they are self-taught, and they developed their style as they went along, following the rock muse wherever it led them. Maureen, for example, took a few guitar lessons, but never tried playing bass till she joined a band.

I think that's the best way to learn, because you don't have any prejudgments about what you're playing. You're not self-conscious about it, so you just go ahead, try things. Part of the reason we sounded like we did was it was raw, you're playing dadadadada, 'cause you're not sure what else to play. And then you just get better at playing and songwriting.

Kat: *It's like you say to yourself, "I would like to hear music that sounds more like this." And then it's like "Well, I guess we'll have to create it then, 'cause it's not out there." The bottom line is if you can make yourself happy. That's the hardest thing. Because we're pretty picky.*

The Babes music has taken them further than they ever expected. There have been two albums on Warner/Reprise, the sort of major label that few punk bands ever get near, and a book on their lives and music from Random House. They tour Europe and Japan, as well as all over the United States, and Lori has even moved on to producing other local bands on her own recently formed record label. Still, she makes no bones about the continuing difficulties of the rock 'n' roll life.

We're doing pretty well; the snowball's big now, and we've been rolling and rolling and rolling. Not in the dough, though, just snow. We're getting snow jobs all over the place. You know, everyone thinks it's all fun, but it's really hard. It's very monotonous when you're on the road. It's a lot of organizing, and a lot of no sleep, and a lot of not being really able to take care of yourself the way you'd like to. And, I don't know, just a lot of work—getting to the venue after driving five to six hours average every day, you know, and setting up. And what it boils down to is about playing an hour set.

Kat: *That's how worth it it is. I mean in music, it's like you're only there an hour, maybe an hour and ten minutes, and it's like "See what we go through to play the one show?" One hour out of twenty-four hours a day.*

As soon as Kat steps onstage, it is obvious what she means. The tiredness and hesitancy fall away, and she is transformed. Silhouetted by the colored lights, with the sound system blowing them up into giants, the Babes are on top of the world.

I live it high cost of livin' tell me why give it all
Inside you gotta head high one size fits all
Head ride you decide
Sweet sweet ride
Sweet sweet ride

The lyric is all but incomprehensible in the sonic barrage. When the words do come through, the language can get as harsh as the music, a fierce show of strength that occasionally breaks to reveal a pained vulnerability. The music, though, is the real message, and the listeners react to it with their bodies. Lori, who often speaks of being inspired by the traditional, spiritual pulse of African and Native American drumming, might call them a tribe, and that is how the band welcomes them in the set's only cover song, a celebratory, all-embracing sing-along of Sister Sledge's disco anthem, "We Are Family." With the first notes, dozens of people surge up onto the stage, around the band members. One bearded and wool-hatted fan grabs a drumstick and clashes along on Lori's cymbal. For a moment, the divide between band and audience is gone, and the room is full of Babes of all sizes, shapes, and genders.

We're so lucky, Lori says. *I really like the level we've always maintained. I mean, we have our fans, people come to see us, and we weren't just like this huge thing that blew up one day and then we would just be gone. We just play, we do what we want to do and no one bothers us, and that's just really great.*

Kat: *When we don't practice I get really uptight and depressed. And then, when we practice, like as soon as we start to play, ahhh, I'm not depressed about anything anymore. It's an emotional release. It's good for you. Everyone should do something like that.*

Lori: *It's a form of release. Like, some people box, some people break windows. My dad was a marathon runner. But just playing drums... You know, most of the people I know that sing pretty songs, like, "la la la la," I'm sorry, but I think they are total bitches. I would not ever want to hang out with them. It's like, "Here's my chance to pretend I'm really nice," so they play that music. But just because you're abrasive and loud, that doesn't mean that you're angry and you hate men, or you hate people and want to kill everyone. It's very therapeutic to be able to release things, and that's what we do. All three of us are very nice women, and we enjoy what we are doing. And we are going to rock the world!*

◆◆◆

Soul Asylum rehearse in their Minneapolis warehouse space.
Inset: (left to right) Dave Pirner, guitar; Sterling Campbell, drums; Dan Murphy, guitar.

Soul Asylum
The Birth of a Twin Cities Rock Band

Minneapolis and St. Paul have been full of young rock bands from the 1950s on, but the scene bubbled underground, rarely surfacing in a way that brought it to the attention of out-of-staters. The explosion came in the early 1980s, when Prince stormed his way to the top of the charts. Suddenly, the music business focused on the Twin Cities, and found a wealth of bands there, waiting to be discovered. In the late 1980s, the Replacements hit nationally, then Hüsker Dü and Soul Asylum.

As befits people on a scene that existed for so long outside the national view, the Twin Cities musicians are a close-knit bunch, going to each other's gigs, partying, and hanging out together. Dave Pirner of Soul Asylum shows up to see Babes In Toyland at First Avenue, to chat and wish them luck, and when they talk about friends and bandmates it sounds as if they are discussing not a musical scene but an extended family.

Today, Soul Asylum are national stars, but they still rehearse in an old warehouse in a run-down neighborhood, alongside the new crop of young players. Their music has changed with the years, the songwriting and arrangements becoming more sophisticated, but in between tunes, lead singer and songwriter Dave Pirner and guitarist Dan Murphy recall what it was like when they were starting out as just another bunch of enthusiastic Midwestern teenagers.

Dave: *At first, you hear things on the radio and you think that's where music comes from. Then I remember the day that I started discovering that there's all these local bands playing around. You look at that, and you go, "Oh, that's how you do it."*

Dan: *I was very influenced by a lot of the bands that I saw: Suicide Commandos and Curtis A and the Fingerprints and the Wallets and the Suburbs and then later there's the Replacements and Hüsker Dü. It's always been a really thriving music city and I think you soak a lot of it up whether you want to or not.*

Dave: *And it's kind of a revelation when you're fifteen: Wow, you can just do this here. You don't need anybody else. You don't need to sit around and wait for the guy from Hollywood to call you up and say, "I've got an advance for you," so you can buy some gear. You go out and get a job and buy an amp, and then you just go down in the basement and set your stuff up and have fun.*

Dan: *We spent our formative years practicing in our bass player's mom's garage. We were there for two or three years. And you know, we didn't have any big aspirations or anything, it was just a hell of a lot of fun. We'd just get together and piss off the neighbors. At first we were called Loud Fast Rules, and that's what we were trying to do, be louder and faster than everyone else.*

Dave: *When we were starting out, you know, our goals were so immediate that by the time we actually got our first gig we were like, "Wow, this is it!" We really felt pretty much like that was as far as you went. And then, just organically and gradually, five more people came to the show every time we played, and here we are.*

Dan: *I remember the first show we ever did, we played at this Sons of Norway lodge, which is kind of like—I don't know what kind of rituals go on in that hall, and I don't think I'd want to know. It was kind of like an Elk's Club situation. And we did our first show and the police came and busted it up. It was perfect.*

4

Folk Songs in the City: JOHN KOERNER

This duck goes into a bar, sits down on a bar stool. The bartender comes up, says "Can I help you?"

The duck says, "Yeah. You got any raisins?"

The bartender says, "Raisins? No, we don't have no raisins. This is a bar. Forget it."

So the duck goes away. Comes back the next day, sits down on the stool. Bartender says, "What would you like?"

Duck says, "You got any raisins?"

Bartender says, "Hey, I told you yesterday, we don't have any raisins. This is a bar. Forget it."

Duck goes away. Comes back on the third day, sits down on the stool. Bartender says, "What would you like?"

Duck says, "You got any raisins?"

Bartender says, "OK, that's it." He says, "If you come back here one more time and ask for raisins, I'm gonna nail your bill to the wall."

Next day the duck comes into the bar, sits down on the stool. Bartender says, "What would you like?"

Duck says, "You got any nails?"

Bartender says, "No."

Duck says, "Oh, good... Got any raisins?"

It is around eleven in the morning, and the winter sunlight is dimly visible through the small window in the door of Palmer's. Other than that faint glow, it might as well be eleven at night, or three in the morning. The room is dark and quiet, wood walls and a few tables, a long mahogany bar with a few early customers drinking their breakfast. John Koerner is behind the bar, filling the sparse orders, greeting the regulars, and telling an occasional joke. Koerner's speaking voice is soft, with a wry edge and a typically midwestern fondness for understatement. He enjoys talking with the customers, but can also sit quietly, drifting off into his own world.

Around noon, another bartender comes in and Koerner moves around to the other side of the bar, settling down behind a blackberry brandy. In the background, people wander around, reorganizing the room for an afternoon concert. Palmer's no longer has an entertainment license, but it is very much Koerner's home turf, so for filming purposes it is closing down for the afternoon and all the regular customers are being invited for a private party featuring Koerner and the cream of Minneapolis's folk sidemen.

In Minneapolis, and among folk and blues fans around the world, "Spider" John Koerner is a legend *(I got that nickname 'cause I'm one of these long, skinny guys; I'm pretty close to being the skinniest guy, height for weight, in town).* In 1962 or thereabouts, with Dave "Snaker" Ray and Tony "Little Sun" Glover, he formed one of the defining groups of the early acoustic blues revival, Koerner, Ray, and Glover. Other young musicians of the time, including his partners, tended to take the old blues masters as models, singing classic songs from the 1920s and 1930s, complete with the original guitar arrangements and vocal inflections. Koerner was different. He developed a weird, choppy rhythm that was instantly recognizable, and wrote quirky songs that, though they clearly drew on the tradition, were utterly his own. He has gone through a lot of changes in the intervening years, but continues to make his own way, disregarding trends and fashions. Sometimes he even disregards music, devoting himself to amateur astronomy, or just hanging around Palmer's trading stories.

Yeah, I'm not so sure that I am a musician. It's one thing that I did. I've had numerous things happen to me where one day I was one way and the next day I was a little different, and music was one of them. As to why I became a musician in the first place, I'm not quite sure, except that it projects you out into the world. You get to hang out with folks, you get to—if you're lucky—impress folks, including the young women possibly. You party around and have fun playing with your friends, and so on and so forth. I think a lot of musicians get into it that way. I was kind of a lonesome polecat before that.

Koerner was born in Rochester, New York, and came to Minneapolis to go to college. *I came here in '56, and had studied for about a year and half, and one day some guy invited me to listen to some folk music, which he both played and played on records. I was nineteen at the time, and had never thought about music before particularly. So I borrowed a guitar from him, and a Burl Ives folk song book, and within two weeks I could play a few tunes and in six months I played my first job at the engineering fraternity over at the University. That was the beginning of the music roller coaster and the end of my formal schooling.*

That time, the early sixties or late fifties, was the beginning of everything that came later. Exactly why that happened, I don't know. My own theory is that things were

John Koerner and an all-star band of Minneapolis folk stalwarts perform at Palmer's: (left to right) Tony Glover, harmonica; Willie Murphy, keyboards; "Spider" John Koerner, guitar; Peter Ostroushko, mandolin; Dakota Dave Hull, guitar.

a little stiff up until that point, and the loosening up was beginning to happen. And of course, it turned into an explosion by the time it hit the mid-sixties and the seventies. I think part of it was that people were tapping into roots. It developed considerably beyond that, of course, but the folk music for sure, and the blues, were tapping into roots and also a certain simplicity. It got complicated afterwards, but that's what happened in the beginning.

In Minneapolis, there was a core of folk people that wound up being associated with Dinkytown, a small area on the other side of the river. There were people like Dave Ray and Bob Dylan, among others, who became future performers, and a whole bunch of other people: some artists, some musicians, some poets, one thing and another. For me, Minneapolis was a fairly healthy scene and it became home to me. If I hadn't been here, I don't even know if I would have been playing. I think there is an attitude here that you don't get on the East Coast or the West Coast, which I appreciated, and which it's handy to carry with you wherever you go. The Midwest is, well, it's a little rough out here and a little lonesome compared to the Coasts. I don't know exactly how to put the attitude. We know we can put up with these damn winters, for one thing. And a lot of folks like to fish and hunt and all that business, and it's just got a feeling of its own.

I don't know how much of that got into the music, but I'm sure it filters in. The hippie days here, for example, we went through a period of the most interesting bunch of people that I ever saw. We had some very funny things happen, and all quite good-natured. That is one of the things around here that has usually been the case, is that there's a good-naturedness to it.

Anyway, I started out in kind of a general sense as a folk singer, but fairly quickly I ran into Dave Ray, who was interested in the blues. I listened to some of his records and got interested in that myself and later on we hooked up with Tony Glover and we worked on that almost exclusively after a point. When I was listening to the records, I found many of them really sensuous and very poetic, and there were also quite a number of very interesting and sometimes charming blues guys. All of them had some kind of moniker or nickname, whether it was Tampa Red or Blind Lemon or Lightnin' or like that, and what I realized was that if you want to be like those guys you gotta sort of do like those guys. So, although I learned some of their songs, I thought it was also necessary to live the life a little bit and to write your own songs, and that's what I tried to work on.

◆

It is mid-afternoon, and Palmer's has gradually filled up until there is hardly room to breathe. The crowd is amazingly varied. ***It's pretty funky in here,*** Koerner said earlier on. ***We get a lot of people who like to drink and a lot of people who aren't working at the moment. And at night it fills up with other kinds of folks, people from many other countries in the world. We have a group of Eritreans who like to hang out here, for example. We get a number of languages floating through on a daily basis. And for new people that come into the area it's a bit of a testing ground. We try to educate them, as to their manners and how to be interesting and interested. It doesn't always work, but that's the type of place it is.***

The group of musicians surrounding Koerner is only slightly less varied than the clientele. There is his old partner Tony Glover, painfully thin with wispy curls, hunched over his harmonicas. Bearded and white-haired Willie Murphy, a local blues-rock legend, is playing keyboards. After the breakup of Koerner, Ray, and Glover, Murphy and Koerner made one legendary album, 1969's *Running, Jumping, Standing Still,* which merged Koerner's folk-blues with Murphy's New Orleans-flavored psychedelic rock, and the pianist still adds an electric edge to Koerner's sound. On strings are two of the Cities' premier instrumentalists, guitarist Dakota Dave Hull, who has several solo albums, and mandolin and fiddle virtuoso Peter Ostroushko, who along with his solo work plays with the St. Paul Chamber Orchestra under the direction of Bobby McFerrin. Hull and Ostroushko had a duo some twenty years ago, then became nationally known in the house band for *A Prairie Home Companion,* as well as ubiquitous studio players for the local acoustic scene.

Koerner makes sure everybody is in tune with his battered twelve-string guitar, then kicks off the first song, his feet tapping out a shuffling beat:

Ain't no use to sit and cry,
Sail away, ladies, sail away
You'll be an angel by and by,
Sail away, ladies, sail away

Don't you rock'em daddy-o
Don't you rock'em daddy-o
Don't you rock'em, oh, no
Sail away, ladies, sail away

Koerner still has the same off-kilter rhythmic feel he developed in the sixties, and the same unique phrasing. The other musicians, though more technically proficient on their instruments, look to him as the leader, and fall in line behind his spare and funky guitar lines. And yet, the songs are a long way from the blues. The sea chanty segues into a classic cowboy song, then a hobo waltz.

In 1972 I got into one of those change situations, I guess you would call it, and I decided to quit playing music forever. That lasted about a year, but when I started up again I didn't want to go back and do the blues exactly. I didn't know exactly what I did want to do, but there were some folk music books sitting around the house that I was looking through one day, and I started realizing that some of these traditional American folk songs were very good songs, with interesting ideas, if not on the surface, then just below the surface. So my thought was to take my guitar style, which I'd learned from playing bluesy stuff, simplify it somewhat, and lay it over these folk songs. I picked out as many as I thought were interesting, and worked them up in my own way. At the time I was living in Denmark and I got hooked up with a couple of Danish guys, a washboard player and a harmonica player, and we had the American Folk Band. We played around Denmark for about three years and then I brought that back over here.

It was quite strange for some of the audiences when I came back, because they didn't know what the hell I was up to. I can remember the first job I played over here when I played just the folk music. I was used to doing it by this time, but the audience was not used to it and I realized after a while these people are looking at me, you know, like, "What are you doing?!" But I stuck with it, and it got more and more interesting and more solid. And, after ten years or so, it started to pay off pretty good, and I wound up being one of the few people who still does traditional folk music.

All these songs, they're very good songs. No one knows who wrote most of them, and they've been around for a long time and worked over by the public in general, and it's interesting because you wind up getting an idea of the attitudes and ideas and experiences of people from that other time. That, to me, is one of the most interesting things about it. But also, these songs survived because they are good poetry and good stories. And there are plenty of them, so you can choose them according to your own taste.

I came from a background that has nothing to do with folksongs, and have leapt into it as sort of a rogue, but I maintain at this point that I do understand it, not necessarily in an intellectual way, but in a way that makes people feel it. I decided to go right by all the ways that other people do this music, and treat it like my own territory. Part of the idea was to put some balls into it, so that instead of being kind of a coffeehouse-style thing, it would be something that you could boogie out a little bit, and make it interesting to people. I decided that I'm gonna punch this out my own way, and then people, when they hear it, they're gonna feel the folkiness of it and the energy of it, and the profoundness of the material.

In a sense, it's similar to something like Cajun music, where you've got a traditional thing, but it's not for just sitting around quietly, listening. I learn most of my stuff in the bars, and you've got to punch it out in the bars, and that picks people up and livens them up. I'm trying to not put them to sleep; I'm trying to have them feel the power of these songs.

You know, I'm a little lazy at learning things. I never worked really hard at trying to become a fancy instrumentalist, so I wound up relying on some simple things. It's like a pitcher: I've got a few kind of simple pitches that I can throw, and I just try to mix those up. I play mostly off the chords rather than trying to work up and down the fingerboard a lot, so it all comes out with a certain flavor to it. Then, as far as the singing goes, it began to change a few years ago. I don't know what you'd call it–I learned it from playing with Willie a little bit—it's not jazz exactly, but it's like constantly improvising the melody and the phrasing, and, once again, it is done in a very simple way. I'm not an expert at it by any means, but it has all sort of managed to blend together into something that seems to work reasonably well.

As for my sense of time, some of that comes from trying to imitate Leadbelly and the old blues guys, and I'm also kind of heavy on the foot when I play. But I also learned how to enjoy playing with the timing, to get that thing going so it makes it rock back and forth a little bit. I don't know how that worked out, but somehow I got a little bouncy beat that seems to be somewhat unusual and somewhat effective.

As he warms up, Koerner begins to slide in some of his own songs, both old favorites like "Ramblin' Hobo" and the surreal murder ballad, "Creepy John," and new pieces like "Some People Say" and "Everybody's Going for the Money." Especially in the newer pieces, Koerner has created a singular blend of tradition and innovation. The music has the same choppy lilt as his other material, but the lyrics wander in odd directions, musing on the foibles and inconsistencies of modern life in ragged lines that sometimes rhyme and sometimes just go their own way. Odd as they get, though, the new songs dovetail perfectly with the old folk material.

In the writing, I just look for anything that starts to interest me, and then I go for it. When I'm writing, I always think about how somebody might hear it—somebody current—and whether it would be interesting to them or not. And I do sometimes try to make a point of putting in things that maybe are not so much from the old days but are a little bit on the simpler side. I like to put nature in there sometimes, and some quietness, rather than the heaviness that we're struggling with all the time these days.

There was a moment, during his pairing with Murphy, when Koerner seemed poised for some sort of folk-rock stardom, joining the host of other folk-raised singers who were crossing over into the charts. Instead he veered off into his own musical pathway, and he has never looked back. In music business terms, his career has been disorganized to the point of disaster, but measured by the cheers and applause of the crowd in Palmer's he is a complete success, and he seems to have no regrets.

I was never built to be a star; I'm sure of that. Right now, I could use some more work and a good booking agent, but, as far as the general thing goes, I've played it in a pretty casual way and some interesting things have happened along the way. It's been an amazing experience to go through all of this, and I've been able to mix it up with all kinds of people. I shook hands with John Lennon in Soho, and I had wild experiences with crazy, funky people in a number of different countries and so on and so forth. It has just definitely taken me around from one thing to another, so in that way I'm satisfied.

As for the music, I mostly only play when I have to. I've been somewhat dormant, which is another word for lazy, over the past few years, though actually if you write up a list of things I've done, it doesn't look all that bad. I spend some time up in the country, where I've got a shack in the woods. I'm interested in amateur astronomy, so I spend some time studying that, both indoors and outdoors. And the rest of it is whatever happens.

John relaxes in Dave Hull's living room.

Everybody's Going for the Money

John Koerner

Well, everybody's going for the money
They're thinking it makes the world go 'round
This old world keeps turning on and on, yeah
When you're laying underneath the ground

Now, somebody's got a hold on you
They got a hold on your everyday life
A hold on your friends and your relatives too
Yeah, they got a hold on your children and your wife

Hey, they sell you on the television
And they sell you on the radio-o
They'll sell you any old way that they can
And they'll come knocking on your front door

I think I will buy me a wonderful car
Yes, and a TV and a stereo-o
I will drive and I'll watch and I will listen all the time
I won't have to think anymore

Yep, now that we got everything that we want
I'll tell you something you might know
It won't be long until this way of life is gone
It's better that way, oh don't you know

Aw, why sing a song about money?
Why sing about anything at all?
Hey, take your life in hand, now, and steal it from them, man
'Fore they send you to the wall

Yes, and everybody's thinking about the money
Thinking it makes the world go 'round
This old world keeps a-turning on and on
When you're laying underneath the ground

5
Singing the Message: SOUNDS OF BLACKNESS

In the beginning was the beat
And the beat was the rhythm of God
And the rhythm of God is the harmony of humanity
And where there is harmony there is peace
We are the drum
We are the drum
Africa to America
We are the drum
Teach!

There has always been a very active, albeit small, African-American community in the Twin Cities and it's always been very musically prolific, with a lot of talent: r&b, blues, jazz, gospel. I mean, Duke and Count were frequently here. This used to be a real jazz town. As for r&b, there were a line of groups that preceded Prince, that Prince used to sneak into the clubs to see, groups like the Amazers, Maurice McGuinness and the Blazers, Showtime Part 1 and 2, Midwest Express—I could go on and on. Blues musicians as well, and musicians and vocalists in the gospel tradition. Minneapolis could have been a mini Motown.

The thing is, being such a small community, one of two things happens. Either you become totally assimilated into the general culture or you really cleave unto your own. I think that here the latter happened much more than the former. And that's why, when people say "The Sounds of Blackness—with that name and philosophy you'd think you'd be out of Harlem or Chicago or Watts or somewhere," I think, no, for those reasons we emanated from Minnesota.

Gary Hines is a professorial presence. Though his black T-shirt reveals the bulging arms of an amateur bodybuilder, wire-framed glasses give his face a scholarly cast, and his delivery is careful, precise, and even a bit stiff. He is sitting in the carpeted basement office that serves as mission control for Sounds of Blackness, the ensemble of which he is founder and musical director. A Grammy statuette is on the desk behind him, and the walls are

Gary Hines, founder and leader of Sounds of Blackness, directs a rehearsal from his place at the keyboards.

lined with concert posters in several languages and a variety of award plaques.

My interest in music started back in my hometown, Yonkers, New York, at age five. My brothers and I began drum lessons, military drum style, at the Samuel H. Dow Number 1017 American Legion Post, and after a couple of years began marching in parades with the Sam Dow Fife and Drum Corps. My family moved to Minneapolis in late 1963, and I went into junior high school and expanded to more melodic percussion: timpani, marimba, that kind of thing. In my school there was a stage band, a jazz band, a symphonic orchestra—a wide range of music. Then we had our funk/r&b band on the side. Plus, my background in New York included my mother being a jazz singer, and doo-wop on the streets, and the old jukebox in the basement of my father's upholstery shop. All of that eclectic range of music came together and served as a foundation for what was later to become Sounds of Blackness.

The way the group started was that in 1969, a gentleman who is still a member, Russell Nighten, was a student at Macalester College here in St. Paul. Macalester had embarked on a very ambitious recruitment program for students of color, called E.E.O., Expanded Educational Opportunities, and the students formulated a number of different organizations. There was a political group, B.L.A.C., the Black Liberation Affairs Committee; there was a theatrical group called Black Arts Midwest; and there was a seventy-voice singing ensemble called the Macalester Black Voices. Russell was heading that group up, and in 1971, in my sophomore year, he approached me about assuming the directorship, because the director at the time transferred to another school.

They were excellent, even back then, and I was very honored. My goal with the group was to continue the traditions of Duke Ellington and Quincy Jones: to establish a legitimate black music ensemble that performed the entire spectrum of African-American music in its proper context. I wanted to do everything from West African music to field hollers, work songs, spirituals, blues, jazz, gospel, reggae, ragtime, r&b, hip-hop, jazz, rock 'n' roll—the full spectrum. Because it's all a family of music that emanated from an experience: You can't understand the "Glory Hallelujah" of the gospel without knowing about the pain of the blues. And that's the meaning of the name: Each style of the music is a unique sound of blackness, and collectively they are the Sounds of Blackness.

The Sounds sang around the Twin Cities for two decades before getting their break. They became known for their community shows, a regular Christmas program, and an annual concert dedicated to Martin Luther King, Jr., but never found a record company or promoter who shared their unique

Even at a rehearsal, the Sounds of Blackness keep the energy level high.

vision. Then, in 1990, they were signed by Jimmy Jam and Terry Lewis, the Minneapolis production team that had hit with Janet Jackson and other r&b acts, becoming the first group on the team's new Perspective Records label. Their first album, *The Evolution of Gospel,* won a Grammy and spawned two hit singles, "Optimistic" and "The Pressure." They followed up with a Christmas album, also nominated for a Grammy, then 1994's *Africa to America: The Journey of the Drum,* which ranged from a cappella spirituals to rap, included the hit single "I Believe," and was a fixture on the gospel charts for months. Now, they have just released *Time for Healing,* are freshly back from a tour of Japan, and are preparing to head off to Europe.

In a Minneapolis rehearsal studio, Hines puts the group through its paces. Though the recording ensemble swells to thirty singers and ten instrumentalists, on tour it strips down to a compact seventeen players and singers. They crowd the stage, while Hines stands in front, his back to where the audience would be, directing from behind an electric keyboard. He raises his hands, and the group sings a warm, a cappella chord. Then, as his hands crisply mark time, the singers break into a classically harmonized spiritual.

Hold on, jus' a li'l while longer
Hold on, jus' a li'l while longer
Hold on, jus' a li'l while longer
Everything will be alright

Fight on, jus' a li'l while longer
Pray on, jus' a li'l while longer
Sing on, jus' a li'l while longer
Everything will be alright
Everything will be alright

With all the musical styles they have sampled, gospel remains at the heart of the Sounds' work. It is as a gospel group that they are best known, and in some ways the most surprising thing about their success has been their ability to persuade the gospel audience to accept their nongospel admixtures. That audience has often rejected artists, from Sam Cooke to the Staple Singers, whom it saw as trying to cash in on secular trends, but the Sounds have so far managed to escape censure even as they venture into such forbidden areas as blues and rap.

Top: Coré Cotton gets ready to shout. Bottom: Carl Pertile grabs a moment's rest.

During a break in the rehearsal, several of the younger singers sit on the

stage and talk about their music, and its meaning in their lives. Billy Steele is the Sounds' assistant director, and he says that, to him, one of the group's greatest gifts was the bridge it provided between gospel and the whole continuum of black music.

When I was coming up, I always thought it was strange that in high school, when I was learning barbershop quartet and other European songs and choir, nobody would tell me there was nothing wrong with that, but then when I wanted to hear the blues or other songs that actually had a very strong message to them, somebody was there to tell me that that wasn't right and you were not no longer a Christian if you listened to it. That separation is just part of a mentality that's not quite understanding where we come from. And when you start learning where we come from, then you can go somewhere. And that's what the Sounds of Blackness have done. We haven't left the church. The church is one of our forefathers of all music. And all the music we do, we're singing out of a whole positive thing and it's a feel-good music. When you hear the music we want you to feel good. And we do really want to offer a solution to people; to all of the drug problems, alcoholism and all those things.

Coré Cotton is an entertainment lawyer who is also one of the group's principle songwriters and most impressive soloists. She has been leaning forward, listening and waiting for a pause:

I don't mean to jump in, but my emphasis is neither whether it's quoteunquote "Christian" music or "secular" or "sacred" or however you want to classify it. My focus is "What's the message?" Whether it's a message with a beat, whether it's a message with somber tone, whether it's a message and you're jumping up and down and waving your hands, the important thing is that there's a positive message. You have to reach people wherever they are, whether they're in a church, whether they're on the street, whether they're in the club. So it's great to have a different medium and various forms of music, and it doesn't bother me that people say that that's secular or whatever, as long as they're listening and communicating and talking about it.

Carl Pertile studied to be an opera singer before beoming a Grand Champion winner on *Star Search,* then joining the Sounds.

You know, if most of those people knew the roots of the African music, and the African God, and spirit and music—all of that works together. It's all intertwining. The dance and the music, it's all one thing. It's not something like "You sing gospel, so you can't do this." Our lyrics, what we represent is never "Let me lay you down and take you to bed." It's always "Hold on, change is coming," "Feel the spirit inside," "God cares." We're not giving any bad vibes as far as, like, some things on the r&b scene. I mean, the music we do is r&b, but the message we give is universal. It's love. It's "Everybody, let's come together and get on the love train."

Gary cues the drummer, the horns punch out a tight riff, and the Sounds are in motion. Though it is just a rehearsal and everyone is in T-shirts and street clothes, their choreography is as tight as if they were on stage in front of a packed house. Hands move in synchrony, hips sway, and Coré and Carl step forward to trade off lead vocals.

Brothers, sisters
Everybody
Time to listen
Love is calling you
But are you down?
Will you share your love
And spread it around?

I know you feel it
I know you hear it
Why don't you listen
To your spirit
You know it's calling
Stop your stalling
No need to fear it
It's just your spirit

The whole group comes in, swaying and singing together:

Spirit
Feel the spirit inside
Spirit
Feel the spirit inside

Coré is wailing, bending at the waist, her eyes scrunched closed and her mouth wide enough to swallow the microphone. Offstage, she is petite and quiet, but when she lets loose she hits like a hurricane.

I guess the best way for me to put it is, I have a small frame, but I have big things going on inside. I sing from within. It's from my soul. You know, that's just the way it is. Of course, sometimes it's more difficult than others. Particularly when we're traveling and having to do a show every night, it's more difficult. Our, uh, esteemed director often emphasizes the craft, the art of using your voice and not having to push so hard, and pacing yourself. I'm still learning that, but for the most part I just sing what I feel. I feel a lot—I have a big heart—and what I feel inside I push out.

What is most striking about the rehearsal is the extent to which all the singers and musicians seem to be totally engaged in what they are doing. There are moments of show biz—the singers present a practiced goodbye wave at the end of what would normally be their closing song—but the rehearsal is clearly anything but a chore. When Gary takes a break, going outside to make a business call, the singers stay onstage and work on their harmonies. Then, as he stays out, they begin to get silly, switching tunes in midchorus and laughing at the impromptu medley they are creating. "God Cares" mutates into a rocking version of "This Train is Bound for Glory," and the singers bunch together in a circle so that they can hear one another. Then they are jamming on a one-word riff from "Optimistic," the group's theme song. The choreography has fallen apart, and they are dancing to their own rhythm, but the sound is still impeccably tight, the instrumentalists watching the singers and following every vocal cue.

The Sounds are acting more like a family than a professional ensemble. When friends show up, hugs are exchanged and babies are handed over to be kissed. And always, whatever else is happening, the music keeps going on. If the singers stop, then the guitarist and keyboard player go to work on a riff that might fit into a new song. When the instrumentalists take a break, a quartet of singers tries out an a cappella harmony.

The Sounds love what they do, and the ability it gives them to communicate their message to the world. A century later, they are carrying on the work of the first African-American college group, the Fisk Jubilee Singers, who took to the road both to demonstrate the richness of their tradition and to be visible role models for a community. Onstage, they are funky and soulful, but also impeccably dressed and rehearsed. Offstage, many of the performers are successful professionals: engineers, lawyers, or college professors. Now, with the success of their albums and tours, they are reaching out to a global audience, but they seem unfazed by any of the growing pressures and responsibilities. Indeed, Gary will say that this is the day for which he has been preparing ever since he took command of the group twenty-five years ago.

We're often asked the question, did we have any idea that Sounds of Blackness would be blessed in the way that we have, with this level of visibility and and international acclaim. And actually, the answer is yes. We didn't know that it would happen, but we always believed that it could and would. Back in earlier days, we would sit around after rehearsals and talk about what it would be like when—not if—we would travel overseas, when we would be blessed to get a recording contract and win a Grammy and all those kind of things.

What gave us that kind of confidence was just faith: Faith in God, and faith in the rightness and goodness and correctness of what we were doing. Because we always say what comes from the heart reaches the heart. And, you know, awards and all of those things are fine, but they're really very secondary to the kinds of testimony that we get from people when we go different places. I mean, we have perfect strangers come up to us and tell us that a friend or a relative heard our music and it turned their life around from being strung out on drugs or hung up in a gang. Or it helped them through school, helped them between jobs—real everyday things. So, you know, Grammys and Soul Train Awards and all that, they're tremendous blessings that we're eternally grateful for, but nothing beats having people come up to you first hand and telling you, face to face, apart from any cameras or the public view, that your music and your efforts have had a positive influence on their lives.

◆ ◆ ◆

6

Strangers in a Strange Land: WANG CHONG LOR & STUDENTS

Wang Chong Lor's mantelpiece looks like a family shrine. There are pictures of children and relatives regularly spaced along it, and more pictures hanging above, alternating with spread, ceremonial fans. There are also instruments: the arching reed pipes of a qeej, and a variety of flutes and Jew's harps. Lor takes a slim wooden flute down from its place and begins to play. The sound is oddly captivating, wisps of gentle melody broken by tonal shifts that are startling to the Western ear. Through a translator, Lor explains that the Hmong language itself is tonal, and that the notes he plays are also words. As he explains its meaning, the delicate flute tune takes on a new poignancy.

The sun is shining
The birds are singing
And I am so lonely,
Because I came over to this country
I'm here without family, no cousin, no brothers,
Today I am so lonely, and that is why I came
I came to look for you,
To see whether you can take my loneliness away.
I am so lonely in this country,
What about you?

This instrument is a courtship instrument, for talking between young men and young women. So all, always talk about love. When you are coming to court a young woman, when you blow this instrument, then the village that you go into won't think of you as a complete stranger. They would identify that you are coming to their village for courtship, that you are here to seek a bride. And you are a friendly guy, intelligent guy, you're not a hoodlum. You played this so that the family that has the young girl that you intended to court will be expecting you. So they will say, "Okay, some noise outside of my house, it's not a thief." They say, "It is a young man making his approach."

Back in the old days, traditionally, the young men courting a young woman, they don't do it in daylight where the parent can identify them and say "So and so is courting my daughter." They have to go in the evening, because they are very embarrassed

Young qeej players fool around between lessons at the Hmong Cultural Center in St. Paul.

and very shy. So that nobody know who they are, but can identify them with their music. I used the flute to court many young girls in the past, including my wife. At night, you blow the flute and you get very close to the woman's house, so you are separated just by a bamboo wall. So what you do next is, you take the Jew's harp and you pop it open. You pop it several times to make noise. And when you shake it like that, so it pops open, that noise will wake up your girlfriend. She will wake up, and then usually you will serenade her with the Jew's harp. You play a song with very sweet words, like,

Dear darling,
Do you hear me?
Are you very deep in sleep?
If you hear me,
Will you wake up,
If you are interested in me.

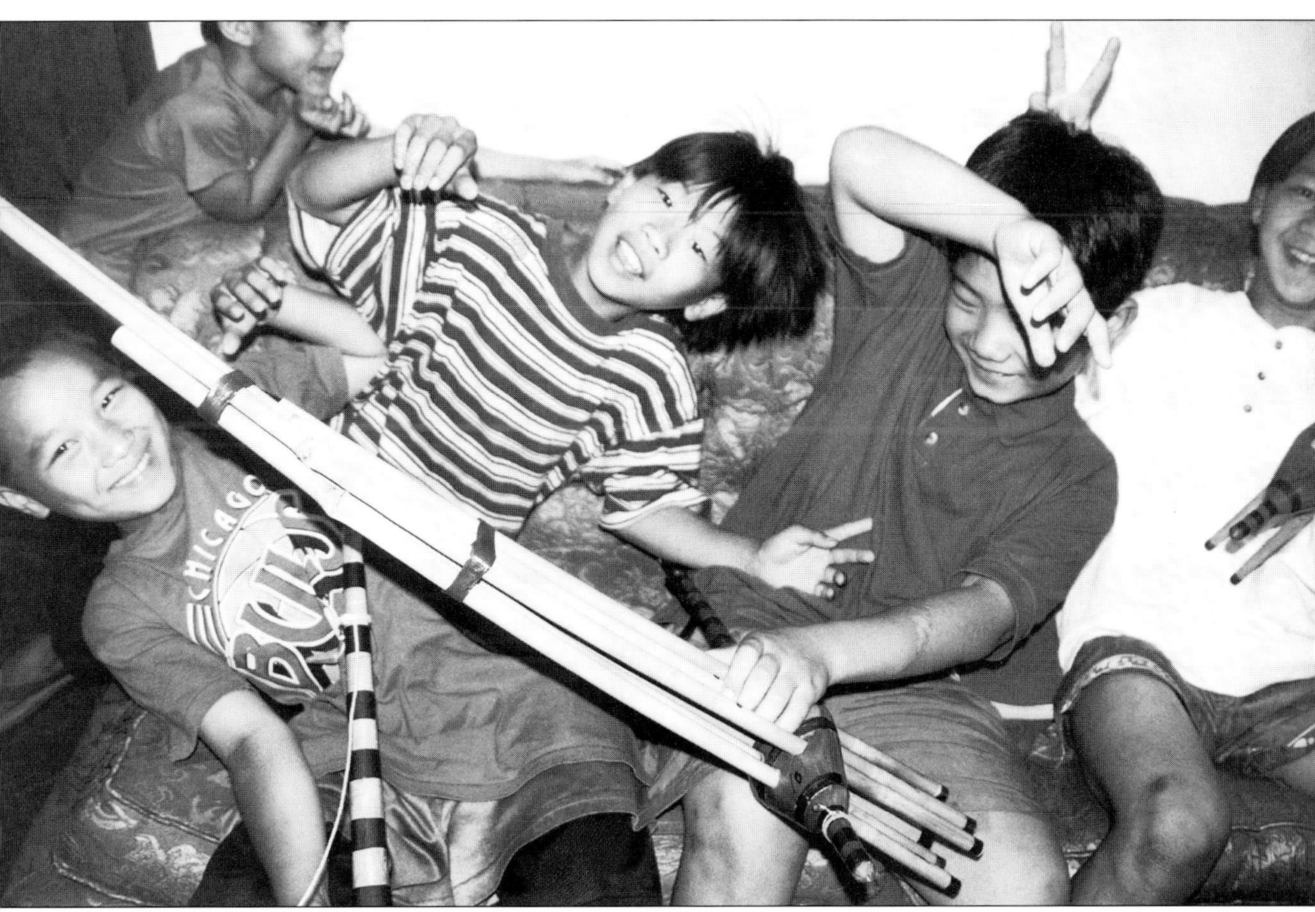

It is a long way from the mountain villages where Lor spent his youth to the quiet St. Paul residential district that is now his home. He came to the United States in 1985, part of a mass immigration of Hmong forced out of their homes in Laos. For centuries, the Hmong had lived in the mountains, resisting the influence of the flatlanders who ruled the country. During the Vietnam War, they were allied with the American troops, helping them navigate the difficult mountain and jungle terrain, and after the war whole villages fled Laos to the refugee camps in Thailand, then came to the States. The Twin Cities are one of the American centers of Hmong culture, along with Los Angeles and Missoula, Montana, and more than 25,000 Hmong have settled here. There are Hmong neighborhoods, Hmong markets, and a cultural center.

Any immigrant group faces difficulties, but the Hmong have encountered unique problems. Most immigrants, whatever country they are from, have some experience of urban life, of the ebb and flow of the modern world. The Hmong, by contrast, were living an ancient, village existence, as their ancestors had for generations, and suddenly find themselves in a completely new world. Isolated mountain settlements have been replaced by a big city on the endless prairie. Older Hmong fight to keep the culture intact, younger people try to find ways to assimilate with the culture around them. For some, music can be a bridge, a way to keep contact with the old ways while absorbing the new. As an elder musician, Wang has made it his mission to educate the new generation of Hmong-Americans.

At first, when I arrived to this country in 1985, I was worried that the culture may be lost and the tradition may be lost. But after 1987 things are becoming more stable, and I have hope that it will keep on going and keep on maintaining itself. It will change in some form or the other, it will not be just the way we did things before. But okay, this is Hmong culture in the Western world, this is how we used to do, and we should keep this, because it's our roots.

When we came to this country, we had to adjust. No matter where we are living, in any country, we have to adjust. There are many things that we can still do here, but we have to let go of the unproductive things and maintain only the good things in our culture. For example, for the funerals, in the past, many families don't use coffins. But here, in this society, we start using coffins. We have to adjust to that, and we believe that that is good. Also, the funeral was usually held in the person's family home, versus now we have to do it at one location, that's the funeral home. In the past, during funerals, many times people just overindulge themselves with wine or alcohol. But now, in this country, that has been slowed down; only certain members who do not have big respon-

sibility in the ritual are allowed to indulge to the very extreme. In the old days, you know, everybody would just go and be happy.

Lor laughs, and goes on to demonstrate some of his other instruments. There is another sort of flute, and the Jew's harp. Then, there is the oldest of Hmong instruments, a leaf from a special plant that Lor has growing in a pot by his back door. He says that to get the proper sound the leaf must first be soaked overnight, so today he will play a second-rate instrument, a banana leaf. Folding it between his fingers, he plays a weird, buzzing melody that dips and quavers. Finishing the musical tour, he sings a final song, in a gentle, high voice.

This song is about the time when Hmong people migrated to Southeast Asia from China. They reached a kind of boundary area, and some decided to stay and some decided to head back to China, and some decide to move further down south through Vietnam. For my family, the Lor clan, they cut a large coin in half and split among the two groups. And so, in the future, they can know each other.

The singing is reminiscent of the flute playing, with the same tonal variations and subtle phrasing. It is hard to see how this simple, quiet style will survive the crashes and bangs of city life, but Lor is doing his best to pass it on and keep the tradition alive.

Every ethnic group and every race in this world has their own music, their own cultures, and this is very important. If we just sit and sigh, and don't use those skills or those talents, then the young people will not know that we do have our own traditional music, our own culture. They may just adopt another, and not have a sense of identity. But if you continue performing, then they realize that, "Oh, we do have our own instruments, our own music, and this is how it sounds. It's not like other people's. And it's our roots, it's our culture."

At the local cultural center, located in a small storefront in a bleak, gray shopping mall, a group of youngsters are learning to play the qeej. A distant relative of the harmonica, or the Chinese sheng, it is an instrument with multiple reed pipes held together by a wooden block at the center. The player blows or sucks air through a mouthpiece leading to this block, and covers holes that force the air through one or more reeds at a time. In the hands of an adept player it can create quite complex melodies, though most sound rather monotonous to the Western listener. In the hands of a roomful of preteens, the massed qeej orchestra produces what even an expert would have to admit is an anarchic cacophony.

Whatever the sound, the qeej class is a lot of fun to attend.

Traditionally, the player is expected to dance along with his own melody, and the kids move in slow, choreographed steps as they play. The center is simply a bare room, with a half-wall dividing the performance space from the front office, and there is barely room to accommodate the after-school class. On the wall, music is written in a unique notation style, and the teacher gestures to it before singing out the melody he wants his students to duplicate. They reply with a welter of notes that bears no recognizable relationship to what he has sung, but he simply nods, smiles, and sings the melody again, watching as his charges circle and dip across the floor.

Wang Chong Lor plays a reed flute in his St. Paul home.

The beginning students look very earnest as they play, but the mood shifts dramatically when two teenagers take the floor. Chue Moua and Meng Vang have been playing for several years, and show a degree of instrumental expertise, but their melodic skill is easily overshadowed by their ability as dancers. They have taken the Hmong tradition and fused it with movements from the American streets, creating a sort of hip-hop qeej style. Meng twirls on one leg, the other kicking out in front or behind as he spins. Chue, wearing a traditional costume hung with metal discs that jingle as he dances, rolls across the floor in a flow of somersaults before ending in a shoulderstand, playing all the while.

Meng: *If you are going to learn this, you must really love it. I see a lot of kids, they come here two or three months and they're out of here. They can't stand it, it's too hard. You have to have the heart for it. I come here normally Monday through Friday, about three or four hours every day. That's how much I give it every day, and then I have to make time for my schoolwork, too.*

I started when I was in my second semester of ninth grade. If I had a personal trainer, it would probably take about two years, but since I just come here to study, normally it will take me about four years to finish everything. There's a lot of things to learn, and many, many songs, each for different occasions. There are special songs for funerals, and special songs for entertainment, and visitation, like going to visit the funeral home. Then you have a special song after a year, when you have to release the spirit of the person who has died. There can never be a funeral without a qeej player, because we believe there is a song that sends the spirit of the dead person to their homeland, to be with their parents and their relatives.

As with Lor's flute playing, the qeej melodies represent lyrics as well as music. For the students, it is almost like they are learning an instrument and a language at the same time.

It's like trying to spell something when you don't know the alphabet. There are notes that are like the alphabet, and you learn word by word. There's different notes, and then you can combine the notes and can say words, but you have to control whether you're breathing out or you're inhaling, because it's the same note but it sounds different so it says something different.

Traditionally there isn't a lot of people that know how to play the qeej. Usually it's just passed on from generation to generation: If your father knew it, then you knew it, but if your father didn't know it, then it's pretty hard to find somebody that'll teach you, because it takes so much time to learn. But now the cultural centers are breaking down the barrier, and giving every kid a chance.

You come here and study, and usually when you graduate is when you are capable of playing for the funeral. That's when you're finished, but then there are still higher levels, if you want to go on. It's like college. If you're able to play for the funeral, that's if you graduate from high school, but then you can go higher. Once you start, it's like a never-ending learning process. There are so many different songs out there, so many different teachers. And then, when you get old, you can create your own song and then teach it down to your students, and they'll have that song to share.

♦ ♦ ♦

The old world meets the new; students show equal interest in an ancient instrument from the Laotian hills and an American soda.

7
The Old Dutchman Polka: KARL HARTWICH

It is midafternoon when Karl Hartwich pulls his new Ranger Bass boat up to the Dam Saloon, just below Lock and Dam 5A, four miles south of Fountain City, Wisconsin. The saloon is a two-decker structure built on a floating wooden raft, with a bar downstairs, a rooftop deck, and another wide, wooden deck in front with lawn chairs, tables, and a jacuzzi. A stopping-off place for local fishermen and barflies, it is a favorite hangout of Karl's, and he climbs out of the boat with his wife, Linda, walks up to the bar, and orders his first beer. It is a local La Crosse brand, Special Export, and will be the first of several this afternoon.

Polka is good beer-drinking music. I think if you go to a polka dance, you almost have to have a couple of beers. I know we do, anyway. And usually if the crowd drinks quite a bit, we sound better.

Linda (defending his honor): *That's not true.*

Karl (looking shocked and insulted): *We don't sound better?*

Karl Hartwich is one of the leading lights of "Dutchman music," a distinctive polka style of southern Minnesota and western Wisconsin. Now in his late thirties, he is a virtuoso on the distinctive box concertina favored by Dutchman players, and leader of a popular band, the Country Dutchmen.

Ever since day one, or actually I suppose year number two or three of my life, my dad and ma took us out dancing to Sylvester Liebl's band, the Jolly Swiss Boys. They were based out of La Crosse, Wisconsin, about thirty miles down the road here, and ever since I can remember I wanted to play with that band. He had some of my relatives in there, and so we were always traveling around to see those guys. It looked like they were having so much fun, and I wanted to have as much fun as they did, so I figured "This is what I want to do."

For my twelfth birthday my parents gave me a concertina. It was a combination birthday and Christmas present, so I didn't get any Christmas presents that year, but that was okay with me because that was enough. I started my own band right away, and Syl would let me play during intermission at their dances. We'd set up my band for about a half hour, when they were taking their breaks, and that helped us an awful lot. So from there on I just kept playing and playing, twenty-five years now.

Karl Hartwich leads his Country Dutchmen at the Hilltop Lounge's annual polka fest, outside Fountain City, Wisconsin.

I learned just by playing along with records and tapes and the radio, and listening to other old-time bands. Wherever I could get my hands on old-type music, I'd just pick up the concertina and play along with that. I tried to read music for a while but that didn't work. It goes by so quick, and I'm not that quick, so I have to kind of play it by ear. And it seemed to work okay. If I had trouble with a chord, especially on the bass side, I'd go to Syl. He helped me out quite a bit on stuff like that, like if I wanted to play a B flat chord on the C box, I'd say, "Syl, where does this go?" And he'd say, "Come over here, Karly"—he always called me Karly—and he'd show me.

Where I grew up, down in Illinois, there wasn't too much on the radio. There was one old-time show out of Maquoketa, Iowa, and that was only a half-hour show each day, and they played a lot of trash, so you had to pick out the good stuff in between the bad stuff and play along with that. But it was mostly on records and tapes, and of course back then it was a lot of eight-tracks, so you had to learn it the first time because eight-tracks would screw up the second time around.

Dutchman music, also known as German music or simply "old-time,"is just one of the multiple polka styles that pepper the Midwest. It was born, or at least found its first widespread popularity, in the 1920s, when "Whoopee John" Wilfahrt began recording and making regular broadcasts out of New Ulm, Minnesota. Whoopee John was a concertina virtuoso and expert showman, and he became the music's first big star, but the style would get its name from his principle competitor, a New Ulm tuba player named Harold Loeffelmacher. Loeffelmacher had at first tried for a cosmopolitan approach, calling his group the Broadway Band, and later the Continental Band. Neither name carried much weight in rural Minnesota, so he decided to go the comic route and redubbed his band the Six Fat Dutchmen ("Dutch," an anglicization of "Deutsch," was a common term for Germans in nineteenth-century America). The Dutchmen became popular favorites and, as with Bill Monroe's Blue Grass Boys, their name was adopted by competitors and became a generic term for the music.

This music pretty much started with Whoopee John and the Six Fat Dutchman and the Babe Wagner Band and some of those guys back in the early 1900s. They get the word Dutchman or German music because most of those guys were German when they started—well, I guess they were when they ended too—but they really didn't play too many German tunes. Like, around here, when people say there's Polish style and German style, neither one of us plays Polish or German music like you'd hear in Poland or Germany. It's more what you would call a Minnesota-style polka music. And old-timers just in general, a lot of old standard fox-trots, some old country songs that nobody plays anymore, and some Dixieland tunes, and lots of polkas and lots of waltzes, some schottisches—see, that's where that "old-time" comes in, because it covers a lot of ground.

What sets Dutchman music apart, I guess, would be the instruments. Dutchman music usually has more horns, maybe two trumpets and three saxes and maybe a trombone, whereas Polish music would have usually two trumpets and one guy would double on clarinet. And they use an accordion and a concertina together, and a bass guitar instead of a tuba, where with Dutchman music it pretty much always has a tuba. And a Polish drummer, they're a little bit different; they're more like a rock 'n' roll drummer, a lot louder. But the Dutchman music is usually like Six Fat Dutchman—I don't know if anybody who'll be watching this program has heard of them, but I suppose they have. It's a household name, isn't it?

Aside from the tuba, which gave the Dutchman style yet another name, "oompah," the most distinctive instrument is the concertina, a large, square, boxlike instrument. A variation on the German or Anglo concertina, Karl's concertina was built by Christie Hengel, a widely awarded instrument maker in New Ulm, who services many of the contemporary Dutchman players. (In a practice also common among bluesmen, Karl has given his instrument a female name. She is Tina, and he introduces her by saying, "She's kind of a slut—anyone can play her.") Unlike the piano accordion favored by most Polish and other Eastern European polka bands, the concertina has no piano keys, but only an array of buttons on either side.

They're diatonic, which means that you push in and you pull out and you get a different note each way. And whoever invented it must have been drunk because there's no rhyme or reason to those buttons. You've just got to be kind of nuts, I suppose, to play one. It helps anyway.

Karl proved naturally adept on the instrument, and became something of a regional celebrity within months of picking it up.

I have to give my parents a lot of credit. When we started out, my dad had to drive us around all the time because I was only twelve or thirteen years old. We started with a truck and camper, and we threw all the instruments in the back and drove all over Illinois playing. Dad was drumming and singing with us, and my sister was drumming, and my mom played tuba, believe it or not. You don' t see too many women tuba players, and she was good too—still is. I guess she played French horn in college, but she didn't start playing tuba till I started playing concertina. Then we figured, "Well, we've got to have a tuba player," so she thought, "Well, I can do that." And by God, she did a pretty good job. She was there playing with me for the first, I suppose, fifteen years, and she also kept track of the books.

Then I moved out of town and got another tuba player, and I took over the books myself. And boy, was that a mess. I'd keep writing down mental notes, and they'd keep getting lost. But it worked. Now, we've been through a pickup and camper and a Dodge Monaco and a Chrysler New Yorker, six trailers, two buses, one motor home, and three vans so far, and one Ranger boat.

Usually we play between 140 jobs and 180 jobs a year. Sometimes up to the 200 mark, but not too often. Sometimes we play small jobs, like once in a while I'll take a three-piece or four-piece job in some smaller bars, but it's mostly polka fests and regular dances. Especially in the winter, it's all regular dances, because the festivals are just in the summer. A lot of ballrooms, nightclubs, and things like that. Different areas, like we played in Texas two months ago, down by Houston, and then we're going out to Vegas again in September, and then again the Phoenix area in February. I counted up once, and I'd played in thirty states, in Europe and Mexico and in the Caribbean. So we try to get around. We hardly ever play around home. I guess we're not good enough, don't you think? It's kind of like when I started my own band, I figured, "Well, nobody else will hire me so I've got to start my own band." But I showed them, didn't I?

On the bluffs above the river stands the local polka palace, the Hilltop Lounge. The Hilltop has polka bands every week, but this weekend is a special event, the annual polka festival. For three days, the Hilltop will have two bands going all day and well into the evening, one in the dance hall and another out back of the lounge, where the owners have laid down a wooden dance floor under a large, white tent.

It's a pretty good-size fest for a small place. I think last year they had about 3,000 people up there. People drive for 500 miles just to go up there and park their motor home and spend the weekend. Just a nice family-oriented deal. I like it up there. It's a nice hall, air-conditioned, nice acoustics. And the owners are nice folks, Gary and Mary. They've got really good food up there, good burgers, good chicken. So if you're ever in the area and you stop into the Hilltop, mention our name and they'll charge you double.

Sunday afternoon, the scene under the Hilltop's tent is like old home week. The Country Dutchmen are playing right before Karl's old mentor Syl Liebl. Though Syl has turned his band, the Jolly Swiss Boys (renamed from the Jolly German Boys during World War II), over to his son, he still likes to come out and play on special occasions. In this region, at least, he remains a celebrity, and the audience gives him a big hand as he takes the stage.

Syl created another sound on the concertina. They used to just play straight melodies, and Syl started putting in fill-in parts and playing harmony along with the

"It's 90 degrees and they're going every single dance. They're nuts, but we love them."

clarinet, so it sounded like two clarinets. It was really nice, and anybody in the tri-state area, or even more then that, if they play concertina, they play Syl's tunes; they almost have to, he's a standard. In the heyday, when Syl was playing, you couldn't even dance, because the floor was full of people just watching the boys play. It was supposed to be a dance, but he was doing so good they'd just stand there and listen. He'd have about 200, 300 people standing there.

"How many of you was here in 1934, when I was playing?" Syl asks the assembled dancers. Quite a few hands shoot up. Syl's audience has aged along with him, and they cheer and dance when he swings into Whoopee John's old radio theme. In between dances, they sit around on lawn chairs, fanning themselves in the summer heat.

After Syl's set, Karl takes over with his bigger band. Besides himself, there is an electric keyboard, a drummer, two horn players, one of whom also takes an occasional vocal, and, of course, the tuba. The set is mostly polkas, with a few waltzes and one pop number, a medley of the jazz standard "All of Me" and Patsy Cline's "I Fall to Pieces." The highlight is Karl's hit, the "Christmas Toy Polka," which brings out dozens of dancing couples. Except for two little girls who whirl around the outside of the floor, all the dancers look old enough to be Karl's parents, or even grandparents. Polka is a famously family-oriented music, and has lately been attracting an ever-larger audience of young people, but the crowd at the Hilltop is definitely weighted towards old-timers. Many of them are retirees, and devote their entire summers to following the polka circuit.

You'll see people from California and Texas and New Mexico, all over the place. There's an awful lot of people that start going to festivals around the end of May or the first of June, and you'll see them at every single polkafest you play. They'll say, "Where are you going next?" You say, "Frankenmuth, Michigan." They say, "We'll be there." And sure enough, there they are. They just take their motor home and they never go home, they just go to festivals and that's it, they live for it. And some of those eighty-year-old people, jeez, they dance every single dance. I'll get out there and dance about four or five and, jeez, I'm glad I'm playing, it's a lot easier. It's ninety degrees and they're going every single dance. They're nuts, but we love them.

Karl adds that, traveling the dance hall circuit, he does get a younger crowd as well. In fact, he met Linda at a dance in Arizona.

It was kind of funny. We were playing down there in Mesa, Arizona, and that's where she was living at the time, and I saw her dance by the stage with her dad. I'd seen her dad a few times for five or six years before that. I didn't really know him, but he knew me. So she was dancing with him, and she was dancing by with a nice low-cut top on, and I looked down at my piano player and I said, "Keith, see that girl down there? I think I'll marry her." Never talked to her before. So then I went out in the tent and sat down across the table from her, and they had a bottle of schnapps there, so I said, "I would help you with that if you let me." We had a couple of schnapps, and she had that low-cut dress on with a nice little pendant like that, and I said, "Is that a real diamond there?" And we had a couple of dates that week.

Linda: *My father had kept saying, "You have to meet Karl, you have to meet Karl." So he introduced us, and ten days later Karl called me on the phone, from the road, and asked me to marry him. I thought he was kidding. I said, "How long do I have to think about this?" And he said, "As long as you like." And I said, "You're serious." And he said, "Yes, I am." So I said yes.*

Karl: *So then I had to call this girl from Omaha that I was going with, and tell her I was kind of tied up with another girl, we're going to get married. And boy, she wasn't too happy. See what you did?*

Linda: *It's okay. We've been married ever since, six years.*

Even when she was a little girl, Linda's father took her and her sisters out to polka dances every weekend, so she was no stranger to Karl's world. After their marriage, she became the band's financial manager and the person who drives the van when the musicians are too tired or otherwise incapacitated. She will even get up on stage on occasion to sing a waltz or an old pop tune. It is a gypsy existence, but she is clearly happy with her choice.

I like it. You always have a good time, it's good exercise, and you meet a lot of nice people. There are certain situations, I guess, when you're tired, when you finish the end of a job and you find that you have nowhere to sleep, and everyone's hungry and there's no place to eat because everything is closed. It generally works out, though.

Karl: *Oh, yeah. Three in the morning, you're just starting to hit the road, drive another 300, 400 miles. Got six guys in the van trying to find a place to sleep. It's a lot of fun.*

Wry as his humor may be, Karl clearly is enjoying himself. And why not? After all, this is all he has ever wanted to do. These days, he is one of the only Dutchman musicians who can make a full-time living, and to do it he has to put up with the long drives and crazy schedule. Still, in the fickle music business, where a new trend comes along almost every month, the polka world provides a security that most musicians will never know.

This music is going to go on pretty much forever. It kind of dies out in spots at certain times, and then you've got to drive a little further to find it, but then a few years later it comes back to the same spot again. It's just a circle, it keeps going. You never make a lot of money doing it—that's why we're so skinny—but it's enough to live on. And, like Linda said, you get to meet a lot of nice people and get to see all kinds of sights, travel all over the place, and you get paid for what you're doing. Of course, after you put fuel in the tank and eat out a few times, by the time you get home there's not much left in the billfold. But—

Anyone who has spent a little time with Karl knows how that last sentence is going to end:

—it's a lot of fun.

◆◆◆

8

Mexican Roots, American Branches: La Otra Mitad

Another polka is playing, but we are a long way from the sunny hilltop full of retired Germans-Americans. Willie G's is a smoky, dusky bar, lit by neon beer signs. The dancers are mostly in their thirties and forties, dark-skinned, wearing T-shirts and jeans, tank tops or tight, short dresses. Over the accordion, two voices are singing in close harmony.

Voy a cantarles un corrido muy mentado
Lo que a pasado allí en la hacienda de la Flor
La triste historia de un ranchero enamorado
Que fue borracho, parrandero y jugador

It sounds like San Antonio or El Paso, but we are in East Moline, Illinois, and the band is a local group, La Otra Mitad. An older man in front is keeping time with a wooden cabasa, or scraper, as he sings. By his side, a young, bearded man plays blaring, mariachi-style trumpet. Behind him is the accordion player, the only band member who is not wearing a cowboy hat. Electric bass and drums keep the dancers on the floor and, from the back of the bandstand, Henry Rangel sings harmony and holds a steady rhythm on his electric guitar.

The first Mexicans came here for the jobs. They came to this area in the early 1900s, and they worked on the railroads, they worked for the steel companies. When our families came here, they didn't have to swim across the border or anything like that; they just walked across and spread out to different communities where people were hiring, different factories and all that stuff, and they had really good jobs. Most of the jobs were on the Illinois side of the river, working for these big manufacturing companies like Case, Alcoa, the Rock Island Railroad. And then the Iowa side, there's all farms over there, so there's a lot of migrant workers, in Davenport, Muscatine.

I was born right here in Moline, right on the river. We lived in a railroad boxcar converted to housing, in between two sets of tracks. It was for transient workers—Anglo people as well as Mexicans, we all lived together. Then later on, during the Depression, we bought an acre of land for $1,000 and we moved out to the country. We lived in between two farms, which was composed of Belgians and Serbians, and they had their traditions and we got along really good together, and we were raised with their children.

My upbringing, I picked up a lot of their habits. I learned country music and I learned some of your Serbian-type music, Scandinavian, Slavic, German-type music, Belgian. They had their accordions that they brought with them, and they celebrated their weddings and birthdays and stuff like that. And so the music was in me, all the different cultures.

My father was an immigrant from Mexico, and he played in a band with other

immigrants. In order to make money during the Depression, they had to go out to the Anglo-type community, and in order to do that they had to play that type of music. They found out there was a big market in Italian music, so they went out and imitated Italian musicians, and I believe they fooled everybody. They could pass as full-blooded Italians, and no one would know, and they would play the old Italian standards.

Pedro and Henry Rangel of La Otra Mitad, onstage at Willie G's in East Moline, Illinois.

Then the family started getting bigger and my dad had to go on the railroad to make more money. So he laid down his guitar and just had it laying around, and I was attracted to it. I just had the feeling of music in me, so I picked it up.

At that time I was like seventeen years old and rock 'n' roll was big, so I started imitating country, fifties rock 'n' roll. I was doing Johnny Cash, the Ventures, the Champs. Three of us, descendants of immigrants, started out together, and then we picked up some other musicians. One happened to be a black kid who I went to school with and he played sax, and then we played with an Anglo-type kid who played drums, and then another Anglo kid on tenor sax. We formed a real nice rock 'n' roll group, and we started playing for community dances, out in parks and debutante balls and different clubs, and later on as we got better and better, we started moving into nightclubs. And that's how I really got started in music.

The band has finished the polka and eases into a slow Mexican ballad. Then the cabasa player switches to trumpet, and with a brassy blare the band kicks into a rocking blues. It is a classic jump sound, the hot r&b that gave birth to rock 'n' roll. The older dancers jitterbug, while the youngsters dance freestyle or head to the bar for another beer. Then, as quickly as it began, the song is over and the cabasa player is singing another *corrido,* the song of an immigrant ready to die for *"Un Puño de Tierra,"* a handful of land.

After a while, there was too many bands, rock 'n' roll bands, that popped up. They'd come from all over the state or the Midwest, and the competition was getting too much, so we decided to relax more and to do Mexican music. There wasn't that much Mexican culture or music going on at that time, so there was a big demand for those bands. We got together with other people like us, immigrants also, and tried to pick up the tastes of the people that were here. There's a big influence of Puerto Ricans and bands from Chicago around here, so we started doing tropical-type music with brass. Big orchestra music like maybe Tito Puente and Xavier Cougat and bands like that.

That was in the early sixties, and it was going okay for a while, but then we were getting other new immigrants. Our bands were playing for the people our age and older, people from the first wave of immigrants to come up here, and we were still playing their music, which was music that dated back to the Mexican Revolution and big band standards. Meanwhile, we were getting this influx of newer Mexican immigrants, mainly migrants. There were younger people, and the music that they brought in with them was like Southwest, Texas style. It came from Mexico, but it seemed to us like it was Americanized, because they were bringing in organs and piano players and accordion players.

We started listening to these other groups, and we said, "We'll try to do some of that stuff, because we like their music, too." At that time different events were happening in this country, the new type of movements, political and all that stuff, and it could be identified with this newer type Mexican-American music. So we tried to play it, but we didn't have the musicians for it. We still had the brass in there, and I said "This isn't going to work at all." So eventually our old group broke up, and we got some younger musicians and started integrating with them. They said, "Let's do this newer stuff," and we said, "Okay, we'll do it." Anything in order to get into that market.

So we started looking for different musicians, and finally—there aren't that many accordion players around here, but we found one and he happened to be Italian, and he'd been playing Latin before, so we added him to the group. And so the transition was forming, and we were going along with the times.

The band swings into a Columbian *cumbia* beat, and the dancers start to swing their hips.

Ay, que bonito bailen las hijas de Don Simon
Ay, que bonito bailen las hijas de Don Simon

Suddenly, the keyboards cut out, the rhythm section goes into overdrive and, unlikely as it seems, the trumpet and cabasa players are rapping in a quirky Spanglish about the three dancing daughters of Don Simon, then exhorting everyone to join in the fun:

Hey, where's the party, dude?
Hey we all want to know
Follow me cuando terminamos *this song*
Y nos dijan que son hijas de Don Simon!

Henry laughs at the reactions some of the group's innovations have produced.

The older people, sometimes, they are culturally shocked or socially shocked. They say, "Wait a minute, this isn't Mexican music. It sounds too American." They go back to the revolutionary days, or what their moms and dads used to play for them on their record players or stereos. Then we talk to the younger people, and they don't like some of the older stuff. They say, "We know that music, but we can't identify with that. We're trying to integrate with the American community, going to school and working in different businesses and organizations, so we've got our own type of music." And they said, "This is what you guys should be playing, and we'll hire you for that, but we don't need a band that plays this older type music."

So we can play for the older and the younger people. We play also to the interracial type, different cultures, mixed weddings. They hire us because they know we play everything. John, the accordion player, he's Italian, but he's playing like a Mexican, even better than some Mexicans. You know, the music is so universal that we can all pick up each other's music. I could do German polkas and keep that rhythm or else I can play American polkas and play that rhythm, and I'll surprise everybody and make my guitar sound like a banjo.

We don't even notice; I mean, we take all this for granted. They can pick up our music and I can pick up theirs, but any musician could do it, anybody who really

La Otra Mitad: Henry Rangel, guitar, second from left.

appreciates music. Just three years ago we had an Irish kid play in our group and he could sing a couple of Mexican numbers. He learned in college, and he could sing Spanish songs really great, like those marachi-type singers from Mexico. And when we played our Italian jobs, he could sing in Italian, and the Italian people were very impressed with him. So here was Irish, Mexican, Italian, all three of us playing together, and we didn't think too much of it. We were just friends.

That's the way it is all over this community. We know all these different people, because we all work different jobs around the area. One of our brass players is retired from one of our local factories, John Deere. He was the safety coordinator over there. And the other brass player is a younger-generation-type horn player, and he works at one of the local factories, a glass company, here in the outskirts of Davenport. Our drummer is a supervisor in the same factory. John, the accordion player, is a maintenance person, apartments and high-rises. And Pete, our bass player, he's had different injuries, and so he's kind of semi-retired.

Everybody around here is all different races, and we go to their jobs or we go to their functions, their celebrations, and political events and everything. Sometimes I'll say, "What's that guy doing in there? He doesn't like Mexican music, does he?" And they'll say, "No. . . . Looks like he's going to dance, though, like he's having a good time."

We've played some Croatian jobs, playing some Croatian music mixed up with

a little bit of country and a little bit of rock 'n' roll, because we have Croatian people who were born here, so they appreciate the other stuff too. We played for a Jewish wedding not too long ago, so we did "Hava Nagilah" and stuff like that. We play some Irish numbers, "Danny Boy." Right now that's the way our band is. Anybody who requests any kind of number, no matter what country it is, we'll play any type of ethnic music.

Happiness, celebrations, that's what it's all about. That's just so universal. We go into different communities up and down the river, across state, and we see where people are mixing and the different cultures are mixing together. It seems like it's become more and more of an integration-type thing. So we play that type of music, and surprisingly it's not scary, it's good. We're losing some culture to other cultures, making one pure culture impure, but it's good. We see the harmony, both musically and in the humanity.

◆◆◆

Top: Manny Lopez; lower left: Dude Lopez; and lower right: trombonist Jeffrey Clauss.

9

Davenport Jazz: MANNY AND DUDE LOPEZ

Across the river from Moline, in Davenport, Iowa, it is the beginning of the annual Bix Weekend, celebrating the region's favorite musical son, Bix Beiderbecke. A banner is stretched across Brady Street, marking the starting line of the "Bix 7" road race, an officially sanctioned runners' event that draws contestants from all over the world. Several thousands runners are milling around, waiting for the signal to take off. It is early, but the July heat is already oppressive.

Manuel "Manny" Lopez steps to the microphone, trumpet in hand. Tilting the instrument skyward, he plays the call to post, then takes a surprising left turn into a hot jazz break, a quick taste of syncopated improvisation. "Bix himself couldn't have done it any better," the announcer comments, and the runners are off.

Like the members of La Otra Mitad, Lopez is the son of Mexican immigrants and started out playing their music, but his career has taken a quite different direction.

In the early sixties there was a guy who came out with a band, it was Herb Alpert and the Tijuana Brass. The connection, for me, was that the music sounded Latin. So I started listening to his music, and any chance I got I would buy one if his albums, save up my birthday money or whatever. I would listen to them and learn his tunes, and that gave me a goal: "Today I'm going to learn this tune or that tune." I would practice for hours and hours. My folks never had to say, "Get up to your room to practice," because I was always doing it anyway. But I was enjoying it.

During Bix Weekend, Manny is working pretty much around the clock. Within minutes of getting the runners off on the Bix 7, he is out under a tent at the side of the race course, leading his band through a set of Dixieland

standards. There is another gig that night, then a few hours sleep before he has to get up and play for a jazz liturgy at a local church. Then there are the day's festival events, and finally his regular Sunday night show at the 11th Street Bar & Grill.

This is a big weekend for any musician in the Quad Cities. People will kill to get a band, they don't care how good they sound—they just want a band that is going to be playing something that sounds like jazz. So everybody gets to work this weekend, and that's great. I wish they could work every weekend. A lot of these guys need to be working more. I feel very fortunate that I have a house gig, so I can say "I know I'm going to be playing at least one time a week."

Lopez's band is a quintet, with trombone, keyboards, standup bass, and his son Manuel Lopez III, familiarly known as "Dude," on drums and occasional vocals. On stage, they are all neatly dressed in white shirts and matching, patterned vests. Manny is a relaxed and enthusiastic frontman, laughing easily and giving all the band members plenty of room to stretch out. Dude is a jaunty presence, slim, with a short beard and sporty cloth cap.

Dude: *I think we really take advantage of the fact that we have something like this, that we can share something that a lot of mothers, daughters, fathers, sons can't do. And that it's something as powerful as music—music is a powerful thing to a lot of people. It moves people in a way that nothing else can. We are making good music and making people happy, and we're doing it together, so that's something really special, but we really don't even think about it. We've always played together, ever since I was little, so I just kind of grew up with it. But when we're on, you know, we respect each other.*

Manny (laughing): *And he's my best/worst critic.*

Dude: *Yes, I am.*

Manny: *If I'm off, he'll let me know: "You missed that, didn't you, Dad?" I'll hear that in the background. Here I may be struggling on a tune, and I know I'm struggling, I'm just dying. And he's there, "Dad, you missed that, didn't you?"*

But it's great. This is something that we can do together, and I don't know, it's just a great time.

Bix Beiderbecke's most famous portrait, taken in Davenport in 1921, wearing a tuxedo for the first time in his life as he prepared to play for a bank opening in Moline.

Dude: *You know, the youngest memory I can really remember is one day, it was before I was five, and Dad had this trumpet and I remember him putting it up against my lips and me playing it for like three seconds or something like that. I don't know if there was a mirror by there or something, but I remember looking and seeing how red my lips were. And I thought to myself, "I'm not going to go through life having red lips all of the time when I'm playing."*

But Dad's younger brother, my uncle Pancho played drums. He never really said "Come and try these out," but for some reason I was really attracted to them. So I just started playing on my own. I mean, I was down in the basement with them, being around that music and listening to them play, and I kind of picked it up.

Manny: *He started playing with us when he was about five years old. He would sit in—Pancho would take a little break and Manuel would sit in for a couple of tunes.*

Dude: *When I really started getting serious about it, I was probably like about ten or eleven. My uncle Pancho, he went on the road with a Top 40 band; he was probably about sixteen years old, seventeen years old at the time. And after he left I joined the band. It was playing the Mexican music and the American music, but it was all stuff that I had grown up with and heard, so I just jumped right in it and played the tunes. It was nothing to me to do that. And I played for about the last three, four years of that band.*

Manny: *I started that band when I was about eighteen, the summer after I graduated high school. At that time, I had Pancho on drums and my other brother, Paul, on guitar and singing. Most of the time we weren't playing any bars or anything, it was Mexican weddings and anniversaries and what they call a* quincenera, *which is when a girl turns fifteen, kind of like a debutante thing. It was a fun band, we always had a great time, and we played for about fifteen years.*

Then one year my brother Paul got an offer to go on the road with a band, so he left the area, and I didn't want to go through the hassle of trying to find somebody to replace him, another guitar player who could sing in Spanish and still play rock 'n' roll—because we had to play some rock 'n' roll; I mean, we were playing weddings. So I just kind of let it go for a little while and freelanced here and there.

Bix Beiderbecke & the Birth of Midwestern Jazz

In 1910, a piece in the *Davenport Democrat* announced the discovery of a musical prodigy: "Leon Bix Beiderbecke, age seven years, is the most unusual and the most remarkably talented child in music that there is in this city... [H]e can play in completeness any selection, the air or tune of which he knows."

Bix Beiderbecke was a uniquely midwestern figure. His father's family were German immigrants with a strong interest in classical music; his grandfather, a local grocer, had organized a German men's choir in Davenport in the 1860s. His mother was the daughter of a Mississippi riverboat captain, and a trained pianist and organist.

Bix was picking out tunes on the piano by age four. At first, he imitated the parlor and classical pieces familiar around his home. Then, in 1918, his older brother Charles returned from the First World War with some cash in hand and bought a record player and a bunch of records, including the Original Dixieland Jazz Band's "Tiger Rag." Bix was an immediate convert. He borrowed a cornet from a friend, and spent weeks sitting by the phonograph, learning every lick.

He was not alone. The ODJB had set off a revolution, and soon Bix was showing off his embryonic jazz chops with a group of fellow students at Davenport High. The local kids had an advantage shared by few other northern Americans. Along with records, they could hear jazz as it came up the river on the big pleasure boats from New Orleans. In 1919, the stern-wheeler *Capitol* brought Fate Marable's band to Davenport, with Louis Armstrong on cornet, and both Armstrong and Bix would later recall their meeting. By the time he was eighteen, Bix was himself working on the boats, playing for summer excursions on the *Capitol* and *Majestic*.

Davenport, however, was still a small town, and Bix's music would not come to fruition until his parents sent him off to school near Chicago. They had hoped to get him away where he could concentrate on schoolwork, but instead they had placed him at the heart of the jazz world. The city was becoming home to a wave of New Orleans expatriates, including Armstrong, King Oliver, and Jelly Roll Morton. Young white enthusiasts were soon picking up their licks and, in 1924, the first of these homegrown midwestern groups went into the recording studio. Called the Wolverines, it featured Bix on cornet, and he was on his way to becoming a jazz legend, a status that only grew as he moved into the popular bands of Jean Goldkette and Paul Whiteman, and recorded small-group sessions with a circulating bunch of young players among whom his choruses virtually always stood out as exceptional moments of magic.

The legend, as it happened, would often obscure the music. Especially after his premature death in 1931, many white musicians and historians, eager for a figure they could identify with, would canonize Bix as the ultimate jazz soloist. In reaction, others would write him off as good for a white player, but not a real contender alongside the likes of Armstrong.

By now, the exaggerations have mostly run their course, and most people agree that Bix, while not of Armstrong's stature, was a massively influential player and helped bring a new approach to jazz. His Davenport youth had allowed him to absorb two widely disparate traditions, giving his playing a unique flavor. He retained the complex harmonic influences of his family's German concert music but, unlike most other white "progressives," he had grown up hearing the masters as they came north on the boats, and was a real jazzman. At his best, he played with gorgeous tone, infectious swing, and a range of melodic and harmonic ideas that would help point the way to much of the later course of jazz.

These days, when jazz is centered in a handful of major cities, musicians rarely have a sound that can be identified as regional. In earlier years, though, every region from Texas to San Francisco to Kansas City had their local favorites, and spawned their own styles and imitators. Bix Beiderbecke would draw from many sources, but Davenport provided his roots, and to a great extent he would always remain a product of his hometown on the Iowa riverfront.

Dude meanwhile was in high school, playing in the school jazz band. After graduation, he went on to play in a local pop band, and then a blues group, then got his first serious road gig with a Top 40 dance band.

They used to come into town and play at a club called Sam's Wells-Fargo Lounge, and my dad had gone up there a couple of times just to check them out. So they knew I was a drummer, and they needed a drummer. At that time I wanted a change. I was nineteen, twenty years old, and I wanted to try something different. And this band was a good opportunity to do that. They were in town, they came here a week early and I learned like seventy tunes in one week, and then played here for like a month. Which was really good, because I had family here and it was really hard on the road, being away for the first time.

I remember we went away for a week and I thought I was going to die. It was so different. Because if you're a full-time musician, that's what you're doing, seven days a week. It's not like I'm playing with dad or with other groups on the weekends and then I go back home. This was the big time. So I did that for about a year and a half, and then I just kind of got a little burned out on it. It was a great experience. The musicians I played with were great, and I learned a lot about the business, and I got to see a lot. And then I was done; that was my fun and I wanted to go back home.

Manny: *So then you came back home and told me how I was running the business all wrong.*

While Dude was working his way across the musical spectrum, Manny was devoting more and more time to jazz. Not that a musician in the Quad Cities could afford to be picky. He did any work that came along, backing touring r&b bands that needed an extra horn, playing on a riverboat cruise with the Nelson Riddle Orchestra, even taking an occasional symphony gig.

I'm just a horn player. It doesn't matter what it is. I'm fortunate to be able to read music, so if somebody calls from the Symphony and says, "We need an extra trumpet player," I can say, "Yes, okay, I'll be there." If somebody calls and says, "We're putting this band together for a wedding and we need somebody who knows a few tunes." Okay, I can do that. I'll take my book along just in case, but I think I can fake my way through it. If a Mexican band were to call me today and say, "Hey, we want you to do this thing, our trumpet player is sick," I could do it. If a German polka band called and said, "We're doing a bunch of polkas tonight, we've got music, come and play it," that's fine, too.

I just like to play. But people, for some reason they want to always put you in a category. "You are a jazz trumpet player. You are a classical trumpet player. You are—whatever." They don't understand that you can be both, or try your best anyway.

You know, most musicians are pretty passionate people about what they do. It comes through in their playing. They are always willing to go to a good jam session and just feel everybody else out and try to fit in. It's pretty universal, I think.

The band I've got these days, everybody has that same attitude: We're here to have a good time. Sure you're going to make mistakes. I mean, we play once a week down here. Sometimes the kickoffs on the tunes are not all together and sometimes the endings aren't all together. But it doesn't matter. We're enjoying ourselves, and the people are feeding off it. If something goes wrong, so what? They're not paying a $25 cover to get in here, we're all having a great time, and they feel that.

Dude: *A little while ago I was talking to someone, and I said, "I wonder if a lawyer gets up in the morning and does his job and feels the same way that I do when I sit down and the song that we're playing is just grooving." Because there's no feeling like that. You just get this warmth and this happiness all through your body. Everything is clicking. And a lot has to do with the people, with the vibe that you are with.*

Up on the bandstand, the group has shifted into a ballad tempo, and Dude is leaning casually into the microphone. "Do you know what it means, to miss New Orleans," he sings, "to miss her both night and day?" His voice has an easy, late-night, saloon feel. The band lays back, framing his vocal, and he caresses each word. The crowd quiets down and listens, fingers tapping gently in time on the table tops.

When my dad got into jazz, that opened a whole new door for me. Because it opened my eyes to the most beautiful songs you've ever heard. I mean some of the ballads, those standards can stand the test of time because they're great tunes. And they have such beautiful lyrics. I mean, this is romance music; these lyrics are just incredible. Some songs, the words don't mean anything, it's just part of the whole sound that you're listening to. But with jazz music, you're singing them and it's like you become friends, and every time you sing a song it's like you fall in love with it more. It's really something cool to do that and feel that.

I love coming in here and watching these people look at me and see how young I am. Because there aren't a lot of young people who get into jazz, not around here. These people are great, and no matter how you are or what moods you're in they're always going to like you. Sometimes I'll come in here with shades, and I'll keep the glass on all of the time just because I'm in that mood. Or I'll wear shirts and I'll have my name painted on them, or I'll have earrings and stuff on my face or whatever. But they never look at me different, because they know what I can do and they respect me for that. They're really cool here, and this was a great place growing up.

We have come to the evening's special tribute. Someone hands Manny a a shiny horn, somewhat smaller than his trumpet, and he holds it up for the audience to see. On loan from a local museum, it is Bix Beiderbecke's cornet, and Manny thanks the museum for "letting us show it off here," then tears into "Jazz Me Blues," one of the first tunes Bix recorded. Dude holds down a steady rhythm, and the band swings with a light, good-time feel.

It is not Manny's first experience with the sacred horn. Last October, the Quad City Symphony premiered a symphonic tribute to Beiderbecke, composed and conducted by Lalo Shifrin, and Manny used the cornet to play the "ghost" of Bix's part from offstage.

It was a great experience; I was very honored to be asked to do this. I have to say, though, it's really just a horn. I'm trying to be honest here. It's a little stuffy; the valves are slow. But some of these people, I'm telling you, they're in awe of this thing. And I suppose maybe I've got a bad attitude about it; I don't know.

Dude: *You have to understand that my dad never grew up listening to a lot of jazz music. It's not that he doesn't respect the past musicians, but he doesn't know their background as much as a person that has studied Bix his whole life. You know, we're really down-to-earth people, and we play the way we play. It's like, if you want to come here and listen to "Jazz Me Blues" played like Bix played it, you're not going to hear it that way. You're going to hear it like we interpret it right now. What we know, what we're living right now, is how it's going to be played.*

Manny: *We're just playing the music. I mean, we can do "Jazz me Blues" Latin if you wanted to hear it. You'd have him do a Latin beat behind it, and the bass player changes his part—A lot of tunes, you can do that with any tune.*

Dude gets a quizzical expression on his face, and starts tapping out a syncopated rhythm. Manny listens, grinning, then starts to sing the old jazz standard, fitting it into his son's arrangement. They try it out for a couple of bars, then collapse laughing.

Dude: *A lot of people would say, "Well, you didn't do it right," but that's the same melody, over the same changes. It's still "Jazz Me Blues"; we're just maybe doing it a little bit different. It's still just as pretty.*

Manny: *And we could do the whole tune like that. But then people would go "Oh my God! You're sacrilegious! You can't do that." But Bix might have been—who knows? He might have loved it. He probably would have had a great Latin band.*

◆ ◆ ◆

"We've always played together, ever since I was little...
When we're on, you know, we respect each other."

PART TWO

The Midwestern

A towboat pushes a barge up the Mississippi.

Crossroads

Of the four regions into which this story is divided, it is in this second that the Mississippi River feels most constantly present. In part, that is because of history. This is where the old river highways, the Missouri, Des Moines, and Ohio, join the Mississippi for the journey south to the main port of New Orleans, and the towns were defined by the river traffic. By this history, if not by geography, the land bordering the Mississippi as it runs through Missouri and Illinois became for many people the center of the United States. In the nineteenth century, it was the divide between east and west, and traces of that division still hold today. West of the river, the prairies begin, the land of cowboy boots, cattle, and myth. East is white America's version of the "old country," the towns that liked to consider themselves as centers of civilization on the border of the barbarous wilderness.

The railroads would supersede the rivers, but for St. Louis they only confirmed its position as a central meeting place, or at least a central switching yard. The city had long been something of a demarcation point not only between eastern and western United States, but also between the northern and southern halves of the Mississippi. With the railroads, it became the place where east-west traffic by rail switched off to north-south traffic, either by rail or river. In later years, when the national migration pattern became as much from south to north as east to west, it was once again an important point on the journey, and a place where some travelers would choose to remain.

The region's music reflects this character. It is geographically north of the Mason-Dixon Line, but Greg Brown and Bo Ramsey talk about the area where they grew up, on the Iowa-Missouri border, as being the northern edge of a "lake" of southern culture. Southern sounds are obvious in the work of most of the artists in this section, from John Hartford and the players at the Hillsboro bluegrass festival to the African-American singers and musicians who settled in St. Louis, to the Bottle Rockets, who fused their parents' country music tastes with the hard rock coming in on the radio.

Though it has both farmland and urban environments, the area around St. Louis provides neither the isolation of the north Minnesota woods nor the burgeoning cosmopolitan feel of the Twin Cities. It feels like a classic, history-book America. At its sunniest, it is the heartland, a place out of Frank Capra movies. Along the once-booming waterfront, it can also seem like a place the modern world has left behind.

Unlike the people we met further north, many of whose families immigrated to the Mississippi region from the old countries, the settlers in this area largely came from other parts of North America. Ste. Genevieve, among the oldest European settlements west of the Mississippi, was one of the chain of towns founded by the French as they moved along the river between Canada and Louisiana. It remained a popular riverboat town, though it would be overshadowed by cities built at the entrances of the other great rivers, St. Louis at the Missouri junction and Cairo at the Ohio. These towns boomed during the western migration of the 1800s, with the traffic that took the Mississippi as a border between home and the unknown, the final civilized outpost before the great trek across the prairies.

By the turn of the century, those glory days were largely past. Mark Twain, in *Life on the Mississippi,* is already looking back with nostalgia on the time before the Civil War and the final victory of the railroads over the river traffic.

Much of the Euro-American music in this section reflects that same feeling, harking back to a previous time: John Hartford to the old steamboat days, the Ste. Genevieve Guignolée to the early French settlers, and the bluegrass and country gospel singers to a legendary past of simple, rural values and traditions.

The African-American artists look back as well, but on a much more recent time. St. Louis became a vibrant center of black culture around the turn of the century, and kept that status through the fifties and early sixties, when it produced Chuck Berry and was home to Ike and Tina Turner. It was the first industrial center on the migration north, the first city where Delta dwellers could feel like they had arrived in a different world. Unlike the Guignolée, looking back to the eighteenth century, Fontella Bass, Oliver Sain, Eugene Redmond, and Henry Townsend can all easily remember a time when St. Louis was a jumping mecca for black musicians.

After the multicultural patchwork of the North, the music we find in the central Midwest feels far more cohesive. As befits the region's position in American history, it exemplifies much of what we think of as "American" music, rather than specifically regional styles. The Guignolée aside, the musicians here represent styles that are found throughout most of the country. Fontella Bass and Oliver Sain have an urban African-American sound of the sort found in Chicago, Detroit, or even New York and L.A., though the music scene in those towns might well have forced them in a more contemporary pop direction; the Bottle Rockets and Greg Brown, rooted as they are in their own places, have much in common with the myriad rock bands and songwriters who grew up as music-making misfits in small towns across America. As for bluegrass, or the church songs of the Boundless Love Quartet, they are ubiquitous in rural areas from Florida to Washington State, California to Maine. With the bustle of the north in the past, and the musical motherlode of Southern culture ahead, this is truly the crossroads and the cultural center of the United States.

1
Prairie Home Bohemian: GREG BROWN

Greg Brown is tromping through the tall grass around the ruins of an old, wooden house, out in the country near the tiny town of Douds, Iowa.

I remember, when we'd come to visit, we'd just pull right up into the yard here. Of course, it was all mowed and everything then. There was a weeping willow here in the front yard; that's what's left of the willow over there, which isn't too damn much. That hill actually still seems pretty big to me, but some of this stuff seems a lot smaller, like the barn. Grandpa built that when I was maybe five or something like that. Now, this house, actually his dad built it in the year of Grandpa's birth, which is 1901. And then Grandpa built that barn and the old shop. Those were built pretty close to each other, probably forty years ago now.

That house would hold an amazing number of people. During Christmas, or during the summer sometimes, there'd be my mother's family and my Uncle Frank and his family and then maybe one of grandma's brothers or sisters—there'd be like thirty people here sometimes. We'd eat off card tables, one out in the front room and one in the living room, and then the big table in the kitchen and a few little kids stuck in the corner. When we'd pull up here, Grandma and everybody'd come out of the house, and it seemed like the people just kept coming and coming and coming.

Greg wanders off down the hill behind the house. He has brought along a friend, an architect and builder, to figure out where he might put up a cabin on his grandparents' land, a place where he could go off and write songs, or just get away to have some time on his own. He might even put in a small pond, stock it with trout, and be able to go fishing in his backyard. As he walks, his conversation wanders back and forth in time, making new plans and remembering what it was like in his childhood.

When Grandpa got married to Grandma, they had an old cabin up there on top of Legel's Hill, it would be about four or five miles. You'd go up that road and then go back in the woods a ways. That was called the "old home place," and that's where my mother was actually born, in that little shack up there. Then when my grandfather's father died, he and Grandma moved down here and helped take care of my great-grandmother, who was still alive when I was a kid. Grammy, she was like a hundred years old or something when she died. Cantankerous woman... sweet, but cantankerous.

Greg Brown, on his front porch in Iowa City.

Back at his house in Iowa City, Brown strums the strings of his old Gibson and sings about those days:

Let the December winds bellow and blow
I'm as warm as a July to-ma-to
Peaches on the shelf, potatoes in the bin
Supper's ready—everybody come on in
And taste a little of the summer
Taste a little of the summer
Come on, taste a little of the summer
My grandma put it all in jars

Greg's voice is deep and thick, with wry corners. The words are nostalgic for rural Iowa, but the phrasing has a lot of jazz in it, and the guitar keeps a quirky, rolling rhythm. His friend and frequent playing partner, Bo Ramsey, sits beside him with a steel-bodied resonator guitar, picking out a spare, bluesy lead.

I just grew up hearing and loving all the music that was in my family, basically. They all loved music. My mother loved classical music and, even though my dad was a preacher—we were Open Bible Church, which was fairly strict—there was never any rule like you can't listen to some kind of music. I mean, I had Jerry Lee Lewis records when I was in second grade.

For me, I never made a lot of big distinctions amongst kinds of music. If something would grab me and move me somehow, then I didn't really care a lot about what it was called, if it was jazz or blues or folk or country or rock 'n' roll, call it whatever you want to. It all seems so connected to me. I think a lot of musicians of this era, you grew up hearing all this stuff. All you have to do is turn on your radio or get a record player. And then, whichever of it you can do something with, if you're a writer and a player, you do what you can with it.

I started out singing in the church. From the time when I was a little tiny kid, like five or six, I'd get up and sing. That was my first real performance—my mother would play the guitar or somebody might play the piano or the organ and I'd sing a church tune. And then when I started playing guitar around twelve or thirteen, it'd be like at a church supper or something like that. I would do gospel music and the old hymns, and then when I started writing songs, which I did pretty early, I'd sing those in church, too. I wrote a lot of those teenage, "what does it all mean, everything is screwed up" kind of songs, and I'd sing those in church, about the meaning of life and stuff.

I never really thought about being a songwriter. I was just one of those kids that made up songs in the back of the car, and made up little poems or playground rhymes. There was never any gap, there was never any point when I thought, "Well, now I'm a writer." I just did that thing that so many children do, and I just never quit.

In his late teens, songwriting and singing were Greg's ticket out of Iowa. He headed east to New York's Greenwich Village in 1969, and became a regular performer at the legendary Folk City. From there, he drifted out to the West Coast, ending up with a job in Las Vegas ghostwriting pop songs, and touring back and forth across the U.S. with a small band. In a few years, he was burned out on the music business. Heading back to Iowa, he began studying to be a forest ranger. His new base was Iowa City.

I got married to a woman who wanted to go to college, and so I moved here with her, and I liked the town so I ended up staying around. I mean, I've lived other places since, but I've come back here. It's got a real good music scene for a small town. When I first moved back here, I didn't play in public for about three or four years, I quit. But when I started again, there was three or four clubs around town where I could play.

You know, being a traveling musician, it seems like it's exotic to people when they find out I'm from Iowa. I don't know what it is—it's like people will say, "Well, where do you live now?"

I'll say, "Well, I live in Iowa."

"You mean you live there?" It's like they can't quite believe it or something.

There was this one club owner in Boston, Bob Donlin, he would always introduce me by saying, "And now, all the way from Iowa—" I mean, when other songwriters got up it wouldn't be like "so-and-so from Illinois, or California." People are where they're from, but Iowa seems strange to people somehow.

If people on the Coasts are surprised that Greg is still settled in the middle of the country, that is at least in part because of his music's hipster edge. He sings a lot of songs about rural life, his childhood and his family, but also plays around with city slang and the sort of subject matter beloved of Jack Kerouac and the beat poets. His guitar work has the funky swing of ragtime blues, and his voice shows the influence of a lot of old blues and jazz singers. Bo adds to this flavor, with a blues-rock touch spawned during years of fronting a local band. On the one hand, Brown's folk pedigree is impeccable, from Folk City to his years as a staff songwriter and performer on *A Prairie Home Companion.* On the other, sometimes he just does not sound very, well, folky. Right now, he is beating out a funky bass rhythm and his voice comes in, talking more than singing, delivering the words with blank, dark alienation:

She's got a slant 6 mind and a supercharged heart
The little princess is singing about her parts
She says "Come hither," but when I get hither she's yon
I was looking for what I loved—whatever it was, it's gone

TV spreads and tension mounts
Like a guy in a bra, it's the idea that counts
It's a picture of a picture of a whore holding a picture of a John
I was looking for what I loved—whatever it was, it's gone

The little towns are lying on their faces
All that's left are fading parking spaces
It's been quite a week, there was a drive-by shooting in Lake Wobegon
I was looking for what I loved—whatever it was, it's gone

There is a brutal quality, an anger and pain in the music that seem pretty far from the elegiac sweetness of much of Brown's work. Brown says that the mix of emotions and voices sometimes perplexes his listeners.

It's a funny thing when you're a songwriter—people assume that when you say "I" you mean, like, "I." And in my songwriting, the "I" is very rarely me. My own approaches do get in there, but I write a lot more about characters, and try to get under other people's skin and tell their tales. And I've had all kinds of mis-understandings. I've got a song called "Oh Lord, I've Made You a Place in My Heart," which is the portrait of a very screwed-up guy. I was playing it out in California once, and there was this woman there who had just been saved recently, apparently, and she completely flipped out. She said, "Jesus saved you, what have you done for him lately?" and went screaming out of the place. If she had stayed and asked me, I would have tried to tell her that the song was a portrait of a soul in pain and certainly not making fun of Jesus or religion at all. But that's the funny thing when you write songs, a lot of times you're telling stories but people take them in odd ways.

The characters in Greg's songs may be troubled or unpleasant, and the language in which he tells their stories is often shaped as much by the urban streets as his rural background. Still, even at his roughest, there is a warm, easy quality to Greg's voice that is sweet and thick as country molasses.

Bo puts his finger on one thing about it:

I always felt like southern Iowa is kind of like where the South finally ends. It's like some of the people have that in their voice, almost a very subtle accent, just a taste of the South.

Greg: *Yeah, if you thought of the South as a lake, or a sea maybe, southern Iowa would be like the north shore. The way of life, in terms of cooking and playing music and telling stories, once you get north of here just a little ways, it kind of dries up. You get into a completely different deal, really.*

Out there in the country, near Ottumwa, where my grandparents are from, everybody played when I was a kid, and it was really more like Appalachian music or—I don't know what you'd call it exactly—hill music or something. A lot of string bands, old fiddle tunes and all. And you know, I've played a lot of different kinds of music, but I still love the sound of an acoustic guitar, and I love the sound of an acoustic guitar and one voice. I mean, I love a lot of sounds, but that particular sound, I just haven't gotten tired of it. Sure, there's times when I don't want to hear it, particularly if I've been to a folk festival or something. But there's something in that sound of just one person with a guitar, or maybe a fiddle—one person and one instrument, particularly a wooden instrument.

I feel there's so much still to be done with that, like it's an open area. I also think, the way I write, my songs really have to breathe. I mean, with my sense of rhythm, it's very hard for me to find a percussionist or a drummer that I can be happy with. I like the rhythm a lot of times to be more suggested than beat out. Bo probably has a different perspective, working a lot with bands, but he knows what I'm talking about—just letting the stuff have a little bit more flow to it than you can if you're playing in a combo. It just seems to be a little more natural to me.

Maybe, even more than the Southern tinge, it is the naturalness that gives Greg's music its unique flavor. He seems completely relaxed as he plays, swaying back and forth, a battered leather hat pushed back from his forehead, a slight smile on his lips. Whether on stage or in his living room, he seems at home with himself and his music.

As he walks through his house, a relatively new acquisition, the rooms seem to mirror his personality. It is a rambling, wooden structure, and has a comfortable, lived-in feel. Walls are lined with books of fiction and poetry, his daughters' pictures are tacked up on the wall, a guitar case sits open on the couch. Out back is a big garden, and Greg has to go out and water it now, before leaving for a gig. As he looks around his yard, it is easy to see why he would have chosen to stay out here rather than pushing his way down the music business fast lane to New York or the West Coast.

It's partly just that feeling of being home. For me, traveling like I have, it wasn't a matter of staying here for my job. I mean, I go other places for my work, and I could live pretty much anywhere in the States that I wanted to. But it's always felt good around here. It's funny, 'cause even most of my family, they took off for New Mexico. The Southwest seems to have a real big pull on my family—the weather's real nice, for one thing—and I love going down there and playing there and traveling and everything, but I wouldn't want to move there.

I think home is a real complex idea. Home is where you hook with all kinds of different things. It's hard to pin down what those are, 'cause you're right inside of them, but it's a whole bunch of stuff. I think, as you grow and you make friends and you live in an area, you eventually have so many memories for so many different hills, and if you're a fisherman like me, the little creeks and ponds and rivers, and friends, and so much builds up over time. It just becomes a very rich thing, and those things I guess are my values: your friends and your family and that feeling of roots or whatever you want to call it. So, I can understand people wanting to move around, for work or restlessness or whatever, but it's just not something I would do. I mean, you can't go and have a cup of coffee with the nice weather.

Greg smiles a wry half-smile, and picks up the guitar for one last song. His foot keeps time as he picks out a bouncy, ragtimey riff:

We used to say "I could walk all night"
And we could and we did
Down a gravel road to that tiny town and a door always open
Now we say "I could walk all night," but it's not true
We can't walk all night, because we don't want to
We want a bed and a blanket and something like breakfast
Sometime tomorrow
We want a bed and a blanket and something like breakfast
Sometime tomorrow
And I sing "Hey, hey; hey, hey;
Who woulda thunk it?
Hey, hey; hey, hey;
Who woulda thunk it?"

Flat Stuff

My friend Carl was the one who said it. We were driving along the Mississippi, and we were coming up out of the river valley into the flatland. And he said, "We're going into the flat stuff now."

Greg Brown

Sundown like a showtune, trumpets play full blast
To create a great impression but it doesn't seem to last
Flat stuff, flat stuff
Way out to the, way out to the setting sun

The muskrat and the bullfrog, the rabbit and the skunk
Old barns full of blue sky, backyards full of junk
Flat stuff, flat stuff
Way out to the, way out to the setting sun

You can't find no river that ain't low and brown
Full of sixteen catfish, who just lay there farting 'round
Flat stuff, flat stuff
Way out to the, way out to the setting sun

Pete hollers to Ruthie, "Open me a beer
And when you get it open, bring it over here"
Flat stuff, flat stuff
Way out to the, way out to the setting sun

The sun looks like a cookie that didn't come out right
The moon looks like a cookie, and someone stole a bite
Flat stuff, flat stuff
Way out to the, way out to the setting sun

When them old boys come through, sometimes I think it would have been best
If they'd said, "Jesus, it's too flat here," and just kept going west
Out of the flat stuff, flat stuff
Way out to the, way out to the setting sun

◆◆◆

John Hartford, fiddling in the main cabin of the riverboat *Twilight.*

2

Riverboats, Fiddles, and Banjos: JOHN HARTFORD

This is called Smith Bay, here, and we're fixing to come down into what is probably the widest part of the Mississippi River, which is just above Lock Number 13. This water's very shallow, so the channel down through here is like a little ditch running through a marsh, almost. There's a fair amount of current; you can see it breaking on that buoy there. Right now we're running hard, 'cause we're hoping to get down to Lock 13 before another boat gets down there. Most of the tows up here are fifteen barges, and that's a double locking, so if we're late we'll have a two-hour delay waiting for him to lock through. Now, we can walk through because we're what they call a "white boat"; we don't have a tow or anything like that. So we can lock through in about twenty minutes, fifteen if we get the lines on quick and get right on the program.

John Hartford is standing at the wheel of the riverboat *Twilight.* The wheel is almost as tall as he is, but he manages it with ease. He is talking about his life and music, and about the old days of Mississippi riverboating, but all the time his eyes remain fixed on the water ahead and he nudges the wheel left or right to keep the boat in the channel. We are heading downstream, toward St. Louis, so he tends to stay near the middle of the river, where the current is fastest. Going up, he would try to keep in the slower water near the riverbanks.

Sometimes I think that learning the skill of piloting a boat is whole lot like learning the skill of playing a fiddle, and vice versa. There's certain feelings and certain things you do, and probably the only way you can do it is to actually do it. I mean, I don't think you can learn it in a school or anything like that.

I always have loved boats ever since I can remember. As a kid in the fifties, I was around them all the time. St. Louis County is entirely surrounded by rivers: the Missouri River running across the top and the Merrimack River to the west, the Perry River south, and the Mississippi River to the east, and the Illinois River coming in just above St. Charles. So it was natural for me to get into the river. Originally, I wasn't gonna be a musician; I was gonna be a riverboat pilot or a captain. I worked on the river, for the Mississippi Valley Barge Line and the Midwest Towing Company. But I got out there and realized that I was maybe a little too artsy-craftsy to do just that. So I wound up playing the fiddle in a dance hall in south St. Louis.

I never really got away from it, though. Back when I worked on the tow boats,

I'd sit and watch the pilots. I never got to steer very much, because I was a deck hand—my main job was to clean up the pilot house, clean out the cuspidors, make ham sandwiches and coffee and stuff like that. But I had a tendency to take my time doing that, 'cause I wanted to watch all I could. Sometimes I'd be in the pilot house and the guy had to go to the bathroom or something like that, and he'd say, "Hold it for a few minutes," and I'd hold it for a few minutes, and then he'd come back.

Then, in 1971, after I'd got off the river and got to playing music, I met Dennis Trome, who at that time was captain of the Julia Belle Swain. *He asked me if I wanted to go to Chattanooga with him and put the boat up for the winter, and I did, and as we left Peoria he asked me if I wanted to steer, and I jumped on the wheel, and I've been on it ever since. I worked on her part-time, when I wasn't playing show dates, and got my license, and it's a labor of love. After a while, it becomes a metaphor for a whole lot of things, and I find for some mysterious reason that if I stay in touch with it things seem to work out all right.*

In between taking his turns at the wheel, John goes down to play in the dining cabin. The *Twilight* is a tourist boat, catering mostly to senior citizens. Right now, it is running two-day cruises, with educational talks about the river, an afternoon lecture by an actor made up as Mark Twain, and a daily concert. Most of the passengers have never heard of John Hartford, but a few gather near the front of the dining area and nod their heads in time as he plays a jaunty fiddle breakdown or sings a song about his early romance with the river, strumming his fiddle in accompaniment and playing a lilting tune between verses:

John Hartford at the wheel of the *Twilight*.

Now I had a teacher when I went to school
She loved the river and she taught about it, too
I was a pretty bright boy but she called my bluff
With her great big collection of steamboat stuff, oh yeah

She had logbooks and bells and things like that
And she knew the old captains and where they were at
She rode the Alabama and the Gordon C. Green
As the Cape Girardeau she was later renamed, uh huh

But her very favorite as you all know
Was the Golden Eagle, Captain Buck's old boat
This old stern wheeler sank and went to heaven
When I was in the fourth grade in 1947, uh huh

Well I know Captain Buck was a mighty sad man
When that old wooden hull went into the sand
And Miss Ferris was sad for sure
But immediately her mind went to work, oh yeah

She did some politicking that was tricky and hard
And she got the pilot house for the schoolhouse yard
And so instead of studying I became a dreamer
Dreaming 'bout boats and the Mississippi River, uh huh

I think the real, true music of the river is just about any kind of music that you can think of, because so many different kinds of people were on the river. I would say that probably every race and kind of person in the world has traveled up and down the Mississippi at one time or other. The original migrations down the Ohio Valley, flatboats out of Pittsburgh and all the tributaries as they settled down the river, that was primarily Celtic or Scots-Irish, so a lot of that music was Scots-Irish. A lot of fiddle tunes and stuff like that. You very seldom see a picture of a flatboat or a keel boat without a fiddler somewhere. So basically the original river music was a lot of breakdowns and hornpipes and things like that.

There's also accounts of flatboats that have people playing bagpipes, which would be nice because you would get a nice echo on the hillside, almost like a steamboat whistle. The flatboats, of course, they didn't have any steam or anything like that, so they would carry a horn, kind of like a fox hunter's horn, and they'd use that for signaling. And then they used to holler a lot, you know, like old boys do back in the country. You can get a kind of a tone going like that, and make a sound that'll get somebody's attention. Of course, sound travels real far on water, 'cause water's flat and smooth so it carries sound well.

The steamboats, most of them carried a little string band up in the cabin, and a lot of the old boats carried brass bands and steam calliopes. And then, of course, the black roustabouts down on the main deck, they had their music as well. I've got a newspaper clipping from the St. Louis newspaper for 1870, an article about the race between the Robert E. Lee *and the* Natchez, *which finished in St. Louis. It has a description of the finish of that race, and it says that, as the* Robert E. Lee *crossed the finish line, there appeared to be a black roustabout sitting in the foretree—which is the little crossbar on the forward jack-staff—playing a banjo.*

I'm not sure what that banjo player would have been playing, but it would probably have been some of the old worksongs, they called them "coonjines." That's no too far off of a sea chanty or a fiddle tune; they're all the same kind of little things, like:

Hey, little girl if you don't dilly daller
Gonna build me a boat and we'll sail it up the river

Just some little kind of a ditty that you could sing while you work.

They played all kinds of music on the river. There's a fiddle tune that they play a lot in Texas called "Shuckin' the Bush," and it's a good tune, but that title has always puzzled me, I always wondered where that was from. And then a while back I was riding on the Delta Queen, *we were going up the river one night and it got foggy, and that old pilot said, "Boys, I think if it gets any foggier, I'll just choke me a bush for the night." And I suddenly thought, "That's where that name comes from." I'll bet you that was a flatboat tune–probably what it means is, "Let's pull those flatboats in and tie up for the night and break out a jug and a fiddle and have some tunes and little dancing."*

Then there were the lead calls. In the early days, these rivers all had bends and the bends all have upper and lower bars and then they have the crossing zone, so a lot of times they'd send somebody out in a little john-boat to sound along the bar and find out where the low place was where a boat could get over. The lead line was a line with knots in it designating how many fathoms there were. The first fathom was marked off with feet, and then the next fathom was just marked off by a fathom—two fathoms is "mark twain," which is where Samuel Clemens got his name. Then three fathoms, which is eighteen feet, there isn't any boat out there drawing eighteen feet, so anything above that's "mark three," and then above that they usually just say, "no bottom."

Basically, these old calls, they would sing them, 'cause you could sing a lead line and it would carry further than if you just yelled it out. Most of the old-time leadsmen were black, and each of those guys had kind of a little particular slant on what these lead line calls were, but the basic principal of it was, the deeper you got the more ornamented you'd make the call. So, like, if you were at mark one, it would be just "Mark one."

John sings out the words in a smooth baritone.

Then mark twain would be kind of like "Mark twa-ain." Then, if you got to mark three, it might be "Ma-ark three-ee-ee," you know, they might really sing some blues into it. And then, if you got over that, you would be getting no bottom, and you might be singing, "No-o-o-o-o bo-ot-to-o-om." And then they'd start singing all kinds of songs about being in love with the captain's daughter, 'cause by that time the pilot isn't paying any attention.

The history is interesting, and John clearly has devoted much of his life to it, but the audience is there for something else. Although he has made a couple of dozen records, written hundreds of songs, and at one time fronted the most progressive acoustic band on the country scene, John is one of those musicians who will forever be best known for one particular song. In his case, it is "Gentle on My Mind," which was a hit on both the country and pop charts for Glen Campbell back in 1967, and was covered by who knows how many other people.

That song was written at a time when I was writing a whole lot of songs, and it was just the next song to fall out. I never thought it would be a hit or anything like that—if I had, I might have worked on it a little bit more, and I might have ruined it. I recorded it, and the record was doing pretty good. Then Glen Campbell put out a record on it, and the next thing I knew everybody and their little brother was making a record of it. So, you know, I'm very thankful for that song cause it allowed me a certain artistic freedom.

The way it happened was, back in the late fifties and early sixties I kind of got fascinated with writing songs. I love to read, and I got to listening to songs, and I love songs, but it was hard for me to hear lyrics. I always heard songs instrumentally, and then when I would finally get concentrated enough where I could hear the lyrics it seemed like the vocabulary was real narrow and that the words went by real slow. I wanted the words to have variety and color in them, and I wanted them to go by my ear at the speed that somebody would talk. That's changed now, 'cause I understand that that slowness is one of the qualities of songs, but a lot of my early songs had a lot of words in them and the words came by at a pretty good clip—like kind of a breakdown clip. And that's how "Gentle on My Mind" came about.

He picks up a banjo, and starts playing a loping tune. Once the pace is established, the words begin to flow alongside, clicking in time with the banjo notes:

It's knowing that your door is always open and your path is free to walk
That makes me tend to leave my sleeping bag rolled up and stashed
behind your couch
And it's knowing I'm not shackled by forgotten words and bonds
And the ink stains that have dried upon some line
That keeps you in the back roads, by the rivers of my mem'ry
That keeps you ever gentle on my mind
I dip my cup of soup back from the gurglin', cracklin' caldron in some train
yard
My beard a roughening coal pile and a dirty hat pulled low across my face
Through cupped hands 'round a tin can
I pretend I hold you to my breast and find
That you're waving from the back roads, by the rivers of my mem'ry
Ever smilin', ever gentle on my mind

The words are wistfully romantic, but John's delivery is dry and plain. The tone is more conversational than musical, and he adds no theatrical emotion. The effect is oddly touching, as if instead of a practiced performer he was just an ordinary guy chatting with whoever happened to be sitting on the next barstool.

I think style is created by limitations: I do the very best I can with what I've got, and that's how it comes out. I would say that my life in music has been a steady thing of trying to teach my hands and my feet and my mouth to reproduce the sounds that I hear in my head. No matter how hard I would try to imitate somebody or do anything else, it's always gonna come out sounding like me, because of my limitations. And that's where the style comes from. I haven't ever tried to manufacture anything; I just try to sound as good as I can.

When I was coming up, we played what is now called "oldtime" music—we just called it music. My mother and dad used to square dance, and the first time I ever heard that music it just went right through me. I mean, I heard all kinds of different music when I was growing up, but that was the music that really set me on fire.

Then, the music that really made me realize that I loved it enough to try to play it for a living was the first time I ever saw Lester Flatt and Earl Scruggs and Benny Martin and Curly Seckler [among the founding masters of bluegrass music]. They were playing on the banks of the Mississippi River, up there above Chain of Rocks, at a place called Chain of Rocks Park. That changed my life when I saw that.

I started to play banjo for square dances, and play behind fiddle players, and then I played the fiddle for square dances. We would mostly do fiddle tunes, breakdowns and waltzes, and we'd intersperse it with songs. The songs that we played were Bill Monroe, Lester Flatt and Earl Scruggs and the Stanley Brothers, and we'd sing those between the fiddle tunes. We were just playing what we heard and what we liked; it wasn't called bluegrass music then—this is like in the fifties. We just called it music. I used to play in honky-tonks a lot, and I've had guys come up to me and say, "Hey, play me some of that there Flatt and Scruggs music there on that banjer." You know, they didn't know what to call it.

John Hartford is reaching the end of his set. He picks up the fiddle and plays a last hoedown. His feet clog along, beating out a steady accompaniment to the raw, wailing notes. The audience is drifting off, heading out to the deck to watch the river or back to the buffet for another bit of lunch, but John hardly seems to notice. He smiles to himself as the bow finds a new rhythm, then finishes the tune without any sort of flourish, rises to his feet and heads back up to the pilot house.

I'm having the time of my life these days. I'm doing what I love, and if it works, that's great and if it doesn't work, then at least I haven't wasted my time. 'Cause I finally figured out that, if I don't do what's in my heart, the worst thing that could happen would be that I'd be successful at it, 'cause then I'd have to do it again and I wouldn't want to, I'd be trapped in that little box.

But I'm playing the music that's really in my heart, and I'm able to make a living at it. I have a wonderful family; I have nine grandchildren. I'm living in Nashville, and I have a real good relationship with the people that I was very much influenced by when I was growing up. Earl Scruggs is a neighbor of mine, Benny Martin is a neighbor and a dear friend, and we play a lot of music together—not trying to be professional about it, just having a good time. I really love that, and I feel like I'm more fascinated by the craft of playing music now then I ever was. So what more can I say?

◆ ◆ ◆

3
Good Old Family Music: WESTERN ILLINOIS BLUEGRASS DAYS

It is evening, blessedly cool after a blazing day in the campground at Sherwood Forest, a park outside the small town of Hillsboro, Illinois. The campground is full of RVs, and a few people are sitting outside their trailer doors, eating a late dinner or chatting with the neighbors. There is music drifting in the night air, a banjo or fiddle rising over the rhythm of bass and guitar, a voice or two singing with a flat, country twang. There are at least four different jam sessions, spread out around the park so as not to bother each other. The most popular seems to be on a rise just above the hollow that holds the wooden amphitheater. Some eight or ten older men, and a couple of women, are sitting around on folding chairs, playing a mix of guitars, fiddles, bass, a Dobro, and sometimes a mandolin or two, trading off lead breaks and song choices.

The group has no leader, but the most striking figure is a rather small, bright-eyed man in a brightly flowered baseball cap. He is playing a harmonica in a metal rack and accompanying himself on guitar. To his right, another harmonica player is following along, sometimes in unison and sometimes in harmony. These are John Snyder and Charles Brush, and they have been playing together for years, whenever there happens to be a bluegrass festival in the region.

Charles: *The first time that I ever saw John, we were at Lincoln New Salem State Park, near Springfield, Illinois. A friend of mine had gone for a year or two prior to my going up there, and he was telling me about this old man—don't hit me, John—who would sit and play the harmonica from daylight until dark. So I went up with this friend, and we set up camp. The next morning, after we had coffee, he said "Let's go for a walk." We went down the road, and he said, "Now, listen." And you could hear John playing. So we stood out on the street and watched him for a while, and then I went back and had my breakfast. After breakfast, I got on my bicycle and rode back, and I could hear John still playing.*

I rode around there about two hours later. By this time, four or five more was in there with him. And they were there all day long. Then there was a jam session down at the little stage, and here John came down and he played all night down there. So I told my friend, I said, "You were right about him. He can play all day and all night."

A fan chats with Joy Lewis Calhoun,
as Bob Lewis (center) chimes in.

John laughs at his friend's recollection:

I never tire. Not at playing music. I might get tired of listening to somebody else, but I never get tired of listening to myself. It's just a natural gift, you know, some have it and some don't. And I just happened to be one of the fortunate ones that, if I have it, well, I praise the Lord for it. I've been playing all my life. If you would subtract twelve from seventy-nine, that would give you about sixty-eight years, probably? I started when I was twelve. And I'll be eighty in October, and I've played pretty much regular ever since. Played for dances for years—most generally "half and half" dances; that's round dancing, square dancing, and schottisch and waltzes—I'd do that three to five nights a week back when I was younger.

You know, I never drank, I never smoked. I never abused myself, although I worked long hours and worked hard. And when I play the harmonica and the guitar, I just do my thing. I play it the way I want to play it; what you see is what you get. My style is my style, and anybody who cannot accept that, well, they just as well can go find them another jam somewhere. Because I just have that one thing. I do the best I can, and if I can do that, whether it turns out good or bad, then I think I'm a success. And I guess I have to give the Lord credit for blessing me with a good set of lungs, a healthy body, and a sense of timing.

A couple of people are asking if anyone can sing lead on "I'll Fly Away." John is chatting with Charlie, but as soon as he catches the question he is happy to oblige. He adjusts the towel that he keeps draped over the top of the guitar to protect it from his sweat, and launches into a upbeat version of the old gospel number. His voice is slightly cracked with age, but it is still powerful, and rings out over the assembled instruments.

Some glad morning, when this life is o'er, I'll fly away
To a home on God's celestial shore, I'll fly away
I'll fly away, oh glory, I'll fly away
When I die, hallelujah, by and by, I'll fly away

Everybody joins in on the chorus, and Charlie's harmonica keeps up a reedy harmony behind John's vocal lead. Then they are into a two-harmonica version of "Wabash Cannonball." Jim Smith, the Dobro player, takes a couple of breaks, but most of the load is carried by the two "French harps," chugging along at a steam-engine pace.

John is in his element here, and later talks about how he came to learn the instrument. His voice has a dry, small-town flavor, and when he says "harmonica," he pronounces the "o" long: "har-moh-nica."

People have asked me, "Could you tell me, how do you learn to play harmonica?" I always say, "Well, get one. And if you can't play it in a week, throw it away and buy you a set of drums, because you either can or you can't." You can't tell somebody how to play a harmonica. It's just something you pick up and start blowing on it, and if you really want to play it, you will seek the notes out with your tongue, and you will learn. I've seen people blew a harmonica for years on end who still couldn't play hardly a "Yankee Doodle,"and other people can pick one up and within twenty-four hours they're playing a good song. So it's just something that you either have or you don't have.

I started when I was somewhere around five year old. I couldn't even read, I remember, because they sent off and got me one of these harmonicas you could order out of the radio from a fellow named Lonnie Glossom, and I got his book and everything. And I could look at the picture and see that the lips went over the harmonica, but the rest of it I couldn't read, so I threw it away. But my grandmother could play one old song, called "Go Tell Aunt Betsy," or "Go Tell Aunt Rhody, the Old Gray Goose Is Dead." She taught me to play that in about two or three days trying, and then I would try other songs. I run the whole family crazy, I'm sure, running around with the harmonica in my pocket. For me, it's just the only gift of music that I have. I tried playing the guitar, and it didn't work. So I went back to the harmonica, and I've been pleased with that. That's all I can do, so I do my best with it. And I have played for years and years.

I've played bluegrass now about six or seven years, I guess. Charlie interjects. *Up until then it was gospel and just the old tear-jerking country music. And I love all that kind of music. But there's something about playing bluegrass music that gets in your blood. It's just the tempo, the beat of it and everything. Really, it's nothing but just old country, speeded up a little bit in most cases, it's just a little faster tempo to the music. That's what I like real well about it. And I would say that whatever song that you wanted to play, if you played it in bluegrass style, you could say, well, that's a bluegrass song. So many people think that it has to be written back prior to the time that the steel guitar became prevalent on the* Grand Ole Opry, *so to speak. But you can only sing a song so long, you know, and then somebody wants to hear something else. So what we do is, I would say it was a little bit of a mixture of country and the old bluegrass.*

John has been listening to this digression and nodding his assent, while waiting his chance to chime in.

Many bluegrass songs are written from personal experiences. They tell a story of somebody's tragedy or something of that nature, the passing of a loved one or a cavein in a coal mine, or a train wreck or something. I mean, they have something to talk about that people can relate to, particularly older people. And to me it encompasses gospel music, and it includes country music that can be done in a bluegrass fashion. There are so many different types of songs that you can do with the bluegrass flavor, and to say that this song or that song is or is not bluegrass, to me that's going out on a pretty small limb.

You know, most of this music was born and bred in the South; you don't find many of the big-name musicians from our part of the country. Those people, as they worked in the cotton fields and they worked on the railroad, they developed a rhythm. A lot of the musical talent that people have were born and bred out of their occupation, whether it was working on a farm, following an old mule plowing corn, or mining coal, or driving spikes on the railroad, or pounding rocks. They done it with a flair and a fashion, and they developed words to the rhythm that they used doing their job. I think that's how a lot of the songs came about, and then people, particularly if they were natural-born showmen, as a lot of people are, they wanted to develop that showman's artistic ability and apply it to their lives in the form of music.

For me, music has been good to me. I have made a little money playing for dances, but I never depended on it as a livelihood. I always worked. So it is more of an outlet than a means of feeding my family or buying a home or car or something. It was more a way of expressing the way I felt. To most of us who play it on the weekends or things of that nature, we don't even consider the money. A lot of times we go out and play and we never say, "How much can you pay?" or "We've got to have so much to come," or anything of that nature. We're just glad for the opportunity to go out there and express ourselves and bring a little happiness to somebody else and let it go at that. And if we make a few bucks, well, that's fine. If we don't, well, we go anyway.

True to his reputation, John is still playing as we head back to Hillsboro to get a night's sleep.

The streets of Hillsboro are hung with banners celebrating the town's status as "Bluegrass Capital of Southern Illinois." The county seat of Montgomery County, Hillsboro is a classic Middle-American farm town. This weekend, the bluegrass festival is competing for attention with the Olde Tyme Farm Show, and the main square is filled with tractors of all shapes and sizes. The two local newspapers give front-page space to the results of last weekend's 4-H show, with pictures of beaming youngsters beside their prize-winning goats, calves, or poultry.

It would seem like the perfect location for a bluegrass festival, but Jake Feazel and Mac Patterson, the festival organizers, say that at first the townspeople were a bit wary.

Lil' Bob Lewis swings a bass.

Nineteen years ago, there was no bluegrass around here, Mac says. *Honestly, a lot of people didn't know what bluegrass was. Some people used to think we smoked it. And we wanted to get something going. We wanted to give the people in Illinois some good music. So we started nineteen years ago in a place over in Greenville, Illinois. Pretty feeble when we first started. What did we have, 100 people maybe attend our first show? I know we had to take money out of our pockets to pay the bands.*

Jake: *And they weren't top bands. But at that time they were good enough. But it has grown since then. How many years were we there, Mac?*

Mac: *We were there six years. And then we took the show to Belleville, and it just flat didn't work. Sometimes you bomb, and we bombed on that one.*

Jake: *You ever went into a German town where it's all oom-pah-pah and tried to play bluegrass? It just flat didn't work.*

Mac: *But then a guy invited us to come over and look at this park. So we drove up here one Sunday afternoon. That area down where the stage is, it was all grown up with underbrush, but it looked like it would be a perfect spot for an amphitheater.*

Jake: *That first time we brought in a portable stage, just sawhorses with boards on. And it went over pretty good. We realized then that something could be going on here. And we convinced the city people here that something could be made of this. But I remember, when we first came into town, one of the officers of the city said, "There's a couple of shysters coming into town here."*

Mac: *He thought we were coming in just to milk the town.*

Jake: *He praises us every year now—or not really praises us, but he says, "You fellows sure made a liar out of me."*

Jake and Mac are about as unlike a couple of shysters as anyone could imagine. They are country from their scuffed shoes to their feed caps, and completely committed to bluegrass music. Mac, in particular, is a hard-core traditionalist on a mission to preserve the acoustic country tradition.

I was born in 1927. That means I'm seventy years old, aren't I? And when I was just a child growing up, we had the old Philco battery-powered radio. And you didn't use that battery very extravagantly. You had to ration it. But on Saturday night, we all listened to the Grand Ole Opry. *That thing went on from six o'clock to midnight, and that music that you heard in those days was what we're hearing out here*

Hillsboro's Sharecroppers play a tune for the watermelon eaters.

now. You heard some of it over there last night in that jam session where those boys were; that's some of your old, early country music.

I've always been a traditionalist, I don't deny that. And it became even stronger on me after Bill Monroe died. I thought, "Hey, there's nobody to protect this thing now. If we don't, who's going to?" So I guess Jake told me that I got worse, more bull-headed. But I just feel real strong that we have to guard the standard. If you don't have a standard, man, you're in trouble. If you go buy a pound of coffee, you don't want somebody selling you twelve ounces. A pound is sixteen ounces. That's the standard, right? Everything worth anything has standards. And bluegrass is valuable enough that we should guard the standard. I feel very firmly about that.

Somebody asked Bill Monroe one time, "Would you define bluegrass for me?" And Bill said—you know, Bill was just a common guy from Rosine, Kentucky—he said, "Well, it's Baptist and Holiness, and it's country, and it's jazz, and it's played from the heart, and it's from me to you. In other words, I'm playing it the way I feel it, and I'm sharing it with you." That's the way he defined it, see?

Bill Monroe's the guy that put this together. He looked for this sound for ten years, but it never really developed until about 1945, when twenty-one-year-old Earl Scruggs came in with that three-fingered style of picking, picking that big-headed bass-sounding banjo. That turned it around. And Lester Flatt, with that hand-rubbed voice that he had, that smooth baritone. That's when it really became what you'd call bluegrass—five instruments: We're talking about banjo, flat-top guitar, and then you've got to have that mandolin chop in there. Then you've got to have a fiddle to fill those holes in the tune. And then the doghouse bass. I call that big old upright bass the "doghouse." You've got to have that. And it's not really, truly bluegrass unless they've got those five basic instruments. Now, there's a lot of bands carrying electric basses. But you know why they're carrying those? Lazy. They don't want to fool with that big old doghouse. Me, I think it's a sin to play an electric instrument in a bluegrass band.

Around here, we still have a lot of musicians who like that traditional sound. And some of them are just young kids. I think that most of the musicians we've had are self-taught. A good example is Alison Krauss. Alison Krauss grew up right in Champagne, Illinois, just over the hill over here, not very far. Her grandfather taught her to play the fiddle, and she used to go around to all these small gatherings and play. Of course, she developed far beyond what we are now; she's gone on away and left us. But, as a young girl, she was very interested in this. And she got her influence from people in these jam sessions. I think the jam session does more to develop bluegrass musicians than any other single form. That's the reason we are so intent on trying to offer an environment where they want to jam. You see?

By mid-afternoon, the jamming is in full swing. Mac and Jake have driven up a truck full of watermelons, slicing big, juicy chunks for the assembled campers. John and Charlie and their bunch showed up to play along with the chomping and seed-spitting. Meanwhile, the evening's featured performers have been arriving, pulling their busses up behind the amphitheater.

The Bob Lewis Family are among the first to arrive. Bob Sr. parks the bus, and people start pouring out: daughters Joy, who plays mandolin, and Nanette, who sings and trades off playing the upright bass; son Lil' Bob, who plays fiddle, and banjoist Kevin Hendrix, the only nonrelative in the band. Mother Barbara, another singer and the band's "producer" ("She literally produced this family"), is still on the bus, minding Joy's new baby, but will soon come out and start cooking what seems like an infinite supply of hamburgers. While the gang waits for the food, they start tuning up instruments, and soon the jam is in full swing. The Lewises, who are among the top Missouri bluegrass outfits, were a last-minute addition to the festival, after the Ezell Family had to cancel due to a pregnancy, and Rory Ezell, the Ezell's teenage multi-instrumentalist son, has made it down to sit in with them. At the moment he is playing mandolin and, with Bob Sr. strumming guitar accompaniment, the kids take off. Lil' Bob sings the lead, and Rory and Nanette join in on the chorus:

Little girl of mine in Tennessee
I know she's waiting there for me
Some day I'll settle down in that little mountain town
With that little girl of mine in Tennessee

The harmonies have the unique closeness of family singers, people who all talk with the same inflections and vocal quality. The instrumental work is crisp and sure, Lil' Bob fiddling with an infectious, youthful verve, and Joy sending out flurries of notes from her mandolin. They finish the song at breakneck pace. Bob, mops his brow, then comically says "OK, let's do a fast one now."

The kids smile at what is obviously an old family joke, then prove their willingness to oblige, blazing into "Rawhide," a classic Bill Monroe mandolin showcase. Joy and Rory trade leads, with Lil' Bob adding a shuffling fiddle break and Kevin getting shouts of encouragement on a flashy banjo solo. A few more tunes and it's time for lunch and the story of the band.

Bob Sr.: *We're out of a place called Poplar Bluff, Missouri, southeast Missouri. What happened was, I was working in Texas, in the oil fields, and we spent about fifteen years down there. And then when the bottom fell out of the oil fields, we moved back to Missouri, and I already knew how to play the guitar. So I taught my oldest son how to play the fiddle, and then he [Lil' Bob] started to play the fiddle, and the oldest girl learned how to play the guitar. And they just kept going, and everybody just kept learning how to play something.*

Lil' Bob: *We've been doing it as long as I can remember. I don't even remember learning how. I just always did it.*

Bob: *I picked the instrument I wanted each of them to play, and I put it in their hand. He [Lil' Bob] carried a mandolin around with him for a long time, and I'd take the mandolin out and put a fiddle in his hands. And he'd throw the fiddle down, pick up a mandolin. It's been that way all the way up to right now. But now he plays anything you want. He plays the mandolin, the guitar, the fiddle, the bass. And he does whatever he wants to. But anyway, we kept on playing until finally we formed a little group. And we first started doing it just as fun.*

Joy (joshing him): *This isn't fun no more.*

Bob: *I mean, it's still fun, but you know what I'm saying.*

Lil' Bob: *It was a hobby.*

Bob: *Yeah, we didn't get paid for it, we just done it for a hobby. And then people started calling us from farther off and wanting us to come and do a show for them, which we couldn't afford. We had to have a little bit of money. So they started paying us a little bit. And then a little more. Now we're—*

Joy: *We almost got rich, right?*

Lil' Bob: *Yeah, we're rich.*

Bob: *We're back where we started. Working for free.*

All three Lewises laugh. In fact, they are doing pretty well. By now, the family has become more than a musical group; they are all-around entertainers. At the evening concert, they come out in matching suits and present a tight show, with comedy, hot picking, and a clog-dancing showcase by Joy and Nanette. Their material ranges from gospel originals to bluegrass standards, all played with expertise and a lighthearted, good-time verve.

Bob: *We don't do a lot of practicing. I'm usually golfing, and Bob's got him a car now and he's usually out running around, and Joy lives about 150 miles from us. But we're on the road a lot. Last year, we played five days a week, because we took our music back east to the schools. We played Pennsylvania, Delaware, Maryland, Virginia, West Virginia, all the eastern states—New York, Maine. We've been playing about thirty states a year.*

We're trying to keep bluegrass alive. We try to keep everything acoustic. I mean, we can go out here behind a tree and practice with our acoustic instruments, where, if you were a rock 'n' roll player, you'd have to plug in cords and you're there for about two hours rigging up. And all my kids that I've raised has stayed into the bluegrass music. Some of them are in other bands, but they're still where I taught them. So one of the reasons why I like bluegrass is that, so far, it's kept my family together.

The Lewises play a blazing version of "Orange Blossom Special," showing off Lil' Bob's fiddle chops, then exit to enthusiastic applause. The next band is already waiting in the wings, and another after that. The listeners sit in lawn chairs that they have brought down from their campers. Some stay the whole evening, patting their feet and clapping along. Others drift off to check out the jam sessions.

John and Charlie, of course, only last a little while down at the amphitheater. They may enjoy hearing a band onstage, but it cannot compete with the pleasure of playing. With much of the crowd down at the performance, they do not have the listeners they had last night, but that is not what they are here for. For John, in particular, this is a way of life.

To me, it's more than just the music. It's the people that we associate with. Music is a great common denominator. I mean, you might find the president of a bank playing with the janitor, but they're on equal terms playing bluegrass music. It's a great equalizer, because everybody's playing the same type of music and enjoying it. And you will notice that one person will take the lead, then another instrument will take the lead. Then another. And there's nobody trying to be the star of the show. It's just everybody enjoying what they're doing. And that's what it's all about.

It's kind of like a reunion. Like a family, because we are really a family. If one person has a bit of good fortune, it gets around, and we all know it. If one has a tragedy, why we rally around and try to support that person. It's really just a great big family affair. There's no rivalry as far as trying to be better than anybody else. Somebody that's played for twenty years will sit down beside a beginner. Maybe the beginner will feel a little shy: "Well, I don't know how to play very well." "Well, bring your guitar in here, and just sit with somebody and watch their moves, and watch when they change chords and listen."

And that's one thing about playing music. It's fifty percent playing and fifty percent listening. You've got to listen and play with the people around you and not just take off on your own thing, but try to play together and try to complement each other, and make each other sound good. And it's just a good old family reunion as far as I'm concerned. Just a great way for people to get out and enjoy the great outdoors and enjoy music and enjoy one another. And a hot dog and marshmallow over an open fire doesn't hurt a thing, either.

◆ ◆ ◆

The old-time jammers. Charlie Brush, third from left, on harmonica; John Snyder, next to him on guitar in his flowered hat.

JOHN HARTFORD

On the Mississippi's Role in the Origin of Bluegrass

In the early part of the nineteenth century we had cut very few roads, much less highways, and so the only way that culture could really get back into the backwoods was by river. There's a fellow named Bob Wynans who has a theory that I really like: He said that a lot of the blackface minstrel shows went back into the mountains by way of rivers. See, early circuses had what they called "boat shows." A boat show would be a circus that would travel by steamboat. It would go down the river, and it would get off at a particular landing and work the little communities that were close to that landing, and then catch the next steamboat and go on down to the next landing and work the communities that were near there. 'Cause, in those days, you didn't have to go very far to get out of reach of the first landing.

Most of these circuses carried a blackface minstrel act, with a five-string banjo and a fiddle, and so the people in the backwoods would hear this music. They already played fiddles in the backwoods, but they didn't play too many banjos, so then they'd go and they'd make banjos out of gourds and groundhog hides and stuff like that. And then they'd want to sing these minstrel songs, but they couldn't hardly remember them, and what few they would remember they would probably get it wrong, so that would start the creation of new material right there.

Then, for the rest of it, they would take these old Elizabethan ballads, and they would play them in double time, like for instance they'd sing "Lady Mary was a sitting in her high hall door," with that fast banjo going under it. And there you've got what would be the ancestor music to bluegrass, which is generally a slow, loping vocal over a ninety-mile-an-hour rhythm section. I think that music certainly went into the backwoods of America by river, because it was the only way to get there.

ST. LOUIS BLUES

"I walked all the way from East St. Louis, didn't have but one lousy dime."

–Anon., "East St. Louis Blues"

"They say that blues originated in New Orleans but St. Louis had some of the best blues singers that ever there was... The levee at St. Louis was known throughout the country as the origination of blues."

–James "Stump" Johnson, barrelhouse pianist, quoted in Paul Oliver's *Conversation with the Blues*

St. Louis was the first big city on the northern trek up the Mississippi, and became a stopping-off place and sometimes a final destination for hundreds of thousands of African-Americans heading up out of the deep South. It was where the South met the North, and as a result was one of the most fertile musical cities in the United States. In the nineteenth century, the junction of river and railroad made it a tour stop for all kinds of traveling musical groups, from minstrel shows to opera companies, but it was at the turn of the century that it came into its own.

The music that put St. Louis on the map was ragtime. The list of pianists who made the city their base is long, and there were many more whose names are now forgotten. The most famous was Scott Joplin, who was born in Texarkana, Texas, and first published while living in the western Missouri town of Sedalia, but did much of his greatest work in St. Louis. Joplin came to St. Louis in 1885, and spent most of the next decade there. At that time, the river brought a rough-and-ready crowd of roustabouts and traveling people into town, and supported a thriving mess of bars, whorehouses, and nebulously defined "social clubs," all fertile ground for pianists and small bands. It was there, according to many accounts, that the fabled Frankie shot her lover Johnny (or in some accounts Albert) because "he done her wrong."

Joplin worked the "sporting houses," but his aspirations were higher. He wanted to be taken seriously as a classical composer, and as soon as he was able to make a decent income from published pieces like "The Maple Leaf Rag," "The Sunflower Slow Drag," "The Easy Winners," and "Augustan Club Waltzes," he retired from the barrelhouse life.

Other players were otherwise inclined. Louis Chauvin became the new local star, playing at the Rosebud Club, a bar and sporting house owned by another fine pianist, Tom Turpin. More musicians arrived on a regular basis, passing through on their way north or south, east or west. In 1904, when the world's fair came to town, St. Louis became an entertainer's mecca, and it continued to boom through the war years.

Not all of the famous musicians who came through would settle. New Orleans stars like

Jelly Roll Morton and Lonnie Johnson stayed a few months, playing on the excursion boats, then moved on. For a musician with dreams of national success, Chicago or New York were already more likely launching grounds, and would soon become even more prominent with the coming of national radio hookups and the recording industry. Still, St. Louis was a thriving center for black music, a place with big-city industrial jobs that payed decent wages, and yet with something of the relaxed flavor of down home.

Many of the local musicians would remain unknown outside the area. While Kansas City, its western Missouri twin, became a spawning ground for national jazz talent, St. Louis's jazz scene remained largely a local affair. Charlie Creath's Jazz-O-Maniacs were regional stars, and for a while featured Lonnie Johnson on violin, but rarely made it further out of town than a riverboat excursion trip. The best-traveled band, the Missourians, would make it to New York after being taken over by Cab Calloway, but once there they never returned as a group. A thriving local brass tradition, influenced both by visitors from New Orleans and by the local German community and its popular brass ensembles, produced a string of fine trumpet players, but none would get much outside exposure until the later era that produced Clark Terry and Miles Davis.

The blues scene was another story. Though W. C. Handy, who wrote "St. Louis Blues," had only spent a few months there as a down-and-out hobo, he could hardly have picked a better location to immortalize. As the first major industrial center north of the Delta, it became one of the hottest blues centers in the United States. Peetie Wheatstraw, perhaps the biggest-selling blues singer of the 1930s, had come up the river from Ripley, Tennessee, to join the growing scene of pianists and guitar players that included such legendary figures as Roosevelt Sykes, Hi Henry Brown, Charley Jordan, Speckled Red, Walter Davis, St. Louis Jimmy Oden. The pianist, guitarist, and singer Henry Townsend came up from Mississippi in the teens, and was king of the local scene for much of the 1920s and 1930s. Today, he still plays regularly at local clubs, drawing a crowd of adoring fans who greet him with the respect that befits a legend.

Fashions changed with the years, but St. Louis managed to keep pace, largely thanks to regular infusions of new talent from down south. Chuck Berry was a local boy who became a star after joining forces with Johnny Johnson, a pianist trained in the St. Louis tradition of Roosevelt Sykes. His competition would include Ike Turner, soon to find young Annie Mae Bullock and rename her Tina, and another transplanted Mississippian, Little Milton. As soul music became the rage, the local gospel world provided a training ground for singers like Ann Peebles and Fontella Bass.

Today, the St. Louis music scene is a study in contrasts. The strong African-American community continues to produce excellent players and singers, but the ever-stricter centralization of the music industry on the coasts has meant that the more ambitious artists tend to leave town. The new riverboat casinos came in with much fanfare, but East St. Louis remains seriously depressed, at least in economic terms. There is still a bedrock of fine older players, but they spend much of their time talking about the past. When the St. Louis musicians turn out in force, though, at the annual blues festival or for a special benefit concert, they show a wealth of talent that few other American cities could match, and their voices provide a living history of twentieth-century African-American music.

4
Poetry and the Drum: EUGENE REDMOND AND SYLVESTER "SUNSHINE" LEE

The words "black" and "art," or "black" and "culture" were not used widely together until the 1960s. When I was a child, you know, people would be trotting off to their little ballet classes and you'd hear "The Flight of the Bumblebee" coming out of the windows of the various homes. When you said "culture" then, it was like "Ah-hem, pardon me." That was the way it was. The root, the folk black culture was not accepted by the middle-class black people, and there was no formal black culture.

Katherine Dunham sort of stepped into that. She came into the city at a time of rebellion—that can't be underplayed. I mean, the black power movement, it had to be given a major role in the black arts movement. Because people started to perform under the banner of being black people. It just was incredible. Miss Dunham came in, and helped give it a theoretical frame of reference. People started using the word "black" in front of "poem" or "black" in front of "gospel," or "soul" in front of "music," or "soul" in front of "food."

It transformed this entire community. I mean, you couldn't walk five or six blocks in East St. Louis in the sixties and seventies and not hear drumming coming out of somebody's basement or somebody's second floor apartment, or a school, you know, or see some African dancers.

Eugene Redmond is standing out in front of the Katherine Dunham Dynamic Museum, housed in a somewhat run-down old mansion in East St. Louis, with his old friend Sylvester "Sunshine" Lee. The whole neighborhood is run-down, with streets and houses badly in need of repair. Young people hang out on street corners, looking bored. Eugene and Sunshine seem anything but depressed, though. They have seen East St. Louis in better times, but also see potential in the people around them, and they have made it their mission to harness that potential. Eugene is a poet, and he does most of the talking. Sunshine is a drummer, leader of a traditional African drumming circle. Both are longtime associates of Katherine Dunham, whose dance company set New York on fire in the forties, and who went on to found a school in East St. Louis as a beacon for black culture and a living demonstration of the talent wasting untapped in America's inner cities. Sunshine says that he is himself a product of Dunham's influence.

Sylvester "Sunshine" Lee leads his class of young drummers in East St. Louis.

As a young boy, I had a chance to go to one of their performances. I think it was at Roy Junior High School, which is down the street, right across from her house. I was watching the drummers play, and it kind of fascinated me. I said, "Man, I want to be a part of that." I seen my little friend that was a part of it and he was saying to me, at that young age, "I'm traveling with Miss Dunham. I'm going places. I'm going to Houston, Texas." And as a young guy I wanted to be able to travel, too and see what the world is about. So I got interested in the drum.

That particular year, she had this instructor, Mor Thiam, he was an African from Senegal who played with the National Ballet of Senegal and he was great. He was a fast drummer; you couldn't hardly see his hands. And for some odd reason, I became one of his pet drummers. I guess it was because I would always smile and say, "Show me this rhythm again." And I would take it up and beat on tables, I would beat on chairs—I ran my mother basically out of the house, you know, trying to learn how to play the drums.

As for Eugene, he was already a promising young poet when Katherine Dunham established her center, but he says that she changed his life.

I had some very severe literary training. In high school I had two years of Latin, and then I had undergraduate and graduate training, so I was pretty well steeped in the Greco-Roman-Hebraic-Christian canon in literature. Miss Dunham put me in touch with the African, Asian, Indian, indigenous island continuum. I learned how to songify the words, how to look at a poem as not a fixed object on the page, but as a script that could be read in various ways and be performed as a book, as in a musical.

The training I received under Miss Dunham changed me as a writer and changed my writing. Because I started writing performance text. I learned how to choreograph a poem—without dancing in a stereotypical sense. It was a much richer part of the art of performing. I learned how to turn an optical text into an acoustical text. How to turn static literature into what we call the archival literature of gesture.

In East St. Louis you have a very storied tradition. Storied in the sense of levels, and storied in a sense of tales. It is one of the blues centers of the world and one of the jazz centers of the world, one of the gospel centers of the world. Blues, because it is part of a network of cultures along the Mississippi River that were influenced by the Delta sounds, by New Orleans sounds, by the Memphis sounds. Jazz because of our proximity to Kansas City and Chicago and St. Louis. This was also one of the major railroad centers; right near where I grew up in the south end of this city, there were fourteen sets of tracks.

We had all kinds of industry: We had three packing houses here for several decades, the railroad yards and steel foundries, glass factories, box factories, chemical plants. And what you'd call industrial folklore grew up, came out of that work environment, and that influenced the music as well. Of course, some of the greatest lyrics have to do with work. And love, you know. And what happens perhaps to your love while you're at work.

Eugene and Sunshine are laughing. Standing on the sidewalk, they look like a couple of neighborhood guys, and Eugene's precise speech and careful turns of phrase slide easily into street patterns.

You know, the song implication of language is very normal for people of African extraction. It seems that there's a ritual greeting and a ritual good-bye. In East St. Louis, it's like not, "Good morning, how are you doing?" but "Hey, what up? And not "Goodbye," but "Check, dude. Later. Alright." So it's the musicalization of the heys, and in East St. Louis that's very rich. People play the dozens—'s all the verbal sparring, verbal fencing, verbal boxing, verbal gymnastics. And that's very, very central to the music.

Later that afternoon, in a large room at the Katherine Dunham Dynamic Museum, Eugene and Sunshine are putting their words into practice. Sunshine is surrounded by five young men, all dressed in African clothing. He and three of his students play djembes, the big, tapered drums popular across much of West Africa. The other two play double-sided barrel drums. Sunshine is clearly the leader, but he gives the others plenty of space. He is completely caught up in the music, his tongue lapping out of his mouth as he concentrates on the rhythm, shouting encouragement, then breaking into a big smile as he hears a sound that pleases him.

You don't beat a drum. You know, most times you hear someone say, "I love to see you beat a drum," but we correct them right away. You do't beat a drum, you masterly play a drum. Because there is parts to that drum—four, five parts that you need to know to be able to play. Because, as you can see in our class, each sound is different, and you have to learn each sound to be able to know what the're saying. You have to say it with your mouth before you play them. We say if you can say it with your mouth, it relays down through the arms, through the body, and you become one with the drum.

After Mor Thiam had to go back to Africa, Miss Dunham brought another drummer. His name was Kwazi Fedoo, and he was a masterful drummer, too. He taught us what the talking drum is about. He said, "You know the sound of elephant?" I said, "No." He said, "Big elephant, you know how they walk?" I said, "Yeah." He said, "Make the sound with your mouth." I never knew what he was talking about. So he made the sound, "boom, tagitty ding ding tikka boom!" He showed us all of the sounds of the animals in Africa: the lions, the tigers, the leopards, all of it, the deer. I became a student of

Eugene Redmond reading.

Kwazi Fedoo and we played hours and hours and hours, and I became a good drummer, a sufficient drummer.

In fact, that particular year, Miss Dunham gave me the name Sunshine. I was working with the Urban League, Manpower and I would come down there every evening to play with my little shirt and tie on. And Miss Dunham told her assistant, she said, "Arthur, go get that boy that make these girls smile." So Arthur would say, "What you talking about, Miss Dunham?" She say, "I don't know. The boy always sitting by you." He say, "Uh, Sylvester Lee?" She said, "I don't know his name, but it should have been

Sunshine because he makes them girls smile." So when Arthur came and got me at the Urban League he said, "Miss Dunham gave you another name." The minute I walked into class, she said, "Okay, your name now is Sunshine." So I took that as my artistic name, and now the majority of the people in East St. Louis know me as Sunshine.

As the drummers play, Eugene is standing at the side of the room. He is dressed somewhat professorially, in a brown corduroy jacket, set off by a round, West African kinte cloth hat, and he is dancing to the drums. The dance is all his own, a sinuous series of mimelike movements that are the introduction to his poetry. When he feels the moment is right, he takes his place in front of the drummers, and begins to read. He holds the book open in his hand, but only occasionally glances at the page. Most of the time, he is looking out at the listeners, and his face and body are constantly in motion, moving with the rhythm of the drums and of the words. Sometimes he is speaking softly, sometimes shouting, sometimes singing.

Eugene Redmond and Sylvester "Sunshine" Lee

Milestone: The Birth of an Ancestor.
For Miles Dewey Davis III, 1926 to 1991, In Memoriam, In Futuriam.

Dressed up in pain,
the flatted fifth began its funereal climb
up the tribal stairwell:
grief-radiant as it
bulged and gleamed with moans
spread like laughter or Ethiopia's wings.
Mourned its own percussive rise
became blues-borne
in the hoarse East St. Louis air

bore witness to the roaring calm
the garrulous silence
the caskets of tears
the gushing stillness:
the death of the Cool
became the birth of an Ancestor.
Let's hear it again:
the death of the Cool
became the birth of an Ancestor

The drums, which had quieted somewhat as he spoke, rise to a crescendo behind him as he smiles and listens, his head moving with the beat.

When I was growing up, East St. Louis had dozens of clubs, all over the place. From the deep south end and the clubs like Town Talk all the way over to the north. Right down the street this way, the Club DeLisa, and then out on Missouri, the Blue Note, and down near where Miles Davis's family lived at Fifteenth and Broadway, where his father had a dental office downstairs and the family lived upstairs. That was a business district and an entertainment center. They had a bunch of clubs there, and they changed names and hands over the years.

In fact, just about four blocks away south of here is where Chuck Berry used to play, the Cosmopolitan Club, right on Seventeenth Street, four blocks down on Bond Avenue. I used to go through there selling papers or doing something else, you know, trying to make something as a teenager. Because I was underage, the bouncer let me stand at the door for a while, 'cause he understood that I needed to be in there, to hear the music. The same thing at the Vets Club, which was two blocks down, two blocks west, and about, eight or nine blocks south. That was a great club. Miles Davis played there, Albino Red played there, Quartet Très Bien, Jimmy Smith. Leon Thomas sang there, Joe Williams sang there, you name it.

In East St. Louis, for several generations, everybody wanted to play a musical instrument. It was just what you wanted to do. Everybody wanted to be able to play a musical instrument, and everybody wanted to be a boxer. I'm talking about males now. Miles Davis boxed, you know. That was him. And if you were a woman, you wanted to sing like Billie Holiday or Bessie Smith or Ma Rainey or Dinah Washington or Ruth Brown. Depending on the era, you know. Sarah Vaughn, Ella Fitzgerald. There were just hundreds of girls, practicing, humming with their boys. Musical culture dominated the overall culture, and I think that's one reason why we produced so many musicians, so many singers.

Another thing, and this is the real telling irony, the real paradox—W. E. B. DuBois talks about this: We wouldn't have what we call black art or soul art had it not been for segregation and discrimination. I mean, if we hadn't been in those shanty towns and those shack villages next to the railroad tracks, the ones that were vacated by all the European immigrant groups that were heading upwards, as we came up from the South, if we hadn't had our own little place, you wouldn't have snoots, you wouldn't have barbecue, you wouldn't have blues, rhythm and blues, rap, you wouldn't have gospel, you wouldn't have jazz, you wouldn't have the dozens, all the incredible oratory that we have.

We are living in this pressure cooker of racism, of economic pressure, of poverty, of misogyny, of neglect, abuse, you name it. Now, a lot of people don't make it in this compression. We bury a lot of people. You know, if you read the paper, if you look at the news, there's a lot of terrible things that are happening. But the people who do make it are jewels.

The difficulty of life in East St. Louis gives a special weight to the work that Eugene and Sushine are doing. Their art is an end in itself, but also serves a vital function in bringing the community together.

Eugene Redmond and Sylvester "Sunshine" Lee

Sunshine: *I use music as a bait and a tool to bring our children off of the street. We believe in the holistic approach: By training the young children, we can get the whole family, and make that whole family work collectively together. You know, all parents like to follow their children in any sporting event, any dancing events. They always say music can soothe the savage beast, so, if that can relate to us as a people, then we can bring them together through music and songs and dance and through art.*

We have a company now of twenty-eight members: fire-eaters, stilt-walkers, kumpo dancers, drummers. And we travel all over the world. We've been to Africa, Brazil, Mexico. And we are a growing company; we're still traveling. Here in the community, we do marriage ceremonies. We teach people how to get married in a traditional way. We try to put that holistic thing together where drumming plays a part in it. How to jump the broom with the drums, instead of the piano grinding and, you know, "Here Come the Bride." We take that whole myth out, and create an African ceremony, through drumming and dancing.

Eugene: *We're not just sitting on our laurels. We're still trying to come back to a greatness that we once had. Black people have a great past, like all the other major wings of the human family. Every culture has a great past, and hence every culture is capable of incarnating or reincarnating that past in some way. Without overromanticizing to the point where—you know, everybody wasn't a king, everybody wasn't a queen. And some of the kings and queens participated in our unfortunate situation here too. But the idea is to get back to some of that greatness.*

A young customer at Annie's Restaurant in East St. Louis

Sunshine: *You know, this is not just about the music and the dance. We say tradition is a way of life. Art is a way of life. We teach art as the way of life, the way we live as a race of people.*

◆

River of Bones and Flesh and Blood

Eugene Redmond

River of Time:
Vibrant vein,
Bent, crooked,
Older than the Red Men
Who named you;
Ancient as the winds
That break on your
Serene and shining face;
One time western boundary of America
From whose center
Your broad shoulders now reach
To touch sisters
On the flanks

River of Truth:
Mornings
You leap, yawn 2,000 miles,
And shed a giant joyous tear
Over sprouting, straggling
Hives of humanity;
Nights you weep
As the moon, tiptoeing
Across your silent silky
Face, hears you praying
Over the broken backs
Of black slaves who rode,
Crouched and huddled
At your heart in the bellies
Of steamships

River of Memory:
Laboratory for Civil War
Boat builders
Who left huge eyes of steel
Staring from your sullen depths;
Reluctant partner to crimes
Of Ku Klux Klansmen;
River moved to waves
Of ecstasy
By the venerable trumpets
Of Louis Armstrong,
Dizzy Gillespie,
And Miles Davis,
Homeboy

River of Bones:
River of bones and flesh–
Bones and flesh and blood;
The nation's largest
Intestine
And longest conveyor belt

River of Mississippi:
River of little rivers;
River of rises,
Sometimes subdued
By a roof of ice, descending finally
On your Southward course
To spit
Into the Gulf
And join the wrath
Of larger bodies

5
Rhythm and Blues Man: OLIVER SAIN

It's Thursday night at BB's Jazz, Blues and Soups, a small club on Broadway in downtown St. Louis. The room has a smoky, late-night feel: dim lights and brick walls decorated with old posters of blues and r&b stars. On the small stage, Oliver Sain is fronting his band. He sits at the keyboard, his eyes shaded by a black leather cap, and his fingers pick out a rolling, barrelhouse accompaniment as he sings:

Now, I know you're a good-timing woman
I know you like to go out and clown
But, little girl, I can't afford to let you tear my reputation down
Stop it, Babe—Mama, please stop breakin' down
I don't think you really love me
I think you just like the way my music sounds

His voice is warm and easy, with a trace of Mississippi accent, and he throws in a Delta falsetto on the word "please." Then, as he finishes the verse, he fishes out the alto saxophone that has been hanging at his side, and starts blowing. The horn honks and shouts with r&b verve, and the band kicks into high gear. Two choruses fly by, and Sain's eyes are laughing as the horn wails a high, screaming note, then stutters down the scale to a moaning close. The bass player signals a final, mellow chord, and the crowd applauds.

I started out playing drums, actually, and I think probably the first guy I played with might have been Willie Love. Willie was with the King Biscuit band in Helena, Arkansas, with Sonny Boy Williamson, and he was my stepdad. He and Sonny Boy played together off and on all of their lives, and when I was a little kid in Mississippi I used to come home from the cotton field and hear them on the radio, long before I ever dreamed that I would meet these people. That's kind of weird, but I thought they were the greatest people on earth.

I didn't start playing saxophone, actually, until I came out of the army. See, just before I went in the army, I started fooling around with my roommate's saxophone. Robert Granville—he had a girlfriend across town, so half the time he wouldn't be there, and I would fool around with his alto. I learned the Charlie Parker stuff off the

Oliver Sain onstage, and talking with friends in his dressing room.

Charlie Parker with Strings *album; I would sit down and play that stuff note for note, without knowing what key I was in. That was in Greenwood, Mississippi; we were playing with a guy named Clarence Hines, and Robert was our saxophone player.*

So anyway, I went in the army, and when I came out I went and bought a saxophone, and I learned on my own; I would lay in bed at night and figure out things that I heard musicians say. Like they might say, "It's in three flats"—that was over my head when I was playing drums, but then later on I would figure that out, and I would say, "C has no flats, and one flat is F, and that's four up from C, so two must be B flat, and then so on." I never went to school for music, and I learned to write arrangements that way, just figured out stuff.

I played around with a few different people. I was in Greenville, Mississippi, with Little Milton, and we went up to Memphis and did some sessions. I left Mississippi in I guess fifty-five or fifty-six, I don't really remember. But I left from down there before Ike Turner or Milton came here to St. Louis. I was already in Chicago, and I just kind of heard that they had came here. First it was Ike and then later on somebody said, "You know, Milton moved up to East St. Louis, too." I said, "Wow, they must have found something up there."

In those days in St. Louis, most of the black entertainment was controlled by black social clubs. These people would go out and sell tickets, and they'd have anywhere from three to five to eight hundred people in these things, every week. And there was

Ike Turner performs at the Oliver Sain tribute concert.

certain kinds of bands who did those gigs. They would be big bands, they'd be reading the charts. The union would send over a guy, and the'd say, "Can the band play good?" He'd say, "What do you want? They're union musicians. We'll send them over, you'll like them, they're okay." So this is what people were kind of used to. And some of the bands were good; I'm not saying that there was anything wrong with them. I'm just saying that it was a certain kind of music.

When Ike Turner and them showed up here, it was a whole other thing. They were doing the songs that you heard on the radio, you see what I'm saying? And they were doing their little dance steps and the horns going up and down. People thought "Wow! That's it, man!" And those guys started doing all the big dances, even the snooty-dooty dances with the tuxedos and things. All of a sudden there was a band playing rhythm and blues music—which was unheard of before that. So they changed this whole thing.

It is Sunday night, and Oliver's fans have packed Mississippi Nights, St. Louis's premier music club. Oliver has been having some health problems recently, and an all-star crew has turned out to pay tribute to the man who for forty years has helped hold the local r&b scene together. There is the James Family soul revue, with fancy costumes and immaculate dance steps, old-time bluesman Henry Townsend, and several of Oliver's associates from the glory days of St. Louis r&b: Tyrone Davis, Little Milton, and Ike Turner. The mayor of East St. Louis proclaims the date "Oliver Sain Day," and Oliver's old friends vie to pay him tribute. A high point comes when Ike joins the Sain band on keyboards, trading blues choruses with Oliver, then leaping up to kiss him on the cheek. Ike was king of the St. Louis scene from the late 1950s until he and Tina moved to L.A., but his friendship with Oliver goes back even further, to their days as young men in the Mississippi Delta.

When I first knew Ike, I went and saw his band in Indianola, Mississippi, one night. That was before I even went in the army. We had a band in Greenwood, and we were kind of cocky and young. We had Little Junior Parker singing in our band, and we had M. T. Murphy on guitar—it was a good band. We kept hearing about him, Ike Turner's band from Clarksdale, but we had the attitude, "They ain't nothing, man."

So one night we all bundled up and get in a car and went from Greenwood over to Indianola. We were there kind of early, and they were setting up, and I saw them putting soda pop crates there and tipping the piano up. I said, "What's that all about?" Turned out they set the piano up on these soda pop things so Ike could stand up and play. He had the same band pretty much that he brought up here, I suppose. Had a guy named Johnny O'Neill singing. Willie Kizzard, I think, was on guitar. Man, listen: When them guys started playing we were like... I mean, we were actually... Man, they were good! They blew the roof off it, man. Four horns, and them dancing, the horns flipping and the whole thing. Yeah, it was awesome.

So then I got to know Ike. He was recording a lot of people in the South, Howling Wolf and people like that, and I was involved in some of that a little bit, especially after I came out of the army. And Ike and I have done a lot of records together over the years. We cut some stuff on Fontella Bass, and Tina Turner. I had a thing on Tina called "Let Me Touch Your Mind," which is a good song. Tina and I wrote several songs together.

As I think back today, I really should have stopped doing a lot of other things and just wrote, because I was successful with quite a few songs. Milton and I wrote some great blues songs together, and that stuff is still around, still earning money. I was lucky to get my stuff before people like Little Milton, Tina Turner, Shirley Brown, Fontella Bass, Mitty Collier, Ann Peebles. That was great.

I still write, if I'm recording somebody. I always did do this—I can write under pressure. I'll say, "We need one more song"—zip, zip, zip, it's done. "Don't Mess Up A Good Thing," which Fontella did with Bobby McClure, was actually written in the car between here and Chicago. I used to do funny stuff. I remember once I was talking to Ike and I said, "Man, I got the greatest song for Tina." So Ike was the kind of guy, if you're going to do anything like that, he'd just fly you right out. "We can get the next flight." And I wrote the song on the airplane, because I just wanted to go to L.A. that day, actually.

Little Milton (left) and Nancy James of the James Family (right) at the Oliver Sain tribute.

Oliver smiles at the memory, but his smile is bittersweet. He is sitting in his recording studio, in a ramshackle house beside a vacant lot. The studio is clean and well kept up, the equipment shiny and new, but this afternoon Oliver has the place to himself.

I don't write much anymore, because I don't know who to cut it on. St. Louis still has a lot of real singers and real artists, there's still that wealth of talent, people who hold that standard. But if you record them, can you get it played on the radio? I don't think so. Because you go into the average radio station, this guy is twenty-eight—he's not excited about Aretha Franklin, it don't mean nothing to him. He's listening to this girl who sells zillions of records and you say, "But she's all out of tune." He says, "Sounds fine to me. Everybody likes it, man." That's the thing.

When I started out, I didn't even know what a producer was. I started into that like many people do: You think that the guy at the board is going to keep your stuff together, and actually he's an engineer, he's not a producer. So I learned that I had to go, "Do this." And that's producing. But I don't even think we used the word at the time. Milton and I, we didn't know we were producing anything. We were just going in the studio playing, and telling the guy, "You're out of tune. Do this. Do that." And I just kind of eased into it in that way, and now I have stuff floating around all over the world with my name on it as producer.

My thing is producing real r&b stuff. I'll do some more contemporary things, but I don't get too much into producing rap, simply because I'm not that good at putting the tracks together. Occasionally I'll have a really brilliant thing and it works, but I don't think I could do that every day. But r&b stuff, I could have an assembly line. If I was cutting blues artists, r&b, if I was in a place like Malaco [the Mississippi label specializing in soul blues], man, I could zip along, because that's my thing.

But that's not where it's at today. And it's sad, because around every corner there's some singer who can just blow you away. You go to some church, she's there. But when you get to the record company, they're going to say it has to have this ignorant hip-hop beat on it. So now we lost what she was about. Because a song has to sound the way that song should sound. You want to use modern equipment, maybe certain drum sounds on the drum machine, that's okay—but not going all the way. Because you can mess a good song up by trying to make it more contemporary.

I've had gospel people come in here, and sometimes I have asked out of curiosity,

I say, "Why are you using that synthesizer for, that 'woooo-ooo?' What is that?" She said, "Well, it's gospel, but we're trying to make it more contemporary." I said, "Okay, now, what you're really doing is making it more temporary."

Because now you lost everybody. The person who would like that song, maybe an older person or anybody who would like a traditional-type gospel song, they would love that song if you did it right. But the guy who you're trying to sell it to when you put this ignorant synthesizer on there is not going to buy that song anyway. He doesn't like that song, it doesn't matter what you put on it. And now you messed it up for the other guy too, so nobody wants it. But that's the business.

The whole scene has changed, because that older audience isn't around so much, some of them passed on. So now you have a twenty-four-year-old who never heard of a social club, don't even know what that is. Certainly don't want to hear a band of any description. They just like records. I was playing in a club once, honest to God, and I was standing at the bar, and these young people were standing around and one looked up on the stage and saw them bringing in the equipment, and he was really hurt, man. He told the other guy, he said, "Oh man, they got a band, man." And all of a sudden that started going all over the place, and these kids left there. So I saw that coming.

But personally I don't try to sell my ideas to young people. That's so frustrating, and I see all the guys doing that sometimes: "Oh, you should remember the way we used to... and we did this... and in those days they had..." You won't get that from me. I will not bore some young person trying to explain something, and they don't have a clue of what you're talking about. So I never do that. If they tell me about some new singer who can't sing in tune at all and sells records, if they say that's the best thing in the world, I just say, "I know what you mean."

When I was playing with Milton, that was my formative years, and we all loved each other and we made it work. That's what made the music so good, was that love and respect for each other. But now it's like "Where is the gig? How much is it?" They don't even know you, they don't talk to each other.

There was a time, the average band, they all probably lived in the same house. See what I'm saying? They knew each other, and they were concerned about each other. And until this day, people like Milton or Fontella, we actually concern ourselves with each other. It's family, is what it is. Back then, we would all play if nobody got paid, or we would all chip in together and go buy baloney. I mean, we've done that many times. The bus would break down, we'd walk, carry the instruments. Because we were going to make that gig. But that was a different day. That'll never be again.

Oliver shakes his head, but he is still smiling. With the Mississippi Nights benefit only a couple of days in the past, he cannot say that the old feeling is completely gone. Maybe the audience is a little older, maybe it does not come out as often, but there is still a family of local musicians who will turn out to take care of their own. Oliver is still recording music, working on an album with his old friend Johnny Johnson, the piano player who worked with Chuck Berry on all those classic rock 'n' roll hits. In another few months, the annual St. Louis Blues Festival will roll around once again, and as always it will feature the Oliver Sain Revue, a full r&b spectacular mixing young and old artists in the classic style. Of course, the years have brought change, and much of it is questionable, but Oliver is carrying on as he has since his teens.

I still play a lot. I get out the saxophone to eat, man. Studio, that ain't happening so much, because everybody in the world has a studio now. Every rap group got some stuff in their basement. But I have the band, and we do a lot of private parties, wedding receptions. A few bars, not too many. We go in and do good old r&b stuff, and people love that. So that's still going on. And of course I get to go to Europe and do some work, and we're going to try to do a kind of extended tour early next year, maybe five-six weeks. So yeah, I'm still going. That music is still my bread and butter.

Oliver Sain on piano

6
Saturday Night and Sunday Morning: FONTELLA BASS

Mt. Beulah A.M.E. Church is empty, but Fontella Bass is playing as if there was a full congregation singing along. Her hands hit the keyboard with the force of a player who grew up in a world without microphones, the left rolling a thunderous bass while her right chops out hard gospel chords. Her body sways from side to side with the rhythm, and she shakes her head, eyes closed. Then she throws her head back and starts to sing.

This little light of mine, I'm gonna let it shine
This little light of mine, I'm gonna let it shine
This little light of mine, I'm gonna let it shine
Let it shine, let it shine, let it shine

Sitting in a front pew, her mother watches her appreciatively. Now in her late seventies, Martha Bass is a short, round woman with a smooth, serious face. A gospel stalwart, she raised Fontella in the classic tradition.

My mother had a great influence on me, and if she didn't she would knock it into me. She was a stern person and still is—she thinks I'm still five years old. And she was a great singer. She went out on the road and sang with Clara Ward, and she sang with Brother Joe May. I remember all these people: Wynona Carr, even Mahalia Jackson. I got to know them as a young person, I'm talking about eight, nine, ten years old. These people were coming in and out of the home all the time.

She had a great influence on my life, and then my grandmother really did. My mother was on the road, so I was with my grandmother a lot. Her and I shared gigs together, doing the funeral homes. In the beginning, when I first started really playing music, she was a friend of the mortuary downtown, and every night I would have to play for different funerals and things. I would play the piano and she would sing, and I did that for six, seven years.

The way I got started playing was that Marion Williams, one of the Ward Singers, was a dear friend of my mother's and she would come and stay two, three months at a time. One Sunday, they wanted my mother to sing at the Pleasant Green Baptist Church here in St. Louis and she didn't have a musician, and Aunt Marion said, "You got the greatest musician right here: your daughter." My mother said, "You're

Fontella Bass (below) and her mother, Martha, perform a duet in a scene from *The Mississippi: River of Song* TV series.

right." So they took me to the piano and taught me this song—I guess I was around seven at the time—and I played it for my mother, and I been playing for her ever since.

Martha Bass moves a bit slowly these days, but she pushes herself up from the pew and walks to the railing beside the piano. Leaning on it, she waits for her daughter to start playing. The first chords are slow and firm, a solid foundation with lots of space for a singer to build on. Martha fixes her eyes on a point somewhere above her daughter's head and begins to sing:

I am so grateful that I have Christ, he's in my life
When I am sad, he just cheers me
And when I get lonely, he will my comfort be
That's why I'm so grateful, I'm so grateful
That I have Christ, he's in my life

Martha's voice has thickened with the years, but what it has lost in agility it has made up in soul and power. As she sings, she slowly builds the emotion, her hands gripping the wooden rail in front of her. On the second verse, Fontella begins to answer her. Fontella's voice is smoother and more supple, adding a vibrant, hornlike flavor. She is smiling, enjoying the taste of old times. Her mother, though, seems to be thinking of nothing but the lyric. She is a solid gospel oak, and her daughter's soaring responses just make her sound more rooted and timeless.

When my friends (Fontella responds: *when my friends) and my folk (oh yes)*
Turns against me
It seems I must be all alone
There's a steel support within me
Yeah he is someone who'll carry (who'll carry) this heavy load

As Martha begins the final chorus, Fontella's piano picks up the pace slightly, and her responses are more fervent and closer together. Her mother feeds on her energy, rising to an old-time shout.

I am so grateful (I am so grateful) I am so grateful (yes, so grateful)
So grateful that I have Christ (I have Christ)
He is in my (in my) in my (in my)
He is in my (in my) life—(he is i-in my li-i-ife)

We traveled, my grandmother, mother and I, all through the South. We played every little town in the state of Texas, and we did programs every night in a different town. My mother had a friend, Reverend Taylor, who was a minister in Taylor, Texas. We would be based there and go out to Cross Roads, Slaton, just everywhere. And what we would do every night, we would have a "generation" singing program. That would be my grandmother, my mother, and myself, and when it would come time to give the donation the people would give to the one they thought was most talented. My grandmother always won. We would raise our little fifty, seventy dollars, and she would come up with two hundred. It took me getting older to understand what they were appreciating: She was the root of everything. She had produced my mother, and my mother, me.

We did that until I was sixteen. They were still passing me off on the train as age eleven so I could ride free. I was sixteen and I looked like I was eleven, with pigtails and braids in my hair. Until I got the mumps.

Fontella laughs and indicates her bosom. Though she is a church singer, there is nothing prissy about her. Today, she is wearing her hair straight, short and blond, forming a striking contrast to her dark skin, and she looks far younger than her fifty-some years. When we move over to her house, which is only a few doors down from the church, the living room is decorated with African art that she has collected during her travels. In the dining room is an upright piano, and on the wall above it a framed gold record. Her mother goes off to another room to watch a soap opera, and Fontella seats herself at the keyboard and continues her story.

As I grew older, I naturally was listening to pop music like Little Richard, Ray Charles, Ruth Brown. My aunt used to get up on Saturday morning and clean her house, her walls, dishes, and she'd have the radio on, listening to Muddy Waters, Howlin' Wolf. That was different from gospel, and it grew on me and I wanted that flavor too.

In high school I would do all the talent shows. I played in different clubs like the Riviera, doing talent scout shows, and that is one of the ways my mother found out that I was doing something other than religious music. We had a talent show on a Ray Charles show, before he was to perform, and the group I played for won and my picture came out in the Argus paper, the local paper in St. Louis. Of course, all of my mother's church members reminded her that I was in the Argus playing blues. So that was how my mom found out.

I really enjoyed the music a lot and I knew that I wanted to be a performer. Then one day I went to the "Harlem in Havana" revue, part of the Royal American Show, this carnival that came to St. Louis once a year. I was sitting with my girlfriends, Sophronia and Janice and Deedee, and they sent my name up for me to perform for the talent show, and behold I won, with Nina Simone's tune "I Love You, Porgy."

Little Milton and Oliver Sain heard me there, and they approached me and asked me, if I didn't go with the revue, would I come and play piano for Little Milton, which at that time Oliver Sain was his bandleader. Well, I wanted to go with the revue, but when I got ready to leave, all my friends were crying, and they finally told my mother that I was going to leave, so my mother came down and literally pulled me off the train. I was embarrassed, quite naturally, but I'm glad to this day that I didn't go on that show, because otherwise I would not have known Little Milton and Oliver Sain.

It was 1961, and the St. Louis scene was jumping. Little Milton had one of the hottest bands in town, and he hired Fontella as his pianist. Soon she was taking occasional vocal solos as well, and sitting in with other groups.

Back then, St. Louis had so many clubs: the Moonlight, the Club Riviera, the Sportsman's Lounge, the Paradise Room, the Circus Bar... I guess that made a lot of musicians kind of migrate to St. Louis, whether they were born here or along the Mississippi. I would sometimes be with Little Milton, sometimes with Albert King; they both played the blues but had different sounds and flavors. Then I would go all the way to the big bands, George Hudson, with thirty-three pieces. We worked the Chase Park Plaza. Then I would leave what they called the high ritz gig, and I would go and moonlight at some hole in the wall—a blues joint, like a juke joint, everybody knocking each other over the head with beer bottles. We had great times and different feels in the music, and we created our own sound among ourselves, just by playing together all the time.

Fontella played piano on several records with Milton, then split off to sing lead with the Oliver Sain Revue. In 1964, she and Sain's male vocalist, Bobby McClure, went out on their own and, on Milton's recommendation, signed with the legendary Chess label in Chicago. Their first record, "Don't Mess up a Good Thing," was a solid hit, but the song that really made Fontella's career came in 1965, when she cut "Rescue Me." It went to number one on the r&b charts, and made her a soul star. Unfortunately, Chess followed up with a sound-alike copy, "Recovery," which failed to match its predecessor's success, and the momentum was lost.

My music career was really short compared to a lot of the artists that are legendary like I am myself now. But I chose to not continue, because of personal problems with the record company and not getting royalties. I didn't need to deal with that, because the church was always there for me and always kept me working. I could go outside, but I could always come home and be with my family—which was the church — and they carried me through.

There were some hard times, but over all the years everything I have ever done has been around music. Whether it be gospel, secular, blues, whatever. During the dry spells I did weddings, anniversaries, funerals, commercials, whatever it took. Because this is what I love doing. Music is my life. I am thankful that I have never had to go on a nine-to-five job and tell the boss to shove it. I'm grateful for having music in my life, and it agrees with me, 'cause it never let me get to the nine-to-five—although sometimes I could have used it.

Fontella runs her fingers down the keyboard, and at first it is hard to tell whether the song is soul or gospel. The church has has had so much impact on black secular music, and vice versa, that the two sounds have become thoroughly intertwined.

You can approach secular music the same way that you would gospel, and that's why you hear some people say, "Oh, she has that gospel touch," because someone has that flavor. You know, it is hard to sing in a way that is not natural for you. It has to be there. Some singers are beautiful singers but if you was to ask them to do a gospel number that would be impossible. It is like asking a blues guitarist to play Mozart. So I get a gospel sound sometimes when I am singing blues or rock 'n' roll. But there is definitely a difference. Like if I play "Rescue Me..."

Bass's left hand swings into the bassline of her hit, and she starts to sing, her voice seemingly unchanged by the intervening three decades.

Rescue me, oh take me in your arms;
Rescue me, I want your tender charms,
Cause I'm lonely, and I'm blue...

She trails off, and starts to play a slower accompaniment, with less of an obvious dance beat.

Now, if I was to put a gospel approach to "Rescue Me," you know, I could change it around and get the trembles and the different things a gospel singer does.

Her voice takes on a darker timbre, and she stretches each word, teasing and playing with the melody.

Come on, Lord—rescue me
'Cause I love you,
Cause I nee-ed you,
Please Lord, come o-on and rescue me

You have different flavors, different approach, different kinds of vibratos that you use in your voice. In gospel, you are letting the public know what you're feeling inside, because you're trying to reach out to someone's heart so they can be touched. In the secular world you're doing the same thing, but you have to do it a different way.

You know, all music is about feeling, and in gospel you have to feel the Lord. Now, if I do blues I send out the blues message. Blues makes me happy. I have had plenty of things touch down in my life that can give me the blues, but I get happy when I do the blues. And jazz, I'm feeling just mellow and I want to send that kind of feeling out. But in gospel I want the people who are listening to me to know the Lord. I have to feel him myself and the only way I can feel him is to terminate a lot of the other things in my life, and present that gospel out.

Really, those are my roots. I was a very religious person all my life. I was brought up in the church. I went to Sunday school, B.T.U.(Baptist Training Union), and Wednesday night meeting; Sunday I lived in church all day, from eight in the morning sometimes to twelve and one o'clock at night. When I was with my mother and my grandmother, I made all the music circuits in the gospel field. Then, when I got older, I guess I rebelled—not so much against gospel, but maybe against my parents for being so strict, not listening to the radio or not being able to go to movies on Sunday. But now that I am back to where I started from, I realize a lot of things. That was just my roots. That is where I started, and I love doing secular music and I still will do secular music sometimes, but my choice is gospel.

She starts to play a gentle, introspective melody, tender chords embellished with little classical flourishes. Her voice is equally soft and soothing at first, then gradually rises as the mood catches her.

I don't feel no ways tired
I come too far from where I started from
Nobody told me that the road would be easy
I don't believe he brought me this far to leave me

◆◆◆

Fontella performs at the St. Louis Blues Heritage Festival.

The Bottle Rockets at the Hi Pointe, Festus, Missouri:
(right to left) Mark Ortmann, drums; Brian Henneman, guitar;
Tom Parr, guitar (back to camera); Tom Ray, bass.

7

Loud Music in a Small Town: THE BOTTLE ROCKETS

In a messy room above the Hi Pointe Bar, situated on the highest point in Festus, Missouri, the Bottle Rockets are rehearsing. They sit in a tight semicircle, except for Tom Ray, who stands by his big, acoustic bass. Brian Henneman sits next to a small guitar amplifier, playing lead and singing. Drummer Mark Ortmann plays a single snare drum, and Tom Parr plays rhythm guitar. All have long hair, and all except Ortmann are bearded. The two guitarists wear baseball caps. Henneman counts off the rhythm, and strums the first chord.

A thousand dollar car, it ain't worth nothing
A thousand dollar car, it ain't worth shit
Might as well take your thousand dollars and set fire to it
A thousand dollar car ain't worth a dime
You lose your thousand dollars every time
Oh, why did I ever buy a thousand dollar car?

A thousand dollar car ain't even gonna roll
Till you put at least another thousand in the hole
Sink your money in it and there you are,
The owner of a two thousand dollar "thousand dollar car"

If you've only got a thousand dollars
You oughta just buy a good guitar
Learn how to play and it'll take you farther
Than any old thousand dollar car
If a thousand dollar car was to be worth a damn
Then why would anybody ever spend ten grand?
Oh, why did I ever buy a thousand dollar car?

We started out right here, Brian Henneman says. He is sitting downstairs at the bar, a half-finished beer near at hand. The other guys are hanging out in the background, chatting with friends and listening to the interview. The Bottle Rockets have become pretty well known, but it is still a bizarre oddity to have a film crew in the Hi Pointe, and the regulars are having a ball watching the whole thing. Brian is a bit self-conscious, but he tries to answer all the questions as fully and directly as he can. He talks with a Missouri country drawl, and has a habit of smiling a bit sarcastically after making any serious comment, as if he was worried he might be sounding pompous.

The Bottle Rockets had a band before it, called Chicken Truck, and we started out here in this bar, to no rave reviews whatsoever. That was a country band, trying to be hard core. We thought "Well, we like Buck Owens, let's do Buck Owens songs," and at that time Buck Owens was fifteen, twenty years past. When people were coming out to go listen to bands, they wanted to hear modern songs, but we just didn't grasp the thought of people not wanting to hear Buck Owens. "Everybody wants to hear Buck Owens!"—not necessarily true.

Then, we have this natural inclination to get excited when we play, and when we get excited we'll turn around and turn the amps up—we just can't help it. So we were louder than we should have been, more abrasive than we should have been, and we weren't doing anybody any favors. So we just took a break for a while and licked our wounds and sat at home and wrote a bunch more songs. We were still doing the same country songs—not Buck, but songs that were inspired by the whole Buck Owens experience–and we eventually evolved into the Bottle Rockets and went into St. Louis and started playing. When we got to St. Louis, nobody told us to turn down; I think everybody is deaf up there. We turned the amps up, and it turned into a whole new thing. It was like, there we were, rocking like Aerosmith, playing these songs that were country songs basically, and that's kind of the thing we have been mining ever since.

I guess it's just like rock 'n' roll done with that country attitude. Country is true stories, and if you can't relate to a true story, get the hell out. Like Hank Williams and guys like that, they just told stories. Real simple stories that everyone could understand. I'm a pretty simple-minded guy; I don't want to sing anything I don't understand. So, that's it.

Brian puts on the mock-cheerful voice of a kindergarten teacher: *Story time!*

The Bottle Rockets have been together in one form or another for some fifteen years, but only recently began to get anything resembling national success. A St. Louis band, Uncle Tupelo, which later split into Wilco and Son Volt, attracted some attention with a somewhat similar alternative country/rock approach, and the Bottle Rockets were the next logical band in the style. Unlike the other bands, though, which have the feel of city guys looking for a roots sound, the Rockets are small-town and proud of it. Playing a rock gig in a St.

Louis club, they hit the crowd with a painfully high-volume honky-tonk number, Tom Ray's acoustic bass slapping in the faces of the city listeners, and Henneman churning out twangy guitar licks and shouting an occasional "Hee-yah!" The song is called "Idiot's Revenge."

She likes Dinosaur Jr., but she can't tell you why
Says, "You like country music? Man, you deserve to die"
She got that whacked-off hair, got them second-hand clothes
Got an itemized list of everything she loathes
And she's so political, so sophisticated
She will swear in court that everything's just over-rated...

Well I know there's no balance to the stuff I just sang
She thinks I'm a redneck idiot just cause I talk with a twang
Well, this is my only weapon, man, I know that it ain't fair
She'll never listen to it anyway, so I guess she won't care
And she's so political, so sophisticated
She will swear in court that everything's just over-rated

There is no one like that in the Hi Pointe Bar. The Bottle Rockets' music may not have gone over so well here, but it is home, and this is where the band members relax, drinking beer and writing songs about the girls who waitress at the Chinese restaurant down the street.

This is Festus, Missouri, and actually I live in Crystal City, which is basically the same town except they are divided by a highway or boundary line. It's kinda tricky, because Crystal City is surrounded by Festus and it can't expand. It used to be a lot more rural than it is now. It used to be a small country town way back when. As St. Louis kept growing, they were looking for new suburbs and everybody down here jumped on that train and it just built up. It's not really a suburb, but I'm sure it will be someday.

The whole town of Crystal City was founded on a glass factory and everybody in this town, if you didn't work in the factory you knew someone who did. My dad worked in it; that's just the way it is down here. Then they closed the factory—that just happened recently—and I don't know what the heck they do down here anymore. Build new homes so people won't have to live in St. Louis, I guess. That's what it has turned into. And I'm sure there is other stuff going on down here but now that I am the traveling musician, I can't keep track of it anymore.

We just grew up here, and the Buck Owens aspect came from Hee Haw.

Sunday night you watched Hee Haw, *and you had your choice of Buck or Roy Clark, and I went with Buck cause I was never a big Roy fan. Then, of course, when you hit those formative teenage years, you don't want your friends knowing you listen to Buck Owens: "I'm a rocker like you, man!" So then you listen to the radio station, and we got the stations out of St. Louis—St. Louis is conservative in their choice of rock stuff, but it was great to us: Aerosmith and Boston, Rush, all these bands like that. So you heard all that stuff and picked what you liked.*

The discovery came around seventy-eight, and our link was the TV. You would sit up on Friday nights and watch Midnight Special *or* Don Kirshner's Rock Concert, *and I remember the night I saw Cheap Trick and I was like "Wow!" They were fun! Before, you were listening to Rush, and they were good but not fun. They were serious stuff. Cheap Trick wasn't serious. It was all mainstream stuff, and Cheap Trick was the way out band. For us, that was obscure. Nothing really got too far out.*

Then, when we started going into St. Louis, it was a whole new circle of people who know stuff that you don't know. It isn't that they are smarter than you, they just had more access to stuff. So all of a sudden someone turns you on to a Doug Sahm record—wow! Or a Ramones record, and you think it's pretty cool. It's just like going to a different school. All of a sudden you are in with people that are playing on a different level, and you become aware that there is more out there. So that's what happened.

It's a funny kind of thing, because a lot of this just depends on where you live. Like, for people who live on the West or East Coast, there's this kind of thing where, if we go to New York City and play a rock show, everybody comes out and they are fascinated that there is life "out there." We are that whole section of the country they fly over. They take naps or read magazines while they are sailing over the major bulk of America. So I think they are fascinated to get a report from that mysterious land in the middle. And just as much goes on here as anywhere else. It's just less glamorous to talk about. So I guess that's it. We are reporters from the heartland.

Brian says that last phrase with something between a laugh and a sneer, but his songs often live up to the billing. A new number commemorates the recent flooding of the Mississippi, which left the Hi Pointe pretty much the only spot above ground:

Live in a river town, it's pretty little
It's high on the sides and sinks in the middle
When it rains too much, the river comes down
Fills up the low spots all over town
Get down, river, river get down

Won't you get down, river, river get down
Once again you have messed up this old town
So get down, river, get down

Well, over cross town's where I want to go
To see my honey, but I don't know
Guess I'm gonna have to row
Looks like the Gulf of Mexico down by the Texaco
Get down, river, river get down
Won't you get down, river, river get down
Once again you have messed up this old town
So get down, river, get down

This is where we've always lived, and is probably where we will always live, and all of our friends live here, everybody that we know and ever grew up with. So we aren't making anything up, we're just talking about our buddies, ourselves and stuff like that. Maybe that's kind of crazy, to think that anybody would care to hear about your pals—it's kind of like showing baby pictures. But that's it. I'm interested in it. Talking about all my friends. So there you go.

It's funny, 'cause all the guys that formed the band were the guys that didn't really have a place to fit in high school. We were the freaks, the ones that didn't fit in with the dopers and didn't fit with the sports guys. We kind of worked our way through all of them, and got along fine and enjoyed everyone's company, but never had a place of our own. We all went to different schools in town, some to the Catholic school, some public, and it was weird, we just naturally drifted together from different places. It was like, "Wow, you like that too?" "Yeah!" I don't even know how the band thing started; I guess just the fact that we were weirdos and didn't fit—can't play sports, so pick up the guitar. It was either that or go to work at the factory. Which wasn't a bad thing, but now we're still playing guitar and the glass factory is gone, so I guess we made the right choice.

◆◆◆

The Ste. Genevieve Guignolée singers celebrate New Year's Eve. Inset: An old French grave marker, Ste. Genevieve.

8
Old French New Year: The Ste. Genevieve GUIGNOLÉE SINGERS

***S**te. Genevieve... is a fine old place. It was settled by the French, and is a relic of a time when one could travel from the mouths of the Mississippi to Quebec and be on French territory and under French rule all the way."*

—Mark Twain, *Life on the Mississippi*

"Happy New Year"!

A yellow school bus pulls up in front of a bar, and a plastic cup full of ice and some indeterminate liquid comes sailing out through a window. Then the bus doors open, and a motley crew tumbles forth onto the pavement. There are about two dozen men, in strange costumes and varying stages of inebriation. The leaders are six men in black frock coats, white scarves, and black top hats. Behind them come men in three-cornered hats and uniforms that to a greater or lesser degree summon up the eighteenth century, a man in leather fringe and long, black Indian braids that clash rather bizarrely with his red-blond beard, someone in a huge, furry thing, meant to be either Grizzly Adams or an actual bear, a couple of possible sailors in striped jerseys and wool caps, and one thin, bearded figure who seems to be masquerading as some variety of Oriental potentate. Most are wearing masks over their eyes, though by this point in the evening a lot of the masks are askew and the wearers must push them aside in order to see anything.

They enter the bar and start to sing. The leaders, four singers and two violinists, stand in the middle of the barroom and sing each line first. The costumed revelers circle around them in a slow shuffle, and sing a response.

Bonsoir le maître et la maîtresse et tout le monde du logis
(Good evening, master and mistress, and everyone in the house)
Pour le dernier jour de l'année c'est la Guignolée vous nous devez
(For the last day of the year, you owe us the Guignolée)
Si vous voulez rien nous donner, dites-nous le
(If you do not want to give us anything, tell us that)

On vous demande pas grand'chose—une échinée.
(We don't ask much from you—a backbone)
Une échinée n'est pas grand'chose... de quatre-vingt-dix pieds de long.
(A backbone is not much... one ninety feet long)
Si vous voulez rien nous donner, dites nous le.
(If you do not want to give us anything, tell us that)
On vous demande seulement la fille ainée.
(We are only asking for your oldest daughter)
On lui fera faire bonnes choses, on lui fera chauffer les pieds.
(We will have her do fine things, we will have her warm feet)

On the evening's first few visits the singing was fairly clear, but each visit is repaid with drinks and by now the words are getting a bit garbled. This is especially true because few of the singers speak any French, and they have learned the whole lyric by rote. The group's leader, Duke Bleckler, is largely of French descent, but even he has only a very scanty knowledge of the language.

We don't have that many Frenchmen left. There are a lot of Germans in this bunch now. I'm French, Frank's French—we've got, I'd say, maybe six is French in here yet. The rest of them are German. But anybody can do this, if they really want to go and learn the song. They have to do that, 'cause, you know, we think a lot of that. This started here back in the 1700s–they started doing it when the town was first settled, you know. And it's been going on ever since, passed down father to son, in families.

What it's about, they would go all around the town, and they went through and asked for a piece of meat—forty feet long, if I remember right—which is what the song says. And if the people didn't have a piece of meat to give them, they would ask for their eldest daughter. Take her out, wine her and dine her—which doesn't sound very good, you know.

The Guignolée make their rounds.

Anyhow, when they got all these pieces of meat, then—I think it's on the seventh day—they would have something like a great big barbecue like we'd have now. They'd invite all these people in that give this meat and everything—and even the ones that didn't—

and have a big old party. That's about what it amounted to. It was just a bunch of guys out having a good time on New Year's, which is what we do now.

The custom of wassailing, as it was called in England, was common in medieval Europe, but has few modern survivals. The Ste. Genevieve Guignolée is one of a handful of groups in southern Missouri and Illinois that keep the ancient tradition alive (with, at times, a degree of confusion about spelling; there are, for example, the "Guillonée" of Old Mines and, on the Illinois side of the river, the "Guiannée" of Prairie du Rocher). It is made up of older natives of the picturesque river town, which has become something of a tourist mecca, attracting retirees and tired urbanites in search of a lost, idyllic past. The old houses have a peaceful, old-fashioned feel, and even the noisiness of the New Year's revelers is imbued with tradition. It is a working-class tradition; Duke and several of the other men work at the local cement factory, which provides the group with its bus, while the wealthier residents of Ste. Genevieve, old or new, are expected to set up the drinks, but rarely asked to join the Guignolée. The tradition is passed on within families, from father to son. (Women have traditionally been excluded and, while some towns have broken this rule in later years, Ste. Genevieve remains adamant.)

Duke's son Stephen has joined his father as a song leader.

Since my father's been going for so long, I just kind of picked it up. He would start playing the tape around Christmas, getting ready for it, and it just kind of grew on me, and as soon as he thought I was old enough to go, I went. I started when I was about sixteen, I guess, and I've been going now for like thirteen years. I've been leading for the last five years, because, due to health problems and things, some of the older men kind of dropped out. We lost leaders, people that knew the song really well, and, since I knew it entirely since I was about eight years old, I was kind of a natural choice to go ahead and fill in.

I worked down at the Louis Bolduct House [an old French house that has been turned into a colonial museum], so I grew up with the French tradition and the French heritage down there. The Bolduct House was founded in 1735, when the town was founded, and I worked down there for about five years, when I was like eleven years

old up to the time I was sixteen, working in the herb gardens and things like that. That was fascinating to me, and I took five years of high school French because I was interested in the French heritage and the French language. There are very few people down here that know French, so the verse we sing right now is like watered-down French to you. It's not traditional French. It's the local French as they call it. I prefer to call it paw-paw French.

Having completed the circuit of outlying rest homes, inns, and restaurants, the Guignolée are now in the center of town, and rather than having to ride the bus they can straggle from bar to bar. This is becoming a time-consuming process. Each bar has received the drink order in advance, and has an astonishing line of glasses lined up along the bar, each filled with the appropriate clear or amber liquid. As the singers finish, they step up and drain their glasses, then theoretically move on out to the next bar. By now, though, they are running into old friends and finding other distractions, and it is taking all of Duke's efforts to herd them on to the next stop. The singing, however, has lost none of its enthusiasm.

Qu'elle ait toujours le coeur joyeux, point de tristesse.
(May she always have a happy heart and no sadness)
Tous ces fillettes qu'ont pas d'amour, comment vivent-elles?
(All these young girls who are without love, how do they live?)
Qui ni dort, le jour, la nuit, mais toujours veille.
(Who don't sleep either by day or night, but are always awake)
C'est ses amours qui les réveillent, et qui les empêchent de dormir.
(It is their loves that wake them, and that keep them from sleeping)

The Guignolée have reached their last stop, an old, wood-paneled bar in the center of town. A few wives have come out to meet their husbands and share the end of the celebration, before driving what is left of the revelers home to bed. Tomorrow is New Year's Day, and there is morning mass to be attended. The bus is waiting outside, and the evening is drawing to a close.

Duke wanders over for a final chat.

The other day, this man I know came up to me at work, and he asked me, he said, "I heard something I want you to verify."

I said, "What's that?"

And he said, "Well, I heard as the evening goes on you guys get a lot better."

I said, "We get a lot louder... "

Then, the other day, he said "Well, do you have any extra uniforms?"

I said, "I don't think so."
He pulled out some old stuff, and said, "Well, will this one work?"
He kind of liked to go along.

Duke rounds the gang up, and gets them ready to head out to the bus. Before they go, though, there is one last chorus to be sung.

The leaders start it off:

Nous supplions bien la compagnie de pouvoir nous excuser
(We beg of all the company that you will excuse us)
Si on fait quelque follerie c'était pour nous désennuyer
(If we have done anything foolish, it was to amuse ourselves)
Une autre fois nous prendrons garde si on a le bonheur de revenir
(Another time we will be careful, if we have the good fortune to return)

Then the whole group chimes in, with the other customers cheering and clapping along:

Bonsoir le maître et la maîtresse, et tout le monde du logis.
(Good evening, master and mistress, and everyone in the house)

9

That Old-Time Religion: THE BOUNDLESS LOVE QUARTET

It is a small, brick church in La Center, Kentucky, the sort of quiet, country community that makes one think of a vanished, mythical America of family farms and old-time values. Inside, the Boundless Love Quartet is raising a joyful noise, backed by piano, bass, and harmonica. The singers are a mix of ages and shapes: lead singer Huell Tilley is a tall, thin older man. His long-time partner Aaron "Flip" Mayo is rounder, with a lined, farmer's face. Bass Charles Martin and alto Jill Brewington are a good deal younger than the others, and they add a polished sheen to the others' mellow, hand-carved sound. All four have grown up in the area, singing old-time gospel music.

Charles: *I was singing church music from the time I was a very young boy. I even heard these two gentleman sing when I was a very young boy, though they might not admit it. They were a quartet called the Deacons—*

Flip: *The Singing Deacons.*

Charles:—*and I heard them perform many times. Then, I sang in high school in a quartet, and sang basically all my life in one type of group or another. Sometimes gospel, sometimes barber shop, different forms. But it's a real joy to sing Christian music, especially with people that you love and enjoy singing with. I think we're real close as a group and that makes it a lot better, for me.*

As the group swings into a song, the closeness is evident. The arrangements show a touch of black gospel rhythm mixed with intricate barbershop harmonies, and the voices blend and overlap, pushing one another, the excitement building ever higher. Charles's bass provides solid underpinning, and Flip and Jill fill out the sound. It is Huell, though, who catches the eye. He steps forward slightly, raising a hand, bending at the waist, then rising up and testifying, all of it with a gentle smile on his face.

Huell: *I've been singing, oh, forty-some plus years, I guess. I was with one group called the Singing Deacons, but then we kind of parted the ways and I moved away from here and was gone for about five, eight years. I came back home and they had a program at the church; there was three groups invited to this program, and Flip's sister was there and she said, "Huell, why don't you get your group to sing, since it's our church, to open the program up."*

The Boundless Love Quartet: (left to right) Huell Tilley, Jill Brewington, Aaron "Flip" Mayo, and (inset) Charles Martin.

So we got them together and we sung five songs for them that night, and the Methodist preacher got up, and I will never forget what he said. He said, "These old people are saying if you don't use your talent from God, he's going to take it away from you."

That got me. I just felt in my heart, "Hey, we need to get back into music." I talked to Flip about it, and he agreed, and upon that situation, I decided to put a group together. Then we had a picnic down at Columbus Day Park and I saw Charles down there. He'd been out of this area, and I said, "What are you doing back here?"

He said, "I'm living back here."

I said, "Are you still singing?"

He said, "I've been singing with a barbershop."

I said, "Well, here's what I've got. I've got three singers, I'm looking for a bass; would you like to get back into gospel music?"

And he said, "Yeah, I would."

I said, "All right, there's just two things I expect you to do. When we have a practice, you be there, and when we all decide to have a program, you be there."

He said okay, and now I'm looking for a piano player. That was on a Thursday. Sunday night after church, I go back to the choir room and there's Randy, their sound man, standing out there, and I said, "Come on, Randy, let's get her booked and go sing."

He said, "I don't have any talent, my wife's got all the talent."

By that time Sandy walked in the room, and I said, "I understand you got talent to play the piano."

"Yeah."

"Did you ever play for a group?"

"Yeah."

"Would you be interested in playing for another group?"

"Yeah."

I said, "Okay, I'll see you tomorrow, I'll bring you some songs."

So, within eight days from the time we decided to put this together, we did. God did it. He's the one. I said a prayer, and it was a selfish prayer: "Lord, if you want me back in gospel music, send me the musicians that wants to play and singers that wants to sing." And He did this. So we're back in. That happened five years ago this last October. We've been together since then, and enjoying it.

The group gives the musicians a break and swings into the old gospel standard, "Working on the Building," singing in classic, a cappella jubilee style.

I'm working on the building (working on the building)
It's a true foundation (it's a true foundation)

Holding up the bloodstained banner (yes, I'm holding up the bloodstained banner)
For my Lord (for my Lord)
I'll never get tired (I'll never get tired)
Of working on the building (working on the building)
I'm going up to heaven some of these days (some of these days)
To get my reward (get my reward)

Huell: *The heritage of this type of music goes back a long ways. In fact, it all originated through the rhythm that black people came up with, it's a blues-type thing. The love of this music came immediately after World War II. That's when the Jordanaires and the Blackwood Brothers and Statesmen was prevalent. They'd come to the Paducah area and have what they call an "all-night singing"; they'd just go and they'd sing till whenever. Flip and I and our other group has gone down to Savannah, Tennessee, and we'd get back in here at four, five o'clock in the morning. That was during the late forties and early fifties, and I think this is one of the reasons Flip and I enjoy this music so much; we grew up with this, see, when we was coming up.*

Then another artist would take it off. Elvis Presley did a lot of this type of singing, backed up by the Jordanaires, and they were good at it. They traveled all over the country with it. And the people that I talk to tell me that Elvis preferred to sing gospel music rather than the rock 'n' roll that he did, but he was famous for the rock 'n' roll. That's quite a story right there.

This has always been a good area for gospel music. They have an association of quartets in this western Kentucky area, and last count I had there was forty-four, I believe it was. They have a miniconvention on Thursday, Friday, Saturday night, two times a year here, and there's about ten or eleven groups perform each night for twelve minutes, for three nights in a row. So there are quite a few quartets. In this county alone, I know there's four.

Every group has their own songs they sing. Sometimes we'll get ahold of a song that another group has done, and it just might blow us out of the water, we just can't get it together. So what our group does, we select songs that feel comfortable to us. When we go to a program with other groups, we don't want to sing the same songs over, see, so that's why we diversified our songs. The songs that we first started with we don't sing anymore, because we want our new songs. We sing some songs for young people, and we sing some for the senior citizens, as well as the middle-aged people. So we try to get the spectrum, not just a certain kind of song.

Charles: *We probably know 100 gospel songs, quartet songs that we could sing.*

The band picks up the instruments again, and starts an upbeat rhythm, the piano setting the pace and the harmonica chugging along. Flip steps out front, and sings a solo, his voice slightly cracking at times, but warm and soulful.

When Jesus says to me, "Well done"
And all of my cares are laid by
Hey, I'll lay down my sword
My battles are all o'er
I'm gonna walk them golden stairs when I die

The rest of the group swings in behind him, layering rhythms and harmonies:

I'm gonna walk, walk them golden stairs
'Cause I know my Jesus, he answered all my prayers
I know when he calls me to my home on high
I'm gonna walk them golden stairs when I die

Huell: *It's really hard to get a group together, and to stay together, because it's so easy to put things off. You got to be dedicated if you stay in this business, you can't just say, "I'm not coming to practice because I've got an ingrown toenail." You make sacrifices. If you don't have the desire and the inclination, you won't have the stickability it takes to stay with it. But this group has that. We've been together now for a good while, and that's when you feel comfortable, because as you practice and sing with the same group, see, you get to have a feeling for what they're going to do, and it just comes natural that way. This group is just like a family.*

Flip: *It's kind of like therapy for me. I mean, when the Singing Deacons were singing, we'd practice every week if somebody wasn't sick. I farm for a living, and some of that's pretty hard work, and sometimes on practice night I'd be so tired I just didn't think I should go. But I'd go on over and sing three or four songs and it would lift me right up. It's good therapy if you love it and enjoy doing it, and I do. I've been doing it for about forty years now, off and on.*

Charles: *I think what we all feel is that God has given us a talent in our voices, and we either use those or we don't, and if we don't use them, my experience is, if you're a musician and you don't use your voice, you lose it. The quality goes away and it isn't long till you don't have the ability to perform the way you would if you did perform all the time. So it's a talent that we feel God has given us and we ought to share with other people. And, as you can see tonight, people enjoy it.*

Flip: *I remember after the Singing Deacons broke up, I really missed it. I missed a lot of blessings. I remember once, when we went to a little church in southern*

Illinois. We went one Sunday night, and I don't know if you've ever had this experience, but sometimes you walk in a church and you can feel the spirit—well, I felt it as soon as we got in over there that night.

The preacher just preached a short sermon and then turned it over to us, and we sang, and I'll never forget this: For the invitation, he wanted us to sing "Amazing Grace." And we sang that and everybody just started getting down on their knees—

Charles: *We sang that song nine times.*

Flip: *And they started coming down the aisle—I don't know how many people were saved. One boy, a soldier boy—he was in Vietnam, I think—he was home on leave and he had to go back the next morning. He made the preacher take him down to the river and baptize him that night. That was just an experience I won't ever forget. Just God working. And we've had a lot of blessings like that.*

Huell: *See, this area through here is known as the Bible Belt, and if the songs we sing can help somebody along life's pathway, we've done our work. We do our thing, and God gets the results. We feel that way about it. The preachers preach; we don't preach, we sing, but we sing the same thing that he preaches.*

Flip: *We're not looking for any personal honor or glory—anyway, I'm not; I'm not going to speak for the rest of you—We want the Lord God to have that, if there's any at all. We want people to enjoy our music, get a blessing out of it, but if they're going to praise somebody, just praise God.*

◆◆◆

PART THREE

The Southern

Steamboats on the lower Mississippi

Fusion

With this section, the Mississippi flows into the deep South, the heartland of the blues and prime breeding ground for rock 'n' roll and soul music. This is by far the most culturally cohesive area of the river. It is farmland, home to cotton plantations that have in recent years turned more and more of their acreage over to rice and catfish farming. Memphis, the regional metropolis, is far less distinct from its rural surroundings than Minneapolis, St. Louis, or New Orleans. Much of its population retains strong country roots, and its musical history has been made less by locals than by folks from the surrounding small towns who came into the city to record and sell their music, just as the cotton plantation owners came in to sell their bales to national brokers.

The plantation system, built with the labor of African slaves and later worked by African-American sharecroppers, spawned a population in which blacks were the majority and, though their political power was brutally curtailed, they were a dominant influence on music. All the musicians to come out of this area, whatever their race, have been deeply affected by black traditions. Also, despite segregation, this is an area where black and white musicians have traded tunes and played together for generations, from the days when Mississippi John Hurt was working at dances with the white fiddler W. T. Narmour to the Stax studio scene that produced the Memphis Horns.

The mixing was by no means easy, and in no way negated the racial problems that surrounded it, but it made for a unique musical world of white blues singers, from Jimmie Rodgers to Elvis Presley, and black country musicians, from the Mississippi Sheiks to Charley Pride. While their music was often marketed in separate catalogues, classified as "race" or "hillbilly," in reality the styles always overlapped. Every black musician we talked to in the Delta spoke of listening to white country music, and every white musician gave credit to the overwhelming influence of the blues. The result is a true fusion music, shared with variations by different generations and ethnic mixtures of players.

One thing that made the Mississippi Delta uniquely productive in terms of music was its relatively new prosperity. It was not until the late nineteenth and early twentieth century that much of it was drained and cleared for farming, and the black workers who streamed into the region formed a younger, less rooted population than in other parts of the deep south. As a result, it was fertile soil for a new musical trend called the blues. The proportion of major blues figures who came out of the Delta was incredible, and the area's style came to define the music's development in the fifties and sixties, through the electric work of native sons like B. B. King and Muddy Waters.

The earliest local blues artists still had strong country dance roots, but by the thirties a new generation had arrived. The blues guitarist and singer Robert Johnson has come to exemplify this generation's music, and his sound has been carried on in its pure form by his protegé, Robert Lockwood, Jr., as well as being adapted into an electric style by Lockwood, Waters, Elmore James, and others. Lockwood became a major influence in the area when he teamed up with Sonny Boy Williamson (Aleck "Rice" Miller, not to be confused with John Lee "Sonny Boy" Williamson) and started a daily live broadcast from Helena, Arkansas, sponsored by King Biscuit flour. The *King Biscuit Show,* which Williamson would continue until his death in 1965, blanketed the area on both sides of the river and helped shape a Delta style that went on to flourish in Memphis, Detroit, and, most famously, Chicago.

The first generation of electric bluesmen were electrifying a style formed in acoustic groups, but by the late fifties a new style had been born, blending the harsh Mississippi sound with smoother instrumental work and vocal techniques adapted from gospel music. Little Milton, who grew up in Greenville, was one of many performers who moved to Memphis and had his first records on Sam Phillips's Sun Records, before heading to Chicago and stardom as Chess Records' soul star of the early sixties. Milton exemplifies the later development of a blues/soul music that continues to attract a large audience in black clubs throughout the southern states. Meanwhile, the Delta has continued to breed a rootsier, rougher sound exemplified by artists like Big Jack Johnson, who learned the classic, acoustic Delta style from his father, then blended it with flavors adapted from artists he heard on the radio. Playing for most of his life in rough Delta "juke joints," he kept a hard, edgy sound that is an interesting contrast to the work of more urbanized blues players.

Blues and the Delta have become virtually synonymous in many people's minds, but the white country tradition was also around, especially on the airwaves. Both Johnson and Milton speak of listening to the Grand Ole Opry as kids, and admiring the singers they heard there. This was part of a long process of cultural cross-fertilization in which, for example, the eastern Mississippian Jimmy Rodgers imitated black blues singers like Bessie Smith, then was imitated in turn by black singers like the Mississippi Sheiks. The music came to a common meeting point in the fifties, with black singers like Chuck Berry, who was considered a "hillbilly" singer by his St. Louis compatriots, and the wave of white rockabillies.

The rural areas around Memphis were as fertile for rockabilly as for blues, and Sun Records became the style's defining label with Elvis, Carl Perkins, Jerry Lee Lewis, and a host of other young, white country boys who had fallen for the lure of r&b rhythms. In Newport, Arkansas, a wide-open strip of bars featured booze, gambling, and hot bands like Sonny Burgess and the Pacers. Like many of his peers, Burgess plays an eclectic mix of material, from country-tinged r&b and blues to blues-tinged country and the occasional gospel song.

Sun Records had a brief heyday, but Memphis really made its name as a recording center ten years later. In the mid-1960s, it became the heart of southern soul music, the virtuoso mix of r&b and gospel that swept the country, but reached its highest expression in the converted movie theater that was home to Stax Records. Wayne Jackson, a white trumpet player, and Andrew Love, a black saxophonist, were part of the uniquely interracial crew that built the Stax sound. (It was a mix that only gradually emerged from the studio. The first Stax hit, "Last Night" by the Mar-keys, was recorded largely by black players, but when the Mar-keys—a name invented for the session—went on the road, the touring group was all white.) The Stax house band, Booker T. and the MGs, was mixed, as were the songwriting and production teams, though all the singers were African-American.

Jackson and Love went on to play at the other studios that soon cropped up to capitalize on the wealth of talent streaming into town, before christening themselves the Memphis Horns and taking their talents out to wherever the work was, becoming the most-recorded horn section in history. In the 1970s, they were regulars at Hi studios as it built another Memphis soul empire on the talents of singers like Al Green, Otis Clay, and St. Louis native Ann Peebles. Peebles continues to live in Memphis, writing songs, playing festivals around the world, and recording new material, and she and the Horns work together to carry on the southern soul tradition.

A lot of talent remains in the area, but it has been some twenty years since Memphis was the center of a major recording scene. The economics of the music industry have changed, and the sort of artists that once came to Memphis in search of national success now head for New York or L.A. The people who have stayed are here because they like the slower, more relaxed pace, or just because it is home. Rufus Thomas, for one, has become so identfied with the town that it is impossible to imagine him living anywhere else. He has become the sage of Beale Street, witness to six decades of musical history, and still plays host to visitors who want to learn about Memphis's rich African-American heritage.

Surprisingly, the recording center for the area has moved south to an area with little history in the music business. In Jackson, Mississippi, Malaco Records has built a black music empire. Its blues artists include Little Milton, but the biggest seller these days is not in "the Devil's music," but on the side of the Lord. The Mississippi Mass Choir has capitalized on the incredible wealth of talent in Mississippi churches to bring together the most popular choir on the current gospel scene. Mississippi Mass draws on the full-throated, searing vocal style that has always been a local specialty, putting some of the state's hottest soloists in front of a huge and tightly rehearsed ensemble, and has dominated the choir field since its inception a decade ago.

Along with Malaco, the area's other big musical news in recent years has been the rise of regional festivals throughout the Delta. After a century of exporting its talent, the region is finally learning how to bring tourists in to support the artists at home. Greenville, Greenwood, and Clarksdale have all been hosting regular blues fests, but the best known of them all is across the river in Arkansas, where the memory of Williamson's and Lockwood's radio show is carried on in the King Biscuit Blues Festival. A free event that draws local families and tourists from around the world to multiple stages, King Biscuit also helps to tie the generations of blues and gospel talent together. Older pioneers alternate with hot, young stars, and favorite sons and daughters return to visit. Levon Helm, who normally fronts the Band, comes every year to get together with old playing buddies and relive the days when he was first hearing blues, trekking in from his home place in Turkey Scratch to sit in the radio station at the feet of the great Sonny Boy.

Though the years have brought a lot of changes, it feels as if there is something timeless about this region. This impression is to some extent illusory—the sleepy, small-town ambiance is in part the result of the mass emigration that depopulated the area after the introduction of mechanized cotton farming—but some is very real. This is still a place where music, food, and life in general have remained close to the earth, and new ways are slow to penetrate. If this is sometimes regrettable, and hard on local residents, it has preserved intact a culture of unique depth and power, and music that no other place on earth can match.

◆ ◆ ◆

1

We Wanna Boogie: SONNY BURGESS

Elvis Presley and all of them was good, but when Sonny started for me, with Kern and Joe Lewis and all of them, after they got together, they had the best band, best drawing card in this country. Their problem was that they never really got out enough. They would leave, say "Sonny's going on tour," and I don't know what would happen, but he'd be gone about a week or two and they'd come back home. But if he'd of went on like he should've—he might not like to hear me say this—but he would have been one of the tops today.

Bob King, owner and manager of the King of Clubs, out on U. S. Highway 67 in Swifton, Arkansas, is standing in his "Hall of Fame," a small alcove full of pictures of acts that have played here over the years: Elvis, Jerry Lee Lewis, Conway Twitty, Roy Orbison, and an array of country stars. There are also several pictures of the man who is standing next to him: Sonny Burgess, a dapper sixty-seven-year-old with a small, white beard and an easy smile, was once the wildest rocker in northeastern Arkansas and he is still going strong. His latest album was produced by Bruce Springsteen's bandmate Garry Tallent, and includes songs by Springsteen, Steve Forbert, and alternative rocker Dave Alvin, a recent friend and collaborator, as well as a slew of contemporary songwriters. Clearly, Burgess is keeping up with new developments in the music world. Today, though, he is on his home turf, and it takes him back to the old days.

I was born and raised out here, about five miles out in the country. At that time it was cotton country, and my family was just a typical farm family. None of them played music, but I had two uncles, one played harmonica and guitar, and the other was a fiddle player. They used to get me to do country dances; we'd play out in the country, like on Saturday nights, you'd go to somebody's house and have a dance. I was their rhythm man, and you talk about getting tired—they'd play those hoedowns for forty minutes, seemed like. And the strings on that guitar were about that high. You'd really get worn out.

Back then it was all country music. Then, when we got the Pacers together, Gerry Grojean was our first manager and he worked at KMBY down here, and of course they had all the records and everything, and we got to listening to dance-type music. This was in the fifties, and there was a lot of rhythm and blues—back then the term was "race music"—which I liked.

Sonny Burgess, rockabilly pioneer. His baseball cap is a testament to his first recording break, for Memphis's legendary Sun Records.

In those days, we didn't get a chance to see the black musicians live; the only black musicians we'd get to see was like Punky Caldwell playing up at Mike's, right above Bob King's there—he had a jazz or pop band and he had three black musicians with him. Then we had a black member of our band for a while, Little Willie, he played drums for us; he's from here in Newport. We played with black musicians, but no big names came in here, you know, like B. B. King, all that bunch. We got to see them later on, in the latter part of the fifties and sixties, but you'd hear him on the radio out of Memphis, WDIA. Our station out here was all country. So you'd hear those mixtures. It was the black artists, rhythm and blues, and you had your churches, church music, and you had your country, and a little pop in there. They all kind of mixed together and I think made what we've got today, really.

I first seen Elvis at a spot down the road here a little ways, Porky's Rooftop. That's when he just had three pieces: him, Scotty [Moore], and Bill [Black], called the Blue Moon Boys. Elvis created something new, and we'd never heard anything like him, you know. He was just a little different from everybody else, and he had everything that a guy has to have to be a star. And he could really sing. I think he was much better than RCA Victor ever caught him on record; I still say that. Back in the fifties and early sixties, he could sing so good, and that group just had a great sound. Man, it's amazing the sound that they got.

When Elvis came over, we said, "Man, we need to go to Memphis." So we went to Memphis and talked to Sam Phillips at Sun Records and he said, "Well," he said, "work up a couple of songs and come on back." So we practiced and we practiced, and we worked up "Redheaded Woman" and "We Wanna Boogie." We practiced up one side and down the other, and never did get them right, you know. But we was wild and having a lot of fun.

On the King of Clubs' stage, Sonny is playing for a room full of old fans. His band is a mix of new and old: Kern Kennedy, the pianist, was in Sonny's first trio, back in the early fifties, while other band members are young enough to be their sons. The set ranges from Sonny's early hits to country and r&b numbers, from old standards to songs from the new album. Sonny takes most of the guitar solos, cutting through the mix with rock 'n' roll energy, and shares vocal chores with various band members. He sings "T for Texas," complete with a Jimmy Rodgers yodel, Hank Williams' "Move It on Over," and Smiley Lewis' New Orleans r&b ballad "One Night of Sin." Elvis recorded the latter song in a censored version, as "One Night of Love," but Sonny does it straight and hard, his voice curling around the lyric with a haunting, emotion-filled whine:

One night of sin
Is what I'm now paying for
The things I did and I saw
Would make the earth stand still

The audience is largely made up of older folks, Sonny's fans from his days as one of the Sun Records rockabilly gang, an elite group that included Elvis, Jerry Lee, Carl Perkins, Johnny Cash, Roy Orbison, and a dozen guys like Sonny, who never went on to major national success but became local legends.

Sam Phillips liked everything to have a feel. I think that was his secret, you know. If you made mistakes it didn't matter—it was whether it felt good. And of course, we could get into a groove like Jerry Lee and everybody else did, and our music was more feel than anything. Sam would just listen to a song and say whether he liked it or didn't. He'd get into it real good, and we were as wild in the studio as we were in person.

I think that's why we never got a really good, clean recording, because it was just like we were playing live, so we never really tried. We didn't know nothing about recording. We'd never been in a studio before in our life, and we didn't have the least idea of what you were supposed to do, and nobody told us. Sam didn't really come in there and say, "Do this and do that." He'd just turn the tape on and say, "Play." And we played like we were playing for an audience, you know; he was the audience.

But man, everybody wanted one of those little gold Sun records, everybody wanted to be on that label at that time. And it made a lot of difference in our lives—we were semistars because we had that Sun record. Not that we got any money; it was just a little bit of money and a lot of fun.

Because so many great records came out of the Sun studio, the classic rockabilly sound has become associated with Memphis. As it happened, though, Elvis was practically the only important figure who actually lived in the city. Most of the rockabillies were small-town boys, Jerry Lee Lewis from Ferriday, Louisiana, or Carl Perkins from Tiptonville, Tennessee. Arkansas was one of the most productive states, with Billy Lee Riley, Charlie Rich, Ronnie Hawkins, and Harold Jenkins, who made his debut as a rockabilly singer at Bob Miller's club before changing his name to Conway Twitty and moving over into country and western–not to mention Johnny Cash, who grew up in Dyess, a New Deal experimental community on the river due east of Newport. Sonny says that the area around Newport was particularly good for musicians.

At that time there was a whole strip of clubs along here, on Highway 67. This used to be the gathering point for all the salesmen that used to make their trips around this part of northeast Arkansas; they made sure they spent two or three nights here in Newport. This was a wet county with dry counties all around it, and it was wide open. The gamblers would come in, and they'd bring the gals and they'd spend the money in town. So it made a pretty prosperous little deal.

We started out playing at Bob's; he would pay us forty dollars to come in and play on a Friday night, so it worked out to ten dollars each. I was working at the box factory then, making forty-five dollars a week and five dollars out for Social Security and stuff like that. So I had forty dollars, and boy when you add that ten dollars to it, I thought I was well off. I had a car—wasn't brand new, but I had a car—and a little money in my pocket. I thought I was rich.

After we got pretty good, we'd play down the road at the Silver Moon Club, Don Washam's place. It was a little different crowd than Bob's. Bob's, you know, was country music. Well, Don wanted a band that was more pop music; in other words, you had to have the saxophone and all that type thing. We came up there, we had to play stuff like "Stardust."

Sonny onstage at the King of Clubs

The Silver Moon Club was famous here in the southern part of the United States. We used to have college kids, lawyers, politicians, everybody came to Silver Moon Club because they had the big bands, like the Dorsey Brothers, Glenn Miller Orchestra with Tex Beneke, Woody Herman, Louis Armstrong was here, Bob Wills, and the Texas Playboys back when he had the big band and was really traveling. When the big bands came in, you'd get what we call the "big wheels" in town. All the rich folks would come out and mix and mingle with us poor folks to see the big bands. Then there was Jerry Lee Lewis, Elvis Presley played here three times, Carl Perkins, Ernest Tubb. Anybody that was in the music business just about has played at the Silver Moon Club or at Bob King's.

It would go all night, sometimes. One o'clock was closing time, but we've stayed in there many a night after hours when they'd just lock the doors. The law didn't bother you back then. Nowadays, they're pretty strict, but back then I don't know whether they paid them off or what the deal was, but they didn't bother you. Don would say, "Lock the door before you leave. Leave when you want to." It'd be daybreak before we'd get out of there. We weren't playing now, it was partying.

We played the Silver Moon on Saturday nights. It was a dollar to get in—at Bob's it was fifty cents on a Friday night—and we'd get usually about a couple hundred dollars. We drew a mixed crowd, a lot of college kids and the other folks, too, because I guess it was the thing that was happening back then. The music was new and different, and everybody wanted to be a part of it.

We had college kids came in from all over. There was a group that was going to school at the University of Arkansas, and they hired us for no telling how many different gigs. Then there was a girl who came here one summer from Louisville, Kentucky—her grandad was a doctor up here at Batesville. She liked us so well that when she had a debutante ball in Louisville, they hired us to come up there to Louisville Country Club. You can't believe it: We go up there, they give us $5,000. Now, that's a lot of money back then. We drive all the way up there, and they've got an orchestra out of Chicago that comes in. This orchestra sets up. We just played thirty minutes, then we drove back to Memphis. The next night we played the Rainbow Terrace in Memphis, another place Elvis used to play there. Nothing but college kids, you know, and teenagers.

We did have a good show. I'd have to say the Pacers was one of the best show groups I ever seen in my life. I guess I've seen everybody in the business, just about, but in our heyday—we only operated about two years with the originals, the guys there in that photograph—it was like watching a three-ring circus. In other words, you couldn't watch just one person, there's something going on with everybody.

It was feel-good music; it made people want to dance. Nowadays, everybody wants to be cool. Everybody wants to be, "Yeah, man," they want to sit around and look cool—and the gals, they got nobody to dance with. That's why this line dancing got popular. It's because those women couldn't get those guys out of the seats to dance with them, so they finally started dancing by themselves.

When Sonny and the boys get rockin', the audience at the King of Clubs is up and jitterbugging like old times. Of course, it is a much smaller audience, but Sonny does not seem fazed by the size of the crowd. He is enjoying himself, and when he kicks off his old hits the years melt away.

Weeeelll, now a redheaded woman's 'bout the meanest thing I know
Redheaded woman's bout the meanest thing I know
Love you a lot if you've got money to show

Weeeellll, a red headed woman make you wish you'd never been born
Redheaded woman make you wish you'd never been born
Make you want to hear old Gabriel blow his horn

I wrote that one about Joanne, my to-be-my-wife; she wasn't at that time. Her hair had a reddish tint to it. And "We Wanna Boogie," that was just a feeling. That became kind of a famous saying. I wrote quite a bit back then. In fact, I've got a lot of songs that I wrote and never recorded. It seemed like I had a little more creativity then than now.

Sonny, Bob, and the other old-timers have hundreds of stories about the wild old days, about bar fights, wild women, and all sorts of hi-jinks: the time Sonny's bass player jumped off the stage at a theatre gig, not realizing there was an orchestra pit between him and the dance floor, or the time a jealous husband trying to spy on his wife fell through Bob's roof onto the bandstand. Sonny joins in, but more quietly than the others, and he is the only one who talks with almost equal enthusiasm about his later life. He quit the music business in the early 1970s, taking a job as a traveling salesman, but got back into it when the Smithsonian put together a group of Sun recording artists as part of a celebration of Tennessee culture at the annual folklife festival on the Capitol Mall.

Jay Orr, he was working with the Country Music Hall of Fame in Nashville, in their archive, and he said, "Well, rockabilly music is a dying type music," said, "Why don't we get these guys together." So he came to Memphis and talked with Roland James, who was working there at the studio, and Sam, and wanted to know if he could put us together to take us up to Washington for two weeks. Well, of course, we all said yeah, and worked around where we'd get off—man, we was all excited. So we went up there and it went over so good—we had a good show, kind of like the Pacers, we had a lot of different little acts going on, everybody had their own little deal. It was little excitement there that they hadn't seen, and it just kind of exploded. So for about six years we were playing all the time. Every weekend, it seemed like they were flying us somewhere to play a festival of some type or other.

Sonny sang most of the lead vocals for what came to be billed as the Sun Rhythm Section, and took a lot of the guitar breaks. The band included bassist/producer Stan Kessler, the author of "I Forgot to Remember to Forget" and "You're Right, I'm Left, She's Gone," and pianist Jerry Lee "Smoochy" Smith, but for a lot of people Sonny was the star, and as the group cut back on its appearances he continued as a soloist.

Stan was real religious, and he didn't like playing the nightclubs, and then Smoochy joined the church, so he decided he didn't want to play as much in nightclubs either. And there's not as many festival deals coming through now as it did, so we kind of stopped doing it. But I said, "Well, I'll still play while I'm still able a little bit." You know, I don't drink and don't even smoke, but it doesn't bother me to go in and play.

I do gospel music as well. I belong to church, and we got a little group called Stranger's Home, we go around and do gospel music in the churches. I'm a Baptist, but I guess my music would be called Pentecostal, because I like the up-tempo gospel music, that's my type. I love playing it, it's good music, makes you feel good. That feeling, you know, in my gospel, I do the same feel as I do my pop music or rhythm and blues, whatever you want to call it—the regular music. It's just the same, just different words.

So as long as it's fun, I'll keep doing it. Once it quits being fun, then I think I need to quit. But you know, it's fun now. I wouldn't want to go back to playing four hours a night, that would get tiresome. But I put this new band together, I got these three boys out of Nashville, and they can really play. So that makes my job easy. And I don't play all the time, but I play as much as I want to.

◆◆◆

2
Beale Street Talking: RUFUS THOMAS

I've seen the lights of gay Broadway
Old Market Street down by the Frisco Bay
I've been over at London, by the Bourse
But take my advice and see Beale Street first
You'll see hognose restaurants and chitlin' cafes.
Things to remind you of bygone days.
You'll see honest men, pickpockets skilled,
And Beale Street never sleeps until somebody gets killed.
If Beale Street could talk, if Beale Street could talk,
Many a married man would take his bed and walk.
Except one or two that never drink booze,
And the blind man on the corner singing the Beale Street blues.
I'd rather be here (that's Beale Street) than any place I know
(And he repeated it, said:) I'd rather be here than any place I know,
And it's going to take the sergeant just for to make me go.
(That's Beale Street!)

Rufus Thomas is sitting in the Center for Southern Folklore, reciting the lyric to W. C. Handy's "Beale Street Blues." He savors each word, and places his emphasis so as to underline the accuracy of certain phrases. Beale Street today is a tourist center rather than the black entertainment district of yore, but Thomas has been coming here for almost eight decades and he has keen remembrances of the old days. If his memory ever lapses, there are plenty of reminders close at hand. Across the street is Handy Park, with a bronze statue of the composer dubbed "The Father of the Blues," and the next corner is the intersection of Beale Street and Rufus Thomas Boulevard.

How about that? That's not too bad, is it? I've got a street named after me, and I also have a monument—all while I'm alive. It's like giving you your flowers while you live, because when you're dead you ain't smelling nothing.

Rufus Thomas onstage at the Memphis Music and Heritage Festival.

I was born in a little place called Cayce, Mississippi, which is around thirty-five miles from here, just below the state line of Tennessee, and my folk brought me up here when I was about two years old. They got tired of farming and they came to the big city of Memphis, Tennessee. And I've been in Memphis since I was two years old.

I started knowing about Beale Street at the age of about six. My first encounter on stage, I was six years old, in the first grade at Cartright Grammar School. I made my debut onstage playing the part of a frog, not knowing that in later years it would become dogs, chickens, penguins and all the like. [Rufus's biggest hits were 1964s "Walking the Dog" and 1970s "Do the Funky Chicken," and his last major chart appearance, in 1971, was "Do the Funky Penguin."] Those animals and me, we've had a great time together.

I don't think I really started coming to Beale Street until I was maybe about twelve or thirteen. I lived a long way from Beale Street, way out south in a place called Lauderdale Sub, the Lauderdale subdivision. During that time everybody walked, there weren't no cars, you didn't even think about cars, and we'd walk to Beale Street from where we lived out there. I was learning how to dance. I wanted to be the greatest tap dancer in the world. Never made that one, but I was a very good tap dancer.

Right across the street there, right next to where the monument is, is where my beginning was on Beale Street: at the Palace Theater, which was "The Show Place of the South." People like B. B. King, Bobby Bland, Johnny Ace, Roscoe Gordon, Rufus Thomas all came from that magic theater. It was a movie theater; they would show pictures and then cut the pictures off and have amateur night. That's where all of the talent would be every Wednesday night. I had a team called "Rufus and Bones." We were a

dance comedy team. We did it all. We sang, we danced, we did comedy, and anything else that an entertainer could do. And we were on the program for eleven consecutive years [c.1940–1951], every Wednesday night.

Back then, Beale Street was the center. See, Beale Street was a black man's haven—I couldn't say heaven, but close. People were coming from far and near, from the river to the railroad, from Arkansas, Alabama, Mississippi, coming to Beale Street. If you had a whole lot of troubles and things were bothering you, come to Beale Street and all your problems were gone. You could have nothing but good times on Beale Street and that's what it was all about.

Beale Street now is not the mecca of black people that you used to see. They'd go to the joints like PW's Club, right here in this neighborhood, they'd be going to the Palace Theater and across the street to the old Daisy Theater. All within one block. This is what made Memphis: one block, or a block and a half, from Third Street back to Fourth. As of today, there is a vast difference. Beale Street now is a tourist attraction that attracts people from all over the world. The two things that people want to see when they come to Memphis: Graceland, Beale Street—or Beale Street, Graceland. But Beale Street is not and it can never be the street of yesteryear.

The change is hardly surprising. There is little continuity in the entertainment world, and perhaps even less in the black entertainment world than in the mainstream. Rufus Thomas, though, endures. He recently celebrated his eightieth birthday with a big bash including guests from throughout his past: B. B. King, for example, who got his start as a guest on Rufus's amateur nights and later followed Thomas onto a DJ spot at WDIA, "The Mother Station of the Negroes."

Rufus tells the story of Memphis music, in a scene from the *River of Song* series.

I've been with the radio, been with WDIA since 1951. It was the first radio station to break from being all-white. It's like the Jackie Robinson story. Bert Ferguson with Nat D. Williams, the first black disc jockey, baptized the water, and since WDIA, they're everywhere now. People who were with WDIA, the white advertisers, they pulled some of the ads off because that was a black voice advertising their product. And then, they found that there was gold in them thar hills and they had to come crawling back, you know. It's the good, old American dollar—money. That's what brought them back, and they're still there, and we're the number one station in this city.

I had a program on Saturday called the "House of Happiness." B. B. King was with WDIA, too. He first had a fifteen-minute program, with Peptikon buying the slot, and every time he started singing that Peptikon song, I'd turn the radio off. He was just that bad: "Peptikon sho' is good, Peptikon sho' is good, Peptikon sho' is good, you can get it anywhere in the neighborhood." But then he got the "Sepia Swing Club" in the afternoon, and when B. B. left, I got the "Sepia Swing Club," and I stayed there for a long, long while, until I started to travel.

Another prominent birthday guest was the generally reclusive Sam Phillips, whose Sun record label had its first success with Rufus's "Bear Cat." The record was billed as "The answer to 'Hound Dog,'" back when the latter song was a hit for Big Mama Thornton and Elvis was an unknown local teenager.

Oh, yeah. I made the first hit record for Sun Studios, and I made the first hit record for Stax Records. I launched two record companies. Now, you've heard a lot of Sam Phillips, what he has done with Elvis, Johnny Cash, Roy Orbison, Jerry Lee Lewis, and Carl Perkins. But before that time, Sam had a stable of black entertainers. And all the time he was looking for a white boy who could sing black, and he found him in Elvis, and as soon as he found him and Elvis started to sound good, he discarded all of his black entertainers. Naturally, you get peeved, you get upset about these things, but life goes on. If you stay in one place, then you don't survive, but with me, it was a matter of survival, and I did, and I'm still surviving.

I don't have hard feelings for Sam. He did what he thought was right, which I think was wrong. But a man has to do what a man has to do. I think personally that it was the wrong thing to do; I don't know how he thought, but I think that he might have thought that maybe blacks and whites couldn't do these things together.

But I was the first and maybe the only black disc jockey that was playing Elvis. I played Elvis because I liked what he had to offer at that time. Elvis was never funky, Elvis could have never been funky at that time with that good, down-to-earth beat that Stax Records had. That was funk, and I would say I was the innovator of that. But Elvis had something that was likable, and I didn't play it just because Elvis was white; I played the music because I liked it. Color didn't have anything to do with it.

Then, a few years after that, Stax came along and proved to the world that people—people, no color, just people who got something to offer to the world in music—can come together for one common cause, and that was music. And they put that stuff together, black, white, any other color that was available and could have that kind of talent.

Stax put together music that was heard from Japan to Mississippi, Germany to Alabama, England to Arkansas, and from Africa to the lowest part of Louisiana. So to tell me that people can't get together, and especially in music, is ludicrous, it just ain't no way for something like that to not happen. Since that time, you heard things like

"Walking the Dog," "Funky Chicken, "Funky Penguin," a whole lot of other great hit records: Booker T. and the MGs, the Staple Singers, all of these wonderful artists: Johnny Taylor, Albert King, all coming out of Stax Records. They made some of the best music that the world had ever known, that ever will be.

Of course, those hits Rufus was listing were his. He gave Stax its beginning in 1960 by cutting his daughter Carla singing a song called "Cause I Love You." Carla's "Gee Whiz" became the label's first major hit, and then Rufus got into the spotlight himself with "The Dog" and it's top-ten follow-up, "Walking the Dog."

When "Walking the Dog" first came into my head, I was at work at the American Finishing Company textile mill, back in the early fifties. I'm on the job, on top of this fourteen-foot vat that was being filled up with cloth, coming over a reel in a continuous roll, and I got me a thing going while I'm laying there. I'm going [snapping fingers] and one of the fellows stopped doing his work to come over there and said, "Ruf', what the hell's wrong with you?"

"Nothing, man. I got a song, man, I got a song going on here."

"A song?" he said. "Man, don't look like no song to me, it looks like you having fits over here."

"No, I'm cool."

And maybe four to five months later, after laying up there watching this job, I'm saying,

Mary Mack, dressed in black,
Silver buttons all down her back,
High, low, tipsy toe,
She broke her needle and she can't sew,
Walking the dog.

Now, I don't know how "walking the dog" got on the end of that song, but I do know where the nursery rhyme comes from, because I played as much of the kid games with the girls as the girls did. I was better than the girls at most of the games; I played hopscotch, I played the jump rope, I could jump faster then any of the girls in the neighborhood. I played them not knowing that in the days to come that the nursery rhymes and the things I'd learned in school, that would come to be in a song.

The other one I used to play was "I Spy," but in the neighborhood, we didn't call it "I Spy;" we heard it as "High Spy," and that's what we called it. That's when you put your hands over your eyes and you count and they'd say,

Asked my mama for fifty cents
To see that elephant jump the fence
He jumped so high, he touched the sky,
And never got back till the fourth of July

Now, we were playing that and counting for everyone to go and hide, but I put "walking the dog" on the end of that. So that's how "Walking the Dog" was born, and I recorded that in 1963, and "Walking the Dog" is almost as popular today as it was yesterday, in 1963, 4, 5, and the like. That's why I can still say I ain't no old-timer—I'm yesterday, I'm today, and I am tomorrow.

I still play right here. Not regularly; I only do Memphis on special occasions. I don't work in clubs every weekend like I used to. Sort of graduated from that, you know. But I perform at the heritage festival that we do for Miss Judy Peiser here at the Center for Southern Folklore every year, and then I do a festival in Italy every year, in Perretta, Italy, where they have a park named after me. That's on the back side of the world from Memphis. So I'm still getting them even on the other side of the world.

I ain't never been an old-timer, and I never will be an old-timer. As long as I live and fifty years after I'm dead, I will never be an old-timer. That's why they call me today "the world's oldest teenager," because all of my music was centered to the younger set, and the younger set took my music and ran with it. And to prove it, if you will see the movie Wattstax, *there is proof that a fifty- or sixty-year-old man can have the young people. This was the Los Angeles Coliseum, 105,000 people, and at least 40,000 people broke the fences down to come on the field to dance to my music. You call that an old-timer? No way.*

"I do know where the nursery rhyme comes from, because I played as much of the kid games with the girls as the girls did."

I never had a face lift yet; I don't have to pull up nothing, don't have to draw up no skin to make me look young. I got this youth from being real. No crow's feet, no none of that stuff. And for an eighty-year-old man, I look damn good.

◆◆◆

The Memphis Horns, Wayne Jackson (top) and Andrew Love (bottom), lay down tracks in a Memphis studio. Ann Peebles (right) listens, waiting for her cue.

3

Memphis Soul Stew: THE MEMPHIS HORNS, WITH ANN PEEBLES

From the first time we played together, there was something about the way our tones blended. His sound and my sound, it was just perfect.

Andrew Love looks over at his partner, Wayne Jackson. As frequently happens, Wayne picks up the train of thought.

We have something that's called "sibling harmonies," although we're not siblings. That's the only way to describe it. You know, you have the Everly Brothers, let's say. They're brothers, and their voices have a certain blend because they have the same harmonies, the same pitches. So they sound like nobody else. And Andrew and I have a certain way that we sound. You can pick us out of a whole room of different horn players. You could match me up with another saxophone player and record it, it wouldn't sound the same—and the same with Andrew. And we've sounded that way ever since the first day we played together, thirty-three years ago.

Andrew is nodding. He is more laconic than Wayne, but is quick to agree.

It sounded so good, we said, "Hey, we might have something here." And then, we had Otis Redding shouting all kinds of horn lines at us, you know.

Wayne jumps back in on Redding's name.

We learned from the best! Otis was amazing; he was the one that we all loved the most as far as being in the recording studio. He put out the most energy and drew the most out of us. If he were back there, really jamming, you could feel it; the whole place was electrified. If he were giving a great performance, you can bet we were giving a great performance, too.

Wayne, on trumpet, and Andrew, on saxophone, were ubiquitous on Redding's records, as well as on thousands of other soul recordings. Memphis in the 1960s was Southern Soul Central, and they were the first-call horn players at every studio in town. Wayne still sounds excited when he recalls those times, especially the days when he and Andrew were among the young players hanging out around the defunct movie theater that was serving as a record store and the studio for Stax records. Everybody jammed together, and after a while coalesced into regular studio groups: the rhythm section, with Booker T. Jones, Steve Cropper, Duck Dunn, and Al Jackson, came to be known as Booker T. and the MGs; the horn players, of whom Wayne and Andrew were the most long-lasting, as the Mar-keys. Both groups, though, functioned less as named recording outfits than simply as backup players for whatever vocalists came through.

We were all very young and nobody knew anything, so everybody learned together. We learned how to plug the cords into the mikes and the mikes into the board and the board into the machine. People were learning how to turn these pots up, and how to make a baffle. [Drummer] Al Jackson was two baffles away from us, across a room the size of a movie theater, so we were actually playing slightly behind him, because the sound was slightly delayed getting to us. That gave us sort of a laid-back horn sound, and that became part of our style.

As Andrew explains, that was before overdubbing became standard.

In those days, we were all in the same room: guitars and horns and Otis Redding and everybody, and everybody played at the same time. You make a mistake, you just keep going.

Wayne laughs.

Man, you couldn't mess up. Because Otis Redding or Sam and Dave or Eddie Floyd or William Bell or any one of those other wonderful artists might be giving the best performance of his life. You wouldn't want to be the one who made a bad mistake and caused them to stop the machines and say "Hold it, we'll roll back. Take it again." You surely didn't want to be that guy. So we all tried very hard to remember for three minutes what we were supposed to do. And we developed a wonderful short-term memory.

Wayne and Andrew have plenty of wonderful long-term memories as well. Both started playing before they hit high school, and instantly took to their instruments.

Andrew: *My dad was a Baptist preacher and my mother was the organ player, so I got my basic training in church. I got my saxophone when I was in the ninth grade, and about a month later I was playing "Amazing Grace" as a solo in church.*

There was a band leader here in town, Gene "Bowlegs" Miller. He graduated from the same high school that I did, and when he needed a saxophone player he would go back to the school and see what young kid is doing pretty good, take him down to a night club and pay him four or five dollars. I was the next one in line, so all of a sudden I was in high school, preacher's son, sneaking down to the night club playing with Gene "Bowlegs" Miller. That's how I got into the business, and it was a long time before my dad found out about it. But before he died he told my mother, he said, "I know you'll be all right; Andrew is going to take care of you." So that's the way it turned out.

Those were the days of segregation, and Wayne grew up in a different neighborhood, over in West Memphis, Arkansas, but he and Andrew were "dropped down on this planet within three days of each other," and, in a lot of ways, his musical background was not that different.

My mother bought me a trumpet when I was eleven, and I just took to it like a duck takes to water. I was good at it, I loved the way it sounded, I liked the way it smelled and felt in my hands; I was just a trumpet player. I got started in the high school thing, and the band director that taught me also was the music director at our church, and I played at church.

Of course, playing "The Holy City" is different from playing "Amazing Grace," but my dad loved black gospel music. He sold insurance way out in the country, and he listened to black gospel music all of the time. And I loved it and enjoyed the feeling of it. You know, in the white churches you get a lot of religious music: [He sings in stiff, stentorian tones] "Rise up, oh man of God, have done with lesser things." That's religious. But gospel music has a tambourine feel, that feel where you want to move your body, stand up and praise God with your whole being and not just your intellect, so to speak. So that's kind of the difference I felt.

I didn't graduate from high school, but I played at the graduation ceremony. I had been playing at the rodeo and in the night clubs—I had a kid, I was a senior here in high school with a not-married girl and a kid, and I was trying to make a living. And so, after the graduation ceremony, I'm the guy that played "Mr. Wonderful," the solo, and "Londonderry Air" and all of this stuff to entertain the crowd. My dad was out in the audience, and my uncle told me later he pulled his handkerchief out and said, "That boy will never make it."

But he lived long enough to see me make it, and he was very proud. After high school I ran across a bunch of guys that called themselves the Royal Spades, and I joined up with them, and we played three-dollar gigs and five-dollar gigs around town and then made a record, changed our name to the Mar-Keys and had a hit. It was the first big record on Stax, I guess.

Wayne and Andrew met at Stax, and instantly jelled. For the next few years, they were part of the bubbling Memphis scene, a rare, interracial island in the midst of a South in the throws of the toughest days of the civil rights battle. The Memphis soul singers were all black, but the backing musicians were a roughly equal mix of black and white. This was an anomaly for its time and place but, looking back, Andrew says that he rarely even thought about it.

In the studios it was "Could you play," not what you looked like. I lived across the street from the Hi Studio. I was really young and couldn't afford a telephone, so I moved across the street from the studio so they could come and knock on my door. And I used to go over there and play on [rock 'n' roll] records like "Haunted House" and several other ones where I was the only black guy in the building. But I could play; that was the thing.

Wayne had the same experience, from the other side.

Many times I was the only white guy; a lot of times. But I think that musicians are a little different from other people. If you're a good musician and you play well, other musicians admire you and hold you in high esteem. They don't really see the color of your skin too much, though other people sometimes do. Andrew and I have been running around this planet together for lots of years and we really have just enjoyed ourselves. With us, the main race issue is racing each other to the bank.

The story I tell about that stuff is my Dairy Queen story. We used to drive to Muscle Shoals all of the time; me, Andrew, Gene "Bowlegs" Miller, and Floyd Newman. That was the horn section: two trumpets, tenor, and baritone. So I'm the only white guy in the car, and just before we get to Iuka, Mississippi, there was a Dairy Queen. We pulled up into the gravel, and this dust rolls by the car, and I look up there as we're climbing out of the car: Well, it has a "colored" window on the side and "white" on the front.

We all just kind of looked at that thing, and I thought, "Well, if I go in the front, you know, I'm going to piss off the guys. And if I go around to the side I'm going to piss off all of those rednecks." So I just reached in my pocket and handed Andrew a five-dollar bill. I said, "Bring me a cheeseburger and a milkshake. I'll meet you right back here." We all laughed; we fell out on the gravel.

Wayne laughs loudly, and Andrew joins in with a deeper chuckle.

We laughed through a lot of situations, just laughed our way on through.

Thirty years later, Wayne and Andrew are still laughing and making music together. Today, they are in the old Onyx (now Easley) Studio, built by their one-time Stax labelmate Chips Moman, working with Ann Peebles. Peebles, who is best known for the classic "I Can't Stand the Rain," had a string of hits for the Hi label in the early 1970s, and Wayne and Andrew played on most of them. By that time, the pair had quit their positions as Stax's house musicians, and had incorporated as an independent unit, the Memphis Horns. Over the next thirty years, they would tour with Stephen Stills, the Doobie

Wayne with pianist Paul Brown

Brothers, and Robert Cray, and play sessions all over the world. They have kept their base in Memphis, though, and when Ann is going into the studio they are still the first horn players she calls.

These guys have their own touch, their own little style. Everything they play on, you can tell, "This is the Memphis Horns. This is has got to be Wayne and Andrew." Because they've got little things that they do that you can't mistake. I like that signature, the I.D. that they have. When we've gone out to play a festival or something, I love for them to be onstage with me. I don't even have to look back, I can just hear them: "Hey, there they are. They're here."

For the purposes of the film project, Peebles and the Horns first recreate a typical recording session, going over their parts on a tune she recorded a few years back, "St. Louis Woman with a Memphis Melody." First, Peebles sits out in the studio, listening to the track on headphones, and sings her part. Then she goes back in the control booth and the Horns play one of their backup lines. If it was a real recording session, they would go on and add a second layer, Wayne putting on a trombone track in addition to his trumpet, and Andrew adding alto or baritone, or maybe both, to his tenor line.

Even the basic, two-horn track they are laying down sounds surprisingly full, and pulses with a sound that by now is part of soul music's genetic code. Though they have not heard the song since they recorded it with Ann, they instantly pick up their parts, sounding as if they have been rehearsing for months. In fact, they have been rehearsing for years, though not on any particular tune. They have three decades of solid experience, and they rely on that to bring them through whatever a producer or singer may throw at them.

Andrew laughs at the loose way he and Wayne like to work. *Every time we do a session, they send us all these tapes, you know, but we don't listen to 'em! So we bring spontaneity to it.*

Wayne: *We bring energy, excitement, because we never listen to the music before we go to the studio. That way we're a little nervous, and—*

Andrew:—*and we put ourselves on the spot. We just throw ourselves to the lions.*

Wayne: *Throw ourselves into the mosh pit of life!*

Andrew: *Sometimes we'd go in there and knock the sessions out so fast that we'd come out and say "Did it again Jesse." Right? Like we were outlaws, Frank and Jesse James.*

Wayne: *I remember once we went to London and made a blues album with a guitar player—I can't remember his name. We left Memphis, flew to London. Off the plane into the limousine, layed down for about three hours and tried to sleep, went to the studio. Did the session in about three hours and said, "When's the next plane out? Can we go home now?" They gave us our money, back to the airport. So we were in London about eight hours. That's the epitome of Frank and Jesse. Ride into town, take the buck, and ride out.*

Andrew: *But we always try to do a good job. We never leave until everybody is satisfied—especially us. We aren't going to mess nobody up.*

Wayne: *The thing is, we've spent a lot of years learning how to do what we do. It's like a pilot flying a 747: You don't know how many thousands of hours he has spent learning to do that efficiently; it looks pretty easy. He's sitting up there in the uniform, looks good, the stewardess is bringing him coffee. But he spent a lot of years getting there.*

We've been doing this a long time, and we do it very well. We pride ourselves on being able to find identification in a song. We'll find a little piece of the melody that the singer sang, and we'll make that the intro on the horns and maybe use it in the ending too. So we've identified the song with something unique about the song. And then put in a little "bop, bop, bop, bop," those little things that we've been doing all of our life, they just fit songs.

Most of the time, we don't even listen to the playback in the control room. We go from the front door to the studio and take the horns out, put the headphones on and start listening to the song. When we hear something, we stop the tape, put our part on, and move on until we hear something else.

This session is a little bit different. After laying down the studio tracks, the three musicians get together in the studio with Ann's regular piano player, Paul Brown, and start jamming on a blues. It is a rarity these days for musicians to record live and, while the Horns take it in stride, Ann is obviously a bit put off at first. Soon, though, she gets into the feel and begins to enjoy herself. The horns start off, playing tight harmony on Thelonius Monk's "Blue Monk," then Ann comes in, improvising on the lyrics of "St. Louis Blues."

She sounds great, easy and soulful, but the surprise comes when the Horns take their solos, something they have very rarely done on record. Wayne plays with a clear tone and lyricism that owes an obvious debt to Louis Armstrong, while Andrew echoes Ann's gospel-flavored vocal with a deep, churchy tenor chorus. After years of hearing them punch out two-second soul riffs, it is a revelation to find what they can do when they relax and stretch out. Listening back in the control room, everyone is excited. The Horns and Ann

"That has got to be Wayne and Andrew. I don't even have to look back, I can just hear them: 'Hey, there they are. They're here.'"

begin talking about doing an acoustic tour, and maybe a whole album with just the three of them backed by piano and maybe a guitar.

The music does sound fine, but even more striking is the feeling in the room. Despite all their years in the business, Wayne, Andrew, and Ann are still completely into what they are doing. Ann, in particular, is enthusiastic.

Today has been really wonderful for me. These two, they're just fun people to be around, and I've always seen that love between them. That's what keeps these guys together is that bond between them, with their music and with them personally. They know each other so well, and you don't find that every day. You don't see two horn players that's been together all this time and still have that love for each other. And know when to leave each other alone—you've got that look now.

Indeed, Wayne and Andrew have been giving each other the fishy eye while listening to Ann's encomiums. Now, all three crack up laughing, before Wayne takes up the thought.

You know, people get along when they have mutual need, mutual goals, mutual responsibility. We had young families—

Andrew: *Got to feed the babies.*

Wayne: *And we had a gift to use to bring all of those people along. So it's worth sacrificing. If I get irritated with Andrew, with something he does, I go to my room and close the door, and I know he does the same thing. Sometimes we sit together on airliners and other times we don't. It's like a good marriage, you know what I'm saying? Same deal.*

I've seen his kids grow up and he's seen my grow up. I mean, when his kid wrecked the Cadillac they had rented for the high school dance ten minutes after they got it, totaled it, my heart was broken. And you know, when things happen to my kids— My daughter Carla would fight you down into the dirt over Andrew Love. Cut your throat in a heartbeat, brother.

Andrew: *And mine the same way with him.*

Today, life has slowed down a little, but the music and the bond are as strong as ever. Wayne laughs over the changes, but both he and Andrew seem satisfied to be where they are now.

We used to carry other musicians with us; once we had six pieces: two trumpets, two tenors, baritone, and trombone. And it was fun. You know, young men need Indians around, tribes of people all moving together and raising dust. Drinking lots of beer. And wearing great-looking suits too, with big, shiny cufflinks. I had a custom-made suit built once a month because I could get it for $125 with a shirt. Those times were really fun, and you didn't care if this guy's kid had got a snotty nose and this guy's wife was leaving—it didn't matter. But time goes by and all of those problems become your problems, and so there came a point at which Andrew and I could do the job easily and cheaper and no problems.

Andrew nods: *And better.*

Wayne: *But I'm gonna tell you all something about me and Andrew. We started as kids and had a good time together, and we never stopped having a good time.*

◆◆◆

Roland

4
Down Home in Mississippi: BIG JACK JOHNSON

Well, if I was a catfish, swimming in the deep blue sea
I'd have all the women fishing after me
Fishing after me, fishing after me

Well, I went to my baby's house and I sat down on her step
She said, "Come on in, Mr. Big Jack, my husband just now left
My husband just now left"

Big Jack Johnson is sitting out in his backyard, wrapping his big hands around an acoustic guitar and playing the oldest of Delta blues. Between verses, he plays sparse, relaxed solos, his left hand pulling off stuttering tremolos then squeezing out a stinging high note. These days Jack spends his time fronting an electric band, and he had to borrow the acoustic for this session, but he has the classic sound in his fingers.

My old man was a violinist, Ellis Johnson. The kind of music he played is the kind of music I just showed you, like "Mama killed a chicken, thought he was a duck , put him on the table with his heels sticking up," and "Corinna" and some old sweet songs, "Old Hen Cackle" and that kind of stuff. Called it "breakdown" music. The way I learned how to do these chords was 'cause I had to play these kind of chords behind him. He'd sing like,

Corinna, Corrina, where you been so long
Corinna, Corrina, where you been so long
It's none of your business, long's you treat me right.

He used to play all that kind of stuff on the violin, like Grandpa Jones on banjo—that old country music. I was brought up on country music, like Hank Williams, Hank Snow, Roy Acuff, Johnny Cash, Red Foley. I know all of 'em. That's all you could hear on the radio then. Weren't no blues on the radio. You wanted to hear some music on Saturday night, that's where you turned: to the Grand Ole Opry in Nashville, Tennessee.

I had several brothers that played guitar: Mike, Arthur, and Ellis was guitar also. They had this big guitar, and it was pretty, man. It had all this color like an apple,

Big Jack Johnson, ready to play

all this big red stuff. Prettiest thing you ever seen. You know, when a kid's young something like that attracts him. When these guys would go to work, they used to have to hang that guitar up on the wall on a big string. And I'd steal it off the wall, man, and the first thing that I learned how to play was this right here:

Baby, please don't go
Baby, please don't go.

Oh man, I thought I was doing something! And then I broke a string. I was scared to death. My brother come home. I was scared to death, man. But he didn't do anything to me, you know, he was proud to know that I had learnt what I had learnt.

Born in 1940, Jack was in the last generation of Delta players to grow up around the string bands and country suppers that had fueled the earliest Mississippi blues. Though history books often miss the fact, most of the older black players in the south were like Jack's father, playing hoedowns and country ragtime. Through the 1940s, country people were still dancing to fiddles, mandolins, and accordions, and blues was just one part of the musical mix.

Back then, we didn't have no electric. They had lamplights in the house. Wasn't no electricity, man. Went to buy coal oil, nickel a gallon. Babe Ruth candy bars, they'd be about that long for a nickel. You had pop, cola for a nickel.

Now you know, the blues started from the cotton fields: cotton chopping, cotton picking, and plowing that mule. That's how agriculture got itself built up, from the cotton site to the cotton pickers, the double shovel to the plows on the tractor. That all had to be done just so we could live. And these peoples sitting out there that gets tired, lonesome, and hungry, they just got together and started humming one day. You know, this one's singing something, this one's singin' something else, and it sounded good. They tried it the next day and it sounded good, and the guy says "Listen, lets you just do it a little bit this way, a little bit that way," and this other guy started singing the bass thing, "boom, boom, boom," this guy in the middle starts singing alto, and now they had something like a quartet.

And then from that to the blues. Took this guitar and made it do what this guy was doing with his mouth, and this "boom, boom" he's doing, they made bass out of it, and this tenor was a horn, alto was a sax. Also took the piano out, took the organ out, everybody in this group had some kind of instruments. And that's what made it different, these people made different parts with their voices, their humming. They didn't even know what to do with the strings, keyboards, drums.

They'd get together on Saturday night and go down in the fields where some guy would be playing one guitar and maybe a have a drum in his lap or something or may have a violin or a mandolin or something playing. And they had this old bad whiskey—back then they didn't have police come on the place. The boss was running things; you know, he had to have his staff to work the next day. The police would have to ask him could he go down and arrest somebody. Now they don't care anymore; they come get you, take you to jail, but they had to ask the boss then—and that's where them blues come from, man, back down in muddy fields where it took a wagon to get out when it rained. Run out of cigarettes, couldn't get out to get none in the rain, and oh, shoot.

Big Jack Johnson

It was in the early 1950s that a new kind of blues hit the Delta. The first hints of it had come over the radio from West Helena, Arkansas, where Sonny Boy Williamson and Robert Lockwood, Jr. began broadcasting their *King Biscuit Show* in 1940, but the real change came with the arrival of B. B. King and Muddy Waters, playing hot, electric styles.

At the time, they were cutting hay, hauling hay on them hay trucks. Guy had a radio inside the truck, he used to have it playing, and this thing come on by B. B. King, "Please Love Me Baby"—"You be my girlfriend, I'll sure be your boy." That damn thing like to run me crazy, man. That and Elmore James doing what he's doing with "Sky Is Crying," and all that stuff. I heard Muddy Waters "Mule Kickin' in my Stall." It sounded real good to me, and I wanted to do these things. I wanted to be B. B., I wanted to be Muddy, I wanted to be Albert King, Elmore James, Jimmy Reed. Howlin' Wolf. So I just got a little bit out of all these guys; I said, "What I'm going to do, I'm going to put all you guys in a sack and I'm going to carry them all with me." So when you hear me play, you might hear B. B. King in it, you might have Elmore, you might have Freddy King, Jimmy Reed. You can hear any of those guys in my picking.

As the conversation goes on, we have moved into Jack's kitchen, where a friend is styling the hair of all the older Johnsons and a few younger ones, heating a curling iron on the gas stove. To coif all the younger ones would take a week. Jack has thirteen children, some twenty grandchildren, and three great-grandchildren, and at times it seems as if half of them are crammed into his house. It is a pleasant, one-story dwelling on a quiet street in Clarksdale, homey and full of young people, except for the formal dining room, where Jack's wife has created a museum of souvenirs, knicknacks, and bright hangings. Jack conducts a brief tour, then sits down in the kitchen to have his hair curled before tonight's gig.

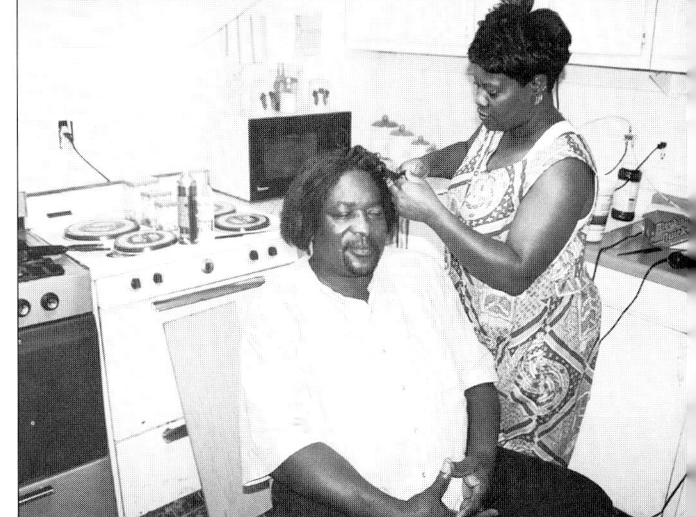

Big Jack in his kitchen, getting his hair done before a gig.

The gig is something a bit out of the ordinary, a reunion of the Jelly Roll Kings, the band with which Jack first made his name in the 1960s. The band started out as the Nighthawks, led by keyboard and harmonica man Frank Frost and drummer Sam Carr.

There wasn't a real blues sound around here till Frank Frost and Sam Carr hit town. Before that, these guys was playing stuff like jazz; had like six, seven horns in the band and this guy was playing guitar, he didn't know anything but chords, and it mostly sounded like jazz music. People'd go out, though, 'cause that's all they had. Until Sam and Frank come to town with the blues. Man, them cats could get it! I tell you. I got with them too, that kind of sweetened the pie a little bit, you know. That's how the blues really got cranked up here. We cranked them up.

The Nighthawks were the hottest band in the Delta through the sixties and seventies. Renamed the Jelly Roll Kings when they recorded their first national album, so as not to be confused with another band of the same name, they drifted apart by the early eighties, and Jack has since toured with his own groups. Once in a while, though, they will do a gig, and it always brings out the local dancers and blues fans.

Tonight's show is in a classic juke joint, a country store that will occasionally hold dances on Saturday night, pushing the grocery shelves aside to create a dance floor and selling beer out of the cooler. It is in Bobo, a tiny settlement outside Clarksdale. Bobo is an old-time, plantation-style cotton farm, complete with the big, white, pillared mansion, visible across a field. These days, though, it is largely depopulated, like much of the rural Delta, and, as he looks around, Jack gets nostalgic.

Man, this place used to be hopping. Back then, they didn't have any cotton pickers, didn't have any chemicals to kill grass 'round the cotton. Had big plantations, and they had to have sharecroppers; somebody had to plow the cotton, somebody had to chop the cotton, and somebody had to pick the cotton. That's why all the big families was coming in there, and that's what made the town. Now, the people are gone, they don't have any more. You've got cotton pickers now, and chemicals to kill the grass and tractors to cultivate the cotton, so that throwed all the big sharecroppers out, you know. The owners sent them away.

When we first came to Bobo, man, you couldn't get in that little town because of all the people out in the country from there. They had three or four stores, and the manager you worked for owned the stores, so when he paid you off in the store, you bought the stuff right there and gave the money right back to him. But we had a good time, man. You didn't know what a doctor bill was. You didn't know what a car note

At the juke joint in Bobo, Mississippi, a grocery store by day. (top) Big Jack plays, while Sam Carr adjusts the amp. (bottom) Some young fans peep over the guitar cases.

was. Something happened to your house, you needed a top on it, you got the top put on. Then, at the end of the year, you got to sell them in. But, hey, when you made your money, you put your money in your pocket. But now you've got to pay a rent, eight, nine hundred dollars. Anything you put your hand on, you've got to pay. Go to the doctor's, you've got to pay for it. You going to get a car, you've got to pay for it.

For a musician, there was a lot of work then, man. You could play here tonight and go two blocks and play for the next guy. Go in the field and play for some other guy. The blues were really squeezing [going great] then around here. Then people started drifting away to Chicago or Detroit, St. Louis, and thought they was going to do better. Thought they're going to the promised land. But they left the promised land when they left here. Really.

They got no land up there. They're stacked on top of one another, ten stories high. Killing and robbing and you can't walk around with three or four dollars in your pocket, you can't go cashing checks. Somebody watching, knock you in the head. You should be here where you can leave your windows up, your door unlocked, and you don't worry. It makes you wonder, man. They don't do that in Chicago.

This is where all the good food is, good fishing. All the peanuts, peaches, sweet potatoes just laying out. Pecans. I went to the city. Yeah, I've seen the city. But I don't want none of them tall buildings. Just something to look at, you know. If I was born and raised there, it'd be a different thing. But I was born and raised down here. So I'm at home, you know.

Jack goes into the store and helps set up the band's equipment. The group consists of him, Frost, Carr, and a young bass player who has hurt his right arm and plays one-handed. When they get everything plugged in and start playing, it almost blows the walls down. Their set is a mix of original tunes, blues standards, and the occasional rock 'n' roll hit. The crowd, packed together in the hot room, drinks beer out of cans and, as the evening wears on, tries to clear some space to dance, or wanders out onto the porch to talk and look at the moon rising over the fields.

Jack is playing with passionate intensity, bending strings in the high, screaming sound that is a Delta trademark. Other guitarists of his age have opted for B. B. King's smoother, more sophisticated approach, but, like Jack himself, Jack's playing has stayed down in Mississippi. His performances are an astute mix of standards, "Baby Please Don't Go" and Elmore James's "Shake Your Money Maker," and his own compositions, which speak of situations common to him and his neighbors. His singing is gruff and insistent, roughly lyrical phrases punctuated by the guitar lines.

I don't want no black rooster in my henhouse after supper at the close of day
I don't want no black rooster in the henhouse after supper at the close of day
I don't want to stay with no woman that won't do a doggone thing I say

I work hard every day, bring home all my pay

I tell her, "What would you do with that money?"
Well, she wouldn't do a doggone thing I say
I don't want no woman that won't do a doggone thing I say
I don't want no rooster in my henhouse after supper at the close of day

The blues makes me feel good, man. It does something to me. Really, it's true. It makes me think about things. You say you hurt and almost lose your mind, the woman you loving has gone, and all that kind of stuff, man, stuff that just gets to you. You can fall in love with that kind of stuff; it makes you feel good. That's what made me play it. And I feel good right today when I'm playing it. Sometimes I be sitting up there, you think I'm sweating and tears will be running down. That's what be happening. Yeah, man.

You know, these last years I've been traveling, that's for sure. Playing 300, 304 days last year. I been all to all these states in here, just back and forth, back and forth. Florida, New York, New England, West Coast, and then the islands of England. Rome, Italy. Amsterdam, Holland. Belgium, Sweden, all those places.

But I'm still related to this—this Delta blues. I didn't change my style just because I went somewhere else. Most guys that played here, left here, changed their style. They don't play like the Delta anymore. But I do. Delta music, it's got a feeling to it. When we was writing these songs, we had a feeling, and when we sang these songs. It's something that makes you feel good inside. Most all the guys that did sing blues, come from the church anyway. And then that's when they started singing the blues. It's just got a feeling in the stuff when you do it from the Delta. That Chicago stuff is fast, you know. They don't have that feel.

A lot of people ask me why I don't go to Chicago, and I tell them there's too many guys up there already, they don't need me. Everybody's kickin in the same stall, trying to get out. Everybody's in a box. This is Chicago right here, this little box, and everybody's in here, trying to get out, but they can't. But I'm already out. And I'm gonna stay out. Them guys are there, all fighting over a gig here, a gig here. Muddy Waters took it up there and everybody else followed. But someone had to stay here. Keep the blues going here, you know. So that's what I did. Hung around right here, and kept that Delta thing going. And I've got to say I'm kind of proud I did, too.

◆◆◆

DELTA LEGEND: ROBERT LOCKWOOD, JR.

Robert Lockwood in the hospitality shed at the King Biscuit Blues Festival, Helena, Arkansas.

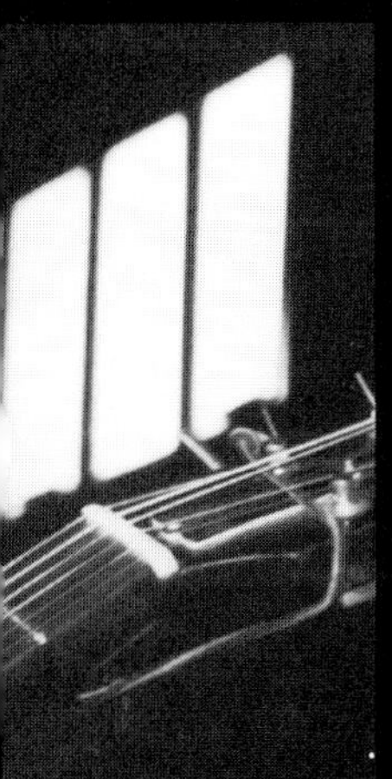

Every year, the King Biscuit festival gives Robert Lockwood something of a hero's welcome, and with good reason. Lockwood was one of the original King Biscuit Boys, playing guitar behind Sonny Boy Williamson on the flour-company-sponsored radio show that brought modern blues to the Delta. That was back in 1941; Lockwood was 24 years old, and already a veteran musician.

I was born down here in Turkey Scratch, Arkansas, about five miles from Marvell. I started playing the old organ at eight, and I started playing the guitar at thirteen. I had a couple of first cousins who played the piano, and that was my beginning. Then, as the time passed, Robert Johnson came into my mother's life and I learned to play the guitar and left the piano alone. It wasn't about the guitar, it was about Robert Johnson. He could play the guitar like you hear me playing it now, and there wasn't nobody else like him—wasn't then and still ain't. (For many years, Lockwood went by the name Robert Jr. Lockwood in Johnson's honor, though he now prefers to be called Robert Lockwood, Jr., after his father.)

I was playing professionally at fourteen-and-a-half, just playing around here with older people. At that time, guitar players were playing a lot on street corners. Making a lot of money, too. I seen Robert sit right out there on the street corner and make $100. But, you understand, he was a recording artist.

By 1941, Lockwood was a recording artist himself, with a double-sided local hit, "Little Boy Blue" backed with "Take a Little Walk with Me." The latter was a reworking of Johnson's "Sweet Home Chicago," and in a quiet room on the festival grounds Lockwood shows how Johnson played it, then how he added his own fillips, reworking it into an individual statement. Johnson not only taught him some guitar, but introduced him to Sonny Boy, with whom he went out on the road in the mid-1930s. Lockwood then headed up north to St. Louis, and finally Chicago, where he made his recordings. He came back to Helena in 1941, a week after Sonny Boy had persuaded the King Biscuit Flour Company to sponsor a regular noontime radio spot.

Sonny Boy had a contract, and I had done recorded records and I had a union card. I think I was one of the first young men down here that had a union card. So the two of us, we were working together. That's why I have to be here every year. It's changed a lot, though. You've got nightclubs down here now. You didn't have nothing but juke joints then, gambling joints. They were gambling in gambling dives, that's what they used to call them. I remember when there was fifteen gambling houses in this city.

A listener suggests that things have come full circle, with all the new gambling houses that have sprung up along the river, but Lockwood scoffs at the idea.

That ain't shit they got over there. That's a trap. Back then, people were gambling and their money stayed here in the area. That over there, they haul it out of there and you don't see it no more. And I don't understand how people go over there and play them damn machines. The machine is set to beat you. People are so fucking dumb.

Even back in 1941, Lockwood had strong opinions, and one was that he was not going to spend his life playing old-time blues in Arkansas.

I always did want to travel. I never had no eyes for living down here. My people own a lot of land down here right now, but I started to play music and started records and stuff, and you know I've just about been all over the world.

I learned how to play by Robert Johnson, and then I went on from that. I always did like harmony, and I listened to Fats Waller and Duke Ellington, King Oliver, several other people who were popular back at that time. My first band I worked with was a black jazz band, and I got off King Biscuit Time *and got on a program called* Mother's Best Flour, *and I hired a bunch of jazz musicians. So then I had to learn how to play that.*

I mean, if you're going to be a musician, why be one type? That's the way I always looked at it. I done worked for country groups, I done worked with jazz, and I worked with blues, I worked with soul, I worked with all that. So I don't see no reason why I should try to play just one thing when there's a million other things to do, you know. When I was recording for other people, they said, "Well, I don't want nothing but the blues." But you don't tell me what to play if you want a recording. That's why I got my own label, yeah. [Lockwood has released an album on Lockwood Records, which he runs out of his home in Cleveland, Ohio.]

Onstage, Lockwood will use his full electric band, and his music owes as much to the big city "jump" style of the fifties as it does to his Delta youth. Indeed, he is dismissive of the idea that the Delta region was special in anything but the number of good musicians who happened to come from the region.

A lot of things was born in Arkansas and Mississippi, you know, a lot of people who was living here that have been successful. But it could have been Missouri, could have been New Orleans, could have been anywhere. Just fortunately, it was in these areas, you know. A lot of real good guys come from down this way.

Lockwood has been living in the North for a long time, but comes back once a year for the festival. He even has had a stage named in his honor, though his annual appearance is made not there but on the main stage, to accommodate the horde of fans. Still, even as he goes out to face the cheering crowd, he professes himself less than thrilled by the belated acclaim.

I think it's a pretty good achievement, but I've been so very underestimated. I'm one of the best underestimated people that there is. That happened because I have never been pushing and grabbing and all that shit. I ain't never done that. When I record, the people I record with, I do my best to make them sound good. And 90 percent of other people just want to be heard. That's a big difference.

I'm still around today because I never participated in what a lot of other people do. I never did participate in dope, nothing but whiskey—but I started drinking that when I was a baby. All them other things—I think I smoked about four sticks of pot in my whole life. And I ain't never done nothing else. And I don't understand how you can get to be an alcoholic because I've been drinking all my life. I drink it when I want and I quit when I want.

As for the state of blues music in general, Lockwood is equally straightforward in his assessment. He is well aware that most of his audience is white, and views the scene with detached irony.

Today, they ain't a lot of young blacks that wants to play blues. Of course, they been misled by you-all [white people]. You don't mind me saying that, right? I'm only telling the truth. You-all said that the blues was bad. I remember when a white boy would get his ass whupped after he was caught trying to play the blues. They used to call it devil music. But now the blues got everybody liking it. I wonder what they'll be calling it now.

◆◆◆

MIDNIGHT RAMBLE

The Midnight Ramble harkens back to yesteryear, when the minstrel shows used to come through Phillips County. After the main show was over, most of the married folks and working folks would go home, and folks like myself would stay for the midnight ramble. It would get a little bit raunchier, and the jokes would get a little bit funnier, the music would get a little bit more risque, and the girls would come out and shake it down a little harder.—Levon Helm, at the midnight riverboat show, King Biscuit Blues Festival. Photos, left to right: Harmonica legend James Cotton, and drummer Levon Helm.
(insets) Members of the Cate Brothers band.

L
M

5

A Blues King Comes Home: LITTLE MILTON

Stand up! Get on your feet! Let's have a nice, warm round of applause as he makes his way to the stage. Ladies and gentlemen, Malaco recording artist Little Milton.

Milton Campbell eases his way through the crowd, pausing to pat old friends on the back, smile at the ladies, and generally revel in the good feeling of a rare homecoming. Milton has been living in cities—Memphis, Chicago and Las Vegas—for several decades, but this is his home turf, Greenville, Mississippi, and the club, Perry's Flowin' Fountain on Nelson Street, is the sort of room where he has spent most of his life. Both the street and the club have changed with the years; the new casinos have taken over the live entertainment field, and the old black club district has gone to seed. The Flowin' Fountain has held on as a neighborhood bar, but has not used its big function room in months. When Milton comes in, though, it is a special occasion, and the old crowd has turned out in force.

This really brings back some beautiful memories of the beginning for me. Back then, I felt like once you got to Nelson Street, if you were an entertainer, then you had really hit the big time. I had a lot of fun back in those early days. The people in that era were fun-loving people and we just had plenty fun, all day long, every day, every night.

I started playing down here when I was a teenager, eighteen, nineteen years old, something like that, but I was into the music long before that. Like it usually is I guess with most of us Southerners, I started out in church, in the Baptist faith. My mom tells me that at a very early age I would be always around singing, reciting what they called little speeches; you might call them poetry now. And I'd be beating on lard cans or what have you, making rhythm, get some sticks and beat on the porch or the steps, singing some sort of song. So she discovered that evidently there was some talent in there knocking on the door, and next thing I knew she had me performing at the church programs.

I remember very distinctively, one time we went to church and they took up a collection, and I guess they must have put three or four dollars or something in this little—I call it a hat, you know, but they had a little thing that they'd carry around and people would put money in it—for me singing. And I said, "Damn, I can make money doing this!" Yeah!

Little Milton hits a lick onstage at the Flowin' Fountain, Greenville, Mississippi.

Milton climbs up onto the small stage, and seats himself on the edge of a stool. His band is already running down a tight instrumental vamp, the horns punching out a soul riff while the guitarist twangs a bluesy solo. Milton looks around him, relaxed, happy, and every inch a star. His hair is neatly shaped, his mustache and yellow aviator glasses frame an easy smile, and his brightly patterned shirt is open to the chest, showing a gold medalion which glints in the lights as he takes the microphone from its stand.

Are you ready? Then you can sit down and groove with me. I've got a little story that I'm gonna lay on you. It's all about me, and it says simply this:

Oh, I once had love and plenty money, mmmm
Some way, somehow, I failed—yes I did
Now all, all I have in my pocket
All I can give account of is a nickel and a nail

Milton is a long way from the sad state of the character in his lyric, but he sings with an understated, slightly amused assurance that reminds his audience that he knows what he is talking about.

When I write music, I write about everyday life, and I write about reality, you know. A lot of times people have asked me, "Did that actually happen to you?" Well, the answer is no, but it could have, and most certainly it did happen to somebody. So somebody out there that hears this, they can identify with it. It don't mean that you're broken-hearted all the time just because you sing about a situation of such. It don't mean that you're hungry because you say, "I'm here, I don't have a lousy dime." That don't mean, you know, that it's you. But somebody somewhere ain't got a lousy dime, and they understand that.

The first part of Milton's show is in the smooth, soul-blues vein that gave him many of his biggest hits. The songs speak of love gone wrong, or the slinky attractions of an illicit affair, and Milton delivers the lyrics with a knowing smile, nodding his head when he is struck by a particularly true phrase. His manner is that of a sophisticated club singer, joshing with the audience and snapping his fingers along with the band as they take an instrumental break. Then, about twenty minutes into the set, Milton reaches back for his guitar, straps it on, hits one note, and the whole mood changes.

Milton is one of the great blues guitarists, and this is where he started, playing for bands around Greenville and Leland. Before going into the next number he introduces Little Bill Wallace, a mentor from his early days, and expresses the hope that Eddie Cusic, his first employer, will be in soon. It is old home week, and recalls the days when Milton was first getting into a blues world that was then the heart of black music.

It's a very unique surrounding in the Delta, and it used to be even more profound than it is today, because you had more people. You had a lot of people that were living on the farms, farmers and sharecroppers and what have you. As you can see when you ride around now on the highways, that don't exist anymore. So that means you got less people, and whenever you got less people, there's less interest and less fun.

In those days, Leland would close down around ten, eleven o'clock and people would have what they called a "house supper." We'd take the table and put it across the door and take the bed down in the front room—there was no living room, the room that you walked into would be the bedroom—so they would take the bed down and then put a table over there, make a counter out of the table to go across the door. Then, when the town would close, people would come by, and my stepdad would serve a little bootleg corn liquor, have some beer, and my mom'd be cooking fish and hamburgers and what have you.

My mom tells a story that one time they had invited this guitar player to come by, his name was Brother Bill. He was playing and I was tucked away in one of the back rooms in bed—it had to be during the wintertime, because I had my long drawers on—and when they looked around, I was standing up right beside him, really into what he was doing with the guitar. Everybody thought that was funny, to have a little kid standing there, rubbing all the sleep out of his eyes, looking at that guitar.

The guitar music always fascinated me, and it still does today. There's just something about it. You know, there are a lot of other instruments, of course, but to me the guitar can do exactly what you feel. If you are good enough, if you're artistic enough, you can make the strings say everything the voice says, even from within. If you just sing it to yourself without saying a word, you don't have to open your mouth, you don't even have to hum; it'll come. The guitar will do that.

That's why I don't sound like anybody else: because I don't feel like anybody else. I feel what I feel, and the coordination from within here comes into my hands, and that's what comes out. I don't know what I'm going to play, which way I'm going to bend the strings and what little oozy thing I'm going to do. When I start playing, it just comes, you know. And a lot of times I've been sort of like down in the dumps, so to speak, didn't really feel like performing, but if I came in and I didn't really feel good that particular night, I'd play the guitar for a while, you know, and everything would just come out.

Milton has rarely stretched out instrumentally on record, but live, it is another story. He often puts the guitar aside for soul numbers, wandering the stage with microphone in hand, but on blues he takes charge, playing chorus after brilliant chorus. His inventiveness is striking. Soaring, sustained bends are broken by skittering, staccato runs that move in surprising directions, then blend into long, lyrical passages where the guitar seems almost to sing. Although Milton insists that the classic, twelve-bar blues is only one facet of his work, it remains the centerpiece of his shows. Tonight, he leads the band into a twenty-minute medley of his recent blues hits. "Catch You on Your Way Down" leads smoothly into "Annie Mae's Cafe," a song he has dedicated to old-time, local hangouts like the Flowing Fountain.

Oh yeah, I can always go down to Annie Mae's Cafe
You can find one in every town (naturally, Greenville's no exception)
You go there after hours to drink a little whiskey
Before long some fool might like to clown
Every town I go to, I can't seem to break away
I can always have big fun when I go to Annie Mae's Cafe

You can get fish, chicken, chitlins (don't forget the hambocks)
While the jukebox plays the blues
If you're out on the town after hours looking for good food, strong drink and plenty fun
There's no better place to choose
Every town I go to, I can't seem to break away
I can always have big fun when I go to—where? Where?

Milton cups his hand behind his ear, and the crowd yells back the tag line. Then he is into another guitar solo, even more inventive than the first. Over twenty minutes, the medley builds and falls with a natural rhythm, carrying the audience along in its flow. Then it is over, and without a pause Milton kicks the band into a highballing "Shake, Rattle and Roll." The transition is perfect, and the crowd is on its feet.

When I was coming up, I listened to all kinds of music. Back in that era you did not have a lot of radio stations, but the ones that you did have, they'd have special programs where you would get to hear people like the great Louis Jordan and the Tympany Five. He had a syndicated program that would come on every evening down here, maybe 6:15 in the evening. So I was glued to the radio every day.

You had all the records on the jukebox. John Lee Hooker had "Boogie Chillun," that was a big, big record. And then smooth, beautiful music—we had Nat King Cole,

Milton is joined onstage by another Delta star,
raunchy vocalist and harmonica player Bobby Rush.

we had Frank Sinatra. A little of all of this stuff. I even got a chance to get involved into the country and western, because Saturday nights, that's what you'd have to listen to, was Grand Ole Opry. That affected me very deeply, because of the lyrics and the melodies, which were simple but soulful, same thing as in the blues. To me, those two are so close, they go hand in hand.

Then you had the "big voice" people, I call them, like Roy Brown, Big Joe Turner, Roy Milton, Jimmy Liggins, Joe Liggins, you had just so many. But my favorite guy was the late T-Bone Walker. This was my idol, and I remember when I lived out here, between Leland and Greenville, in the country, on a farm, sharecropping, and I would sneak out of the fields a lot of times and be sitting on my porch and take a sneak thing at my guitar, you know, and some of the wrong guys would be on the tractors and they'd come by and see me sitting there and they'd stop and tease me, "Hey, T-Bone Walker!" So I said, "One of these days, I'm going to play just as good as T-Bone You Walker, or better." Better, now, that was going a little far, but—

DELTA RADIO

These days, radio tends to be something that comes from the national music centers. Recordings, and often whole programs, emanate from New York or L.A., and beam their way into the most removed reaches of the countryside. Back in the forties and fifties, the situation was very different. Disc jockeys picked their own favorite records rather than having them assigned by a station's music director, and a single could become a huge hit in Memphis, say, even if it never hit anywhere else in the United States. A record on a local label could get local radio play, and fuel a profitable career at least within the listening area of that station.

Aside from the records, there were also live programs. Live music was the original lifeblood of radio, which did not seriously go in for playing recordings until the Second World War, and performers were doing regular shows on local stations through the fifties (in fact, live gospel shows remain a Sunday staple on rural stations to this day). B. B. King started out with a fifteen-minute show on Memphis's WDIA, sponsored by Peptikon, and Sonny Boy Williamson and his band blanketed the Delta with their daily noontime spot for King Biscuit Flour. While King and Williamson went on to become stars, many purely local figures also made their reputation on radio, singing, playing and advertising their evening's gigs in between putting in plugs for their sponsors. Sitting around the Flowing Fountain, Little Milton and his mentor, Little Bill Wallace, reminisce about those days.

I idolized the guy, and I eventually got a chance to perform with him, and then met him, and we got to be decent friends before he passed. To me, that was very special. It's a rarity for you to find your idol and get to not only perform with him, but get to know him and actually hang out together and be friends, you know. He was a great guy.

Then, there were plenty of good musicians right around here in Greenville. You had this man that we called Little Bill, his name was Bill Wallace. He had a group and they were very popular in the Delta and throughout the region, in Arkansas and Louisiana, what have you. And it was "Little Bill and his Singing Guitar." I used to hear him on the radio. Then I used to listen to Sonny Boy Williamson—Rice Miller—and Willie Love, Elmore James, and Joe Willie Wilkins. These were guys that I got to know and got to work with. I lied about my age and they gave me a job. Eddie Cusic gave me my very first paying gig, and I never will forget the first pay that I got: It was $1.50, for playing all night. And that was big money. I was in the big times, finally!

That was a whole different era, and a different time. I remember living here in

Milton: *This was the era of the artists buying radio time. You'd go buy you an hour or half an hour. The radio station would charge you whatever they charged, and what you would do, you would go out and solicit spots. You would go out to different businesses that was up and down Nelson Street, or in Leland, Hollandale, Indianola or wherever, the black businesses that had things that they needed to be advertised. The bandleader that had bought the time on the station would go and solicit these people to give money for spots, and you would advertise that business while you were on the air. And the advantage of that was, you were going to take your band in the studio and you would play live in the studio and they would broadcast your music.*

Little Bill: *Willie Love and me, we had a radio show in Greenville. I was the mastermind of the radio show and Willie Love was the mastermind of the talk. He sure could talk. True Blue Snuff was our sponsor, and Peptikon. He would say on the radio, "Do your mouth get watery and juicy? With the True Blue Snuff, you have to spit quick or drown." And that was a big thing. We'd advertise our dates on the radio. We'd go in like Milton said, we would talk to the sponsors that we was booking our date through, and they would give us a fee for advertising their business. We stayed on the radio two years.*

Milton: *This man, Little Bill, he was one of the masters of this during that era. I used to sit back as a kid and listen to him on the radio, squeezing and pushing the strings on that guitar. And I would say, "Damn, that's Little Bill, that's Little Bill." And all of my little crony buddies, you know, they'd be with me. We'd be trying to hustle some beer, some corn liquor. That was our thing, you know. It wasn't about doing drugs, killing somebody or raping or robbing anybody. It was about having some fun. This guy was in that era, and he was there to give all of us just an inspirational thing, for us to say, "I want to be like him a little bit."*

Greenville, and we would go out and do gigs, and we didn't have a station wagon, had an old car, and we'd have the drums, and the big upright bass was tied up on top of the car, and our amplifiers, and we'd come in like on a Sunday night, Monday morning, and I would put the instruments on the porch, and we would cover them with the canvas or something in case it rained, and they would stay out there all week. Never worried about anybody taking anything. Try that now. Not a chance. These days, you might be in the house sleeping and the whole house be moving—they'll take you and *the house!*

You had a lot of for-real people back then. You had some fools, of course, you're gonna find that anywhere, in any generation. But it was nothing like today. And I'm sure it was like that in a whole bunch of different places, where people felt more safe and more neighborly. Everybody basically knew everybody, and even if they didn't know everybody, they sort of had mutual respect. The human race was just totally different. That's all I can say.

I played with a lot of people back then, but the ones that taught me to be a professional were Sonny Boy, Willie Love, and Joe Willie Wilkins. It was just the four of us, and I was the young kid on the block. They taught me how to drink properly. They taught me how to respect people. They taught me that just because people might scream and applaud for you, and what have you, that you are never any bigger than the people that supported you. You might live a little better, or you might live different, but you're no better. They taught me all these things and, to me, I would have rather come up in that era with these great people than to have to come up the way it is today, with all of the nonchalantness, and no respect, and all of the vulgar stuff in the music. They taught me that that just wasn't necessary—if you had talent, display your talent, and try to give the people their money's worth.

Back then, what we used to do, whoever had a hit record, that's who we tried to sound like; exactly like the record, see? It would get a little confusing sometimes; I remember me trying to sound like Charles Brown, trying to sound like Louis Jordan, and naturally I wanted to sound like T-Bone Walker. But I just kept working, doing what I felt, you know. When I would do a tune of anybody's, I'd just sing it the way I felt like doing it, and I'd do it from within. I just let the whole inner me just sort of flow, and then one day I woke up and Little Milton was born.

Another blues number, and then Milton lets the band take the instrumental lead again as he swings into one of his trademark hits, "Grits Ain't Groceries (All Around the World)." Though the song has been in his repertoire for thirty years, he still makes it sound fresh, and the crowd laughs at the lines as if they were brand new. Next comes a new hit, "Kick the Cheatin' Habit," with a guest appearance by Milton's Delta contemporary and Malaco labelmate Bobby Rush, ending with an instrumental duel, Rush playing fancy harmonica licks and Milton playing them right back on guitar. Then it is time for the closer, a straight-ahead, twelve-bar workout that has become ubiquitous on the current blues scene.

Each of my songs is special to me, you know. But I guess if there's one that I could say has been particularly important for me, career-wise, it would have to be the "Hey, Hey, the Blues Are All Right." That's gotten to be the international blues anthem, so to speak, and that makes me feel kind of good because it belongs to me.

The way I came to write that was, I was on tour in Europe with Magic Slim and his group. I went basically to take care of business, to open some doors for the future, and I was supposed to have been just a guest artist on that tour. I went on a couple of nights, and Slim was supposed to close behind me and it wasn't working out, so the promoter came and asked and then Slim came and asked, would I close the show.

I had a problem there, because I did not have my own band with me, I was playing with Slim's band, so my ability to perform the things that I'm accustomed to doing was very limited. I had to lean toward all the twelve-bar stuff, because the musicians were more comfortable doing that, because basically that's all they played. So I found myself in the very messed-up position of having to close the show and didn't have anything to close it with. So I just started thinking, and I stumbled up on that little groove thing and I started saying to the audience, "Hey, hey, the blues are all right." A lot of them don't speak the English, but if you keep repeating something, they catch on, and they started singing it. It just started catching on, so I'd write a little version every day and try it out the next night, and in about two-and-a-half weeks, I had a song, and it was "Hey, Hey, the Blues Are All Right."

Milton hits a stinging high note on the guitar, and the band swings in behind him.

I got this song I'm gonna sing
I'm gonna sing it just for you
If you dig the blues, I want you to help me sing it too
I want everybody to hear me when I say
That the blues is back, and it's here to stay
Let me explain it to you:
I used to have some woman that meant the whole world to me
But she left me for someone else, left my heart in misery
That's when I found out the blues would always be a part of me

Let me tell you this:
You see, when she left me she gave me the blues
That was the last thing I thought I could use
But now I'm glad she left me, I'm glad she gave me the blues
You see, I went out and found me, I went out and found me someone new
That's why I can say this tonight:
Hey, hey the blues is all right

The audience sings the line back at him: "Hey, hey the blues is all right"
Hey, hey the blues is all right
"Hey, hey the blues is all right"
It's all right! It's all right! Every day and night.

To me, people really do have the wrong concept of what blues is. Now, I don't think anyone has a true definition of the blues, because it means different things to different people in so many different ways. But I know one thing that it doesn't mean. It doesn't mean ignorance, raggedy, evil, drunk, you know, just somebody that's down and out and all they're singing about is their problems. You've got all types of blues. You've got happy blues, some that's sad. It's not just some guy sitting on a corner, on a store porch or in a little dingy joint with patches on his overalls, singing about his woman left him and took everything. Hey, rich women leave rich men as well. Educated men, educated women leave each other, so I fail to see the significance of just the down and out kind of thing.

The image of the blues has been distorted, and that's why some people have a tendency not to want to be associated with it; they think it's talking about ignorance, being drunk, loose in the head, dirty, illiterate. And that's not it at all—it's a very meaningful music and it's a very wonderful heritage. And hopefully history will say that I was able to add or contribute something to the shining part of it, the bright part that makes it worthwhile recognizing.

I think an individual can have some class, whatever type music or profession they might be in. That's the way I was taught and that's the image that I want. There's nothing wrong with coming on stage looking like you're somebody that's successful. You can be clean, you can smell good, you can look good, and if you perform good, you don't have to wear the same sweaty clothes every night. If you've got talent, dress the part, you know. If you're down and out and that's the way you want to do it, fine, that's your thing. But my thing is be a professional at all times.

Like I said before, I've always tried to stay true to the code and pick my material—if I didn't write the lyrics myself, if I decided to accept them from some other writer, I always had a choice—and to make sure that it's about everyday life. I might not sell a million copies, you know, like you do if you come up with some sort of fad or what have you—and I've never done a fad song, never. Million sellers have come very few for me; I think I could say three, maybe. But life is a cycle; what goes around, comes around, and you're blessed if you can just still be here and be competitive and stay in the game.

I've got a thing that I say: If you just keep getting two hundred thousand, two hundred-fifty thousand sellers, get you four of those, then you've got a million sales. And the advantage to that is you're in the ears of more people because you're more consistent. A lot of times you'll have artists that get that one big record and they never get any more. One song is cool, and they might make a lifetime off of that one. They do it in country western all the time; if you're ever a star there, you're forever a star. But in this thing where I am, believe me, you got to constantly keep doing something; you've got to be consistent. And that's what I've been able to do so far. All of the records are not smashes, but they make enough noise to let them know that Little Milton is still alive and well.

◆ ◆ ◆

The barroom at the Flowin' Fountain

6

United in Praise: THE MISSISSIPPI MASS CHOIR

The small, brick church is like hundreds, probably thousands, of other Mississippi churches. In a quiet neighborhood of Vicksburg, it is the meeting place and spiritual home for a small congregation of worshippers who come together every Sunday morning. The service includes a Bible reading, a sermon from the pastor, and songs led by a nine-member "praise group." All of the singers have been performing gospel music since their childhood, and they sound like it. Their voices have an assurance, and a deep, traditional feeling, that would make them stand out in most Northern or Western congregations. In Mississippi, though, this is just regular black church singing.

Mississippi has always had a reputation for being the deepest of the deep South—whether that was good or bad depended on what aspect of Southern life was being considered. When it comes to singing, Mississippi has produced some of the greatest voices in American music. It was only a few years ago, though, that someone thought to consolidate the riches available in the state's churches. That was Frank Williams, leader of one of Mississippi's foremost gospel quartets, the Jackson Southernaires. He got together with a Jackson-based songwriter, David Curry, and they put out word throughout Mississippi that they were looking for people to sing in a mass choir. Curry remembers:

We sent out P.S.A.s on the radio and with the newspapers, and some by word of mouth, because some people we knew they could sing, and we asked people to send in tapes of their voices. We had boxes and boxes of tapes came in, and we examined them, narrowed it down to about 200 tapes, and then we had the people come in and do a personal audition, and we picked from there. We narrowed it down from 200 to

Sunday service at Greater Jerusalem House of Worship, Vicksburg, Mississippi. Doris Miller is at the far left in the choir.

about 150, and 150 has been a pretty good working number for us ever since.

Jerry Mannery, who joined as the choir's business manager, adds a word of explanation:

All of this talent here has never had an outlet. So when Frank put this together, and brought David in, then all of a sudden we were able to get the cream of the crop. We were able to go into Tupelo, Mississippi, and get the Bean family—I mean, they are renowned up there. Or go down to Brookhaven, Mississippi, and get someone like Lillian Lilly; these people that have been known for years.

From Vicksburg came a young nurse named Doris Miller.

I had no intentions of getting involved with the Mississippi Mass Choir. About a month or two before the choir was started, a friend of mine, he liked the way I sing so he told me "You know, they're thinking about starting a Mississippi Mass Choir and I think you could make it." I said "Oh, OK, all right." He's a police officer, so he told me, he said, "Well, come by the station, I'll give you all the information on that."

So, being polite, I went down and got the information and I brought it home and I laid it on my TV, never even hardly looking—I think I looked at it when he first gave it to me and I just laid it down. I wasn't really thinking about it. Then, they were asking for cassettes of me singing a song to send in for an audition, and finally it was getting close to the deadline and I decided to just go ahead. I said, "Well, he went through enough to get me the information, I could go ahead and try it." So I got a friend of mine to go to the church and we taped a couple of songs and I sent them in.

A couple of days later I heard from Frank Williams, telling me to come over for a live audition. I said, "OK, I'll take this thing a step further." So, nervously, I went over and tried out and I made it. Even after I made it, I didn't plan on staying. By me living here in Vicksburg, I would have to travel like forty-five miles to Jackson to even attend rehearsals. But I got started into the first initial rehearsals and got to like it, you know. So I've been with the choir ever since. I guess that when the Lord has something intended for you to do, you're going to do it, no matter what you have plans to do.

Like the other choir members, Doris had been singing her whole life.

I never had any formal training, but I started off singing as a little girl in my church choir. It was just little stuff, but I knew I liked to sing.

And I would sing a lot at home. In fact, it's funny—My sister Deborah and I used to share a room at home, and she was a scholarly type. She loved to read, I loved to sing. She'd be reading and I'd be singing, and she would tell me to shut up. But I guess she did hear something she kind of liked, because when she decided to get married she asked me if I would sing at her wedding. That was my first really outward singing, and after that other people heard me sing and I've been singing for weddings, banquets, funerals, different functions ever since.

Then, I had always dreamt of being in a large choir, where you had the sections—sopranos, altos, tenors—and you could really get into your part. Whereas at my church a lot of the time we're just singing. You know, we sing in unison, we don't have that expertise involved in it. So when I joined Mississippi Mass, I got into that and I just really enjoyed it. It gave me a lot of experience.

The experience was not only musical. To everyone's surprise, the Mass Choir's first album became a huge hit, the biggest seller that its label, the Jackson-based Malaco Records, had ever had. Within five weeks of its release in the spring of 1989, it was the number one record on the *Billboard* gospel charts, and it held that position for an unprecedented forty-five consecutive weeks. Doris still seems thunderstruck by the speed of the group's success.

Oh, boy. I really thought I was just getting into a choir, and we were going to do an album, and probably that album would sit on somebody's shelf, you know? But after it came out and it did what it did—it just really took off—I think it kind of changed all our lives. It's really something, because here I am, just Doris Miller from Vicksburg, Mississippi, and people come up and ask me for my autograph. And I think, "My autograph for what?" It's really amazing to me, the impact that the choir has had on people. All you have to do is say "Well, yes, I'm a member of the Mississippi Mass Choir," and it's like "Wow! You sing with that group?" They look at you differently for some reason, like you've got this power.

It's like you've got something to offer them, and I just try to offer it through prayer, through singing. People are really hungry for something, and we were able to reach a lot of people, just through the album. I have no doubt that the Lord put me in the choir for a purpose. It makes me feel fulfilled when I do this. I feel like I'm doing what the Lord wants me to do. And the traveling and everything, I don't know, it does something to you. We've been together, it will be ten years next year, and the Mass Choir is like an extended family to me now. It's played a large part in my growth spiritually; I've gotten to see places that I never would have seen just on my own, and to meet all kinds of people. It's just opened my world up a lot.

The next Sunday evening, Doris is in a huge, modern church outside

The Mississippi Mass Choir. (top) Regina Thomas is a soloist accompanied by the choir (center); (bottom) choir director, songwriter, and organist David Curry.

Jackson. Dressed in her choir robe, she sways and sings in the soprano section of Mississippi Mass. There are maybe eighty or ninety members here today, more than tour in the road ensemble but fewer than make up the group's full strength. They are old and young, big and small, middle-class professionals and assembly-line workers. The soloists come forward, a different one on each song, and they are excellent, but the choir's real power comes from the massed sound of all those voices, singing out their praises. Doris is in the second row, among the sopranos, joining her voice to the throng.

We aren't professional singers; we are working people: nurses, doctors, police, teachers, all different aspects of the job market. We have people from different religious backgrounds, all different walks of life. The only thing we all have in common is that we love the Lord and we're all coming together for a certain purpose. There's something about singing in the group; there is a energy there, like we're all combined and we've got this one thing we're trying to accomplish. We do have certain ones that basically do the lead singing, and I think a part of me would love to be able to do that—I have done backup lead on occasion, I haven't done a recording lead—but I've learned that we're a conglomerate. We come together and we're supportive of one another. The back is just as important as the front, because everyone has something to contribute.

It is not always easy. The traveling, whether on weekend trips to neighboring states or tours of Europe and Japan, has to be fitted in between job and family commitments. The choir, successful as it is, must plow most of its income back into its infrastructure, keeping the busses repaired, making the next recording, paying the people who work full-time coordinating the tours, so there is little money left over to pay the hundred-plus singers. The rewards are personal and spiritual rather than economic, and that can produce strains at times.

A lot of people can't understand how we do it, and if you really want to know the truth, when I look back over the last almost ten years I don't understand it myself. In the hospital, I've worked with a wonderful group of people, co-workers that have traded days with me, worked in my place, head nurses and supervisors that were very understanding of what I do. The doctors, nurses are always asking me, "What are you doing next?" or "Where did you go this weekend?" Because I work every other weekend, and usually when I'm off, I'm gone.

It affects my church as well. I do take a active role in my church choir, but I'm gone a lot. I think they're kind of used to it now, though, and my pastor understands. But being a part of Mississippi Mass, it requires a lot of understanding on your family's part, your job, your church, because it does affect a lot of people, traveling like that.

We have lost choir members for various reasons. Some get married and move away. Work-related, have to move. I've just never had any of those things to affect me, so I've always been a part of the choir. But I've learned since I've been traveling on the road with Mississippi Mass, a lot of people look at it as like a glamour thing. It's not a glamour thing. It's a lot of work to it. But I am an original member and I've seen different changes come about, and I think I'll always be there. It's become a big part of my life.

Tonight's performance is not a regular church service, it is a concert drawing an audience from throughout Jackson rather than simply the church's regular congregation. Nonetheless, as at all the choir's appearances, the evening includes more than just music. Benjamin Cone, the group's spiritual advisor, comes forward to deliver a sermon, and even holds an altar call, asking people to come forward and accept Christ into their lives. The choir has both a sermon and altar call on each record as well, reminding its audience of its real function, and the members do not consider their mission accomplished when they come offstage.

Instead of "concert," we like to say "service," because we are servicing the Lord. And we can do that anywhere. We sing in all different areas, and I think that's a big part of our ministry. When we are traveling, we sing in restaurants. That's something that Frank Williams got us into when we first got started and we've kept that up for the past ten years. When we stop to eat, a lot of people, when they hear that this is Mississippi Mass Choir, they're so intrigued and they want to hear us sing, and they usually give us real good service. And we usually sing for them, the people sitting in the restaurants and the workers that are working there. And you'll be amazed at how we just touch people.

We are people people. We like to be among the people, and we don't set ourselves apart. Whereas you know, I've been around where other artists don't like to be bothered; they like their privacy—Now, I used that word "bothered," but it's not a bother for us. It's just being among the people. That's a part of Frank Williams's legacy, a part of what he taught us. His whole ministry was about people, about loving people and concentrating on what the Lord wants us to do, not looking at this as being a star performance or something like that. We're always ready to reach out to people, no matter where we go.

The first time we were in Japan, we just went to the crowds and we sang. We were singing to Japanese audiences, and we were singing in English, and you found very few people who spoke fluent English, but yet and still, I guess it's just communicating through song. Like they say, music is the universal language; but these people, it was like they could really understand, they could really comprehend what we were saying. It's like the Holy Ghost did not have a language barrier.

Overleaf: The Mississippi Mass Choir

As the choir raises its unified voices, it is not hard to understand how

its spirit could transcend language. The members not only sing; they sway, clap, shout, and on one song even jump in unison. Like the music, the motions are carefully arranged, but leaving enough room for individual expression to come out. Everyone may hit the same note, or sway in the same direction, but each brings his or her own flavor, and the soloists cut loose with a possessed, passionate freedom. This is part of the choir's strength, preserving its down-home feel, and matches its musical position, on the line between traditional and contemporary styles. It is backed by a tightly arranged band, relies largely on original compositions, and has introduced some modern harmonies into its sound, but it has not lost the old-time, churchy flavor. The technique is formidable, but never overwhelms the spirit, and this is what helps set Mississippi Mass apart from the big-city choirs that have tended to dominate the recent scene.

After the performance—or service—Jerry Mannery and David Curry sit off to one side of the hall and talk about the group's choice of direction. Jerry says that Mississippi Mass's greatest strength has come from its insistence on staying close to its roots.

Our music is what you're going to hear on Sunday morning at eleven o'clock. The other music, the contemporary music has its place, but the Lord gives each one of us a talent and a ministry, and our talent was sticking with the church. We all are fishers; the contemporary artists out there just use something different—we might use bait, they may use tackle—but the idea is to catch fish. It's not a matter of whether what we're doing is better than what another person is doing; it's just that this is the way the Lord has given us: He said, "I want you to use the worm and use the minnow." Others might be using the tackle, but if they're catching fish, praise the Lord. But, for us, we stick with the church music, and that will never go out of style. When it goes out of style, then you'll know the churches have closed up their doors.

As a songwriter, David has gone for the plain, direct impact of the classic gospel standards. Where some lyricists go in for fancy rhymes and catchy concepts, he is just trying to put the Lord's word into song.

See, the thing about other songs is you can actually write a lie, but we like to write truth. You can fabricate on other songs, but in gospel you have to stick with the truth and let it come from the Bible—sort of get a life-changing type message, you know what I'm saying? And I would much rather do the truth than do a lying song, because we want to try to bring anybody, everybody to Christ, and the truth will set you free.

Jerry adds that the task is not always easy.

I think in a sense that it's a little bit more difficult for me to write gospel than it was when I was out in the world, writing secular songs and r&b songs, because, as David said, it has to line up with the truth. You know, a carpenter uses an instrument, a leveler, to make sure that the wall is going up level. If the bubble is not in between that little mark, you know that it's off-center. When you're writing gospel, you have to use the Bible as your leveler, and if it doesn't line up, you have to throw it out. It's not like you're just coming off the top of your head and saying, "Hey, I feel like this is the way it is." What defines the gospel is the word of God. So you have to study, to show yourself or prove that you can rightly divine the word, because if you don't know what doth sayest the Lord, how can you tell people what doth sayest the Lord?

A couple of choir members, listening on the sidelines, nod in agreement. Others have already left, quickly doffing their robes before starting the long ride home. Some have three-hour drives ahead, and make this trip whenever the choir has a concert. Others, living in Jackson or the surrounding towns, can take their time, and they stay to have a bite to eat together and chat. It really does feel like one big, extended family, as children flock around and new babies are admired. Looking around, one has to remind oneself that these "just plain folks" are the biggest draw in the gospel market, and have been for almost a decade.

Doris Miller (center) prays with her fellow worshippers.

There are many explanations for the Mississippi Mass Choir's astonishing and enduring success: it has strong support from its record company, which has produced videos to go with each album and made sure the product got to the stores; it came along at just the right time, when the gospel world was ready for a shot of its old-time, hard-hitting sound; it was formed by some of the most experienced people in the gospel field and had a whole state's worth of talent to draw upon. Nonetheless, if one asks the members for their opinions, they will not cite any of these factors. They might put their responses differently, but all come down to the same thing, a theme that Doris returns to before taking her leave and heading back to Vicksburg.

The Lord just gave us a gift. It's nothing but Him shining through us, because I know it's nothing we're doing. You see a lot of choirs out there that sound real good. Sometimes I really feel like they sing a lot better than we do. But I learned that it's not all about what you sound like. It's what the Lord has in store. It's Him that's doing this. So it's not that we're so extraordinary or anything, it's only the Lord's hands on us. It's all His work.

◆◆◆

PART FOUR

Louisiana, Music

The Louisiana bayous

Where Is King

Louisiana is a world unto itself, and music is a big part of what makes it unique. Or, more accurately, Louisiana is several worlds, each distinct from the others. North Louisiana is part of the deep South; New Orleans is part of the Caribbean; the Cajun country is a sort of Southern Quebec with bayous and a rich African-American heritage; as for the even more isolated pocket of Spanish-speaking Isleños at the Mississippi's mouth, it remains unknown to most Louisianans even today. Each of these regions has its own music and food, two things that tend to go together in Louisiana, and that are valued here as in no other part of the country.

The northern part of the state shares the most with surrounding areas, bordered as it is by Mississippi on the east, Arkansas on the north, and Texas on the west. The northern river region nurtured Jerry Lee Lewis and his cousins, Jimmy Lee Swaggart and Mickey Gilley, performers whose country roots fused with a gospel-blues piano style and Pentecostal vocal fervor. Kenny Bill Stinson, a singer and songwriter who leads bands around the region, continues to blend blues and country in a Louisiana honky-tonk sound.

Our journey briefly abandons the river, moving over to Shreveport to celebrate the birthday of Governor Jimmie Davis. The diversion was not planned; we were going to visit Davis in his Baton Rouge home, but the date turned out to be his birthday and the *Louisiana Hayride* band was holding a reunion in Shreveport to celebrate the occasion, with Merle Haggard joining in, so we headed west. After all, how many states have had a governor who is also a major figure in American music? Davis, who was elected to office in the forties and again in the sixties, was a formative early country star, and—though politically he ran as a segregationist—he was one of the few country figures to record with African-American sidemen. Best known for "You Are My Sunshine," he started as a blues singer before recording a string of country classics, and he is still in good voice and spirits at age ninety-eight.

We move south into Cajun—our north Louisiana interviewees insist on using the term "coon-ass"—country. This is not, strictly speaking, on the river, but by now the Mississippi is fanning out into a true delta and the swamp region can all be considered river-related. Anyway, the music is too good to resist. Throughout southern Louisiana, a music lover is constantly faced with an embarrassment of riches; every style has multiple great exponents, any of whom deserves a documentary all to himself or herself.

The rural French population of south Louisiana has its roots in Acadia (now Nova Scotia), from which the French settlers were driven out by the English in the mid-eighteenth century. They mixed with earlier French Louisianans and new arrivals, and interacted with the black and Native American population. Catholic and francophone, they remain largely separate from their neighbors in the north of the state, and also distrustful of the big-city folks in New Orleans, maintaining a unique cultural belt.

By the time Cajun music was first recorded, in the twenties, it had developed its basic instrumental line-up, with guitar, fiddle, and accordion. For many years, though, Cajun musicians kept pace with outside developments, adding elements of Texas swing and honky-tonk styles. D. L. Menard, "the

Cajun Hank Williams," was the master singer and songwriter of the honky-tonk period, marked by the addition of steel guitar and a new songwriting style that matched what was happening at the time in Nashville. The recent Cajun revival has tended to concentrate on an earlier, "purer" style, but Menard remains one of the music's grand masters, loved by modernists and traditionalists alike.

Zydeco (named from a song, *"Les Haricots* [which sounds like 'zydeco'] *Sont pas Salés,"* "The Stringbeans Aren't Salted"), the music of the region's black francophone population, developed its modern form around the same time as Menard's honky-tonk style. Earlier black and white French styles had overlapped, with Amadé Ardoin, a black accordionist, being considered one of the great early Cajun recording stars. In the fifties, though, as white Cajuns fused country-western elements with their music, black Cajuns brought in a strong r&b and blues influence. The King of Zydeco was Clifton Chenier, who adopted the piano accordion in order to get the full r&b sound, as well as adding saxophone in place of the fiddle. Although Cajun music today is largely a revivalist, "folk" style, zydeco remains the popular music of black rural Louisiana, packing dance halls with young people following the latest trends. Geno Delafose is a special figure in the new scene, a player who has carefully stayed in touch with the tradition while assimilating new developments.

While the Cajun culture formed in the countryside, New Orleans developed an equally distinct world. The major Gulf Coast port, with a history that comprises Spanish, French and American rulers, it is as much a part of the Caribbean as of the United States, and its music has the rolling, African-influenced rhythms of Cuba, Haiti, and Trinidad rather than the sound of the inland South. This is what Jelly Roll Morton used to call the "Spanish tinge," and it continues to underly all the local music.

New Orleans is, among other things, a tourist mecca, and the streets and bars of the French Quarter provide work for more musicians than any comparable stretch of real estate in the country. These range from jazz revival bands to blues groups, Cajun bands, contemporary brass bands, and—on the streets in particular—anyone else who wants to try their luck with the flocks of passersby. David and Roselyn have been making music on the streets of the Quarter for twenty-five years, playing a repertory of New Orleans standards mixed with their own quirky choices.

The first New Orleans music to break out into the greater American consciousness was, of course, jazz. A mix of marching-band music, the sophisticated sounds of the "creole" society orchestras, and a drumming tradition that exists throughout the Caribbean, the early jazz sound is continued today in various forms. Among its most vital exponents is the Treme Brass Band, which maintains the funeral-band tradition, specializing in the old hymn tunes that have long accompanied burial services, played slow on the way to the graveyard and in joyous, danceable celebration on the way home.

The Treme band has also kept up with the times, developing the sort of hot rhythm workouts that mark the recent brass-band revival. Started as a revival of the traditional form, the brass boom has taken on a life of its own, becoming the street sound of young, black New Orleans. The Soul Rebels exemplify the new wave, adding reggae and hip-hop to the classic brass-band sound. Regarded as troublemakers by some of the traditionalist element, the Rebels are proudly bringing their music into the twenty-first century, proving that New Orleans is more than the museum of a glorious past.

Henry Butler is another forward-looking musician, though one who is much more acceptable to musical conservatives. Like other young Crescent City jazz men, including the Marsalis brothers and Nicholas Payton, the city's crown prince of the piano has immersed himself in the history of jazz. He traces the music's evolution from Jelly Roll Morton through modern jazz, but distinguishes himself from many of his compatriots by giving equal weight to parallel developments in blues and r&b. His concerts make vital connections between the concert and popular traditions, something that was common for the early jazzmen but has become rarer through the years. His deep knowledge of history and his uncanny ability to play every style he mentions make him a perfect guide to the history of New Orleans music, and when he teams up with Eddie Bo, one of the idiosyncratic geniuses of r&b, he proves that he can rock as hard as anyone in town.

New Orleans saw a unique flowering in the r&b era. Although many of the local hits never broke nationally, enough did to make the whole world aware of the local talent. From Fats Domino and his peers in the early fifties to the boom a decade later under the guidance of Allen Toussaint, to the rise of the Meters and the Neville Brothers, New Orleans's island-flavored sound was a vital part of the evolution of rock, soul, and funk. Eddie Bo, for example, a pianist in the classic mold of the legendary Professor Longhair and Huey "Piano" Smith, found his work copied by Little Richard, who came down from Georgia to record in the New Orleans studios. In the early sixties, Irma Thomas emerged as the "Soul Queen of New Orleans" and racked up a string of hits, first with Toussaint and then with the New Orleans expatriates who became mainstays of the Los Angeles studio scene. New Orleans is pretty much the only city in America where artists of Thomas's and Bo's generation can still make a good living without adulterating their classic sound, and young and old alike know their music as part of the city's trademark sound.

Part of the reason for Louisiana's richness of cultures is the unusual juxtaposition of its varied ethnic and national roots and the isolation provided by the swamps and bayous. Possibly the least familiar of all the state's isolated cultural groups is that of the Isleños, Spanish immigrants from the Canary Islands who settled some two hundred years ago on the islands at the mouth of the Mississippi. It is here our journey ends, on a fishing boat in the apparently endless, swampy, grass-and-water-lands where the Isleños have preserved a medieval Spanish ballad tradition, adapting it to whatever events happened in their lives. Thus, we come full circle from the Ojibwe of Lake Itasca, back to a culture that has traditionally lived largely on water and survived off the natural world around it.

◆◆◆

1

North Louisiana Twang: KENNY BILL STINSON

Balloons are floating across the river toward Louisiana, big globes of hot air with intrepid riders in baskets underneath. On the Mississippi bank, the cliffs rise up to Natchez, where an annual fair is going on. Along the riverbank is a line of bars, the one-time riverboatmen's gambling, drinking, and whoring center known as Natchez-Under-the-Hill. It has been cleaned up a lot since the riverboat days, though a new casino has brought back the gambling part and a lot of alcohol is still being consumed. This afternoon, it's mostly beer, and the bottles are clicking on wooden tables all along the sun-splashed deck of the Wharf Master's House, a local bar and restaurant. Over in the corner, his eyes concealed by round, black sunglasses, Kenny Bill Stinson is picking out a rocking boogie rhythm and growling a lyric that is clearly close to his heart.

Yeah, I like my rice and gravy and my black-eyed peas
Corn on the cob, I want a big glass of tea
Some okra and tomatoes and some turnip greens
I want some real soul food, do you know what I mean?
Well, I'm going on down to Ma and Pa's Cafe—Mercy!
I want some 'taters and gravy with some chicken-fried steak

Kenny Bill's voice has plenty of country in it, but with an edge that is a long way from Nashville, and his guitar is solidly rooted in the blues.

I come from West Monroe, Louisiana, and I play a blend of country music, blues, rock 'n' roll—whatever I can throw together to make a living. I've been playing music, it seems like, ever since I was a baby. My mother said that I came out singing, not crying, and I've been hollering and yodeling and warbling ever since. I started out just like any kid, beating on the pots and pans around the house and building drum sets out of Tinker Toys and lightstands—getting a badminton racket and putting it around my neck and playing like I was playing the guitar, you know. It's just always been in me, this music thing, it couldn't be denied, so I just had to go after it and do it.

Where I'm from is kind of like a train wreck of country music and blues; they kind of crashed together and blew up there. It was twangy, and it was bluesier than what a lot of other people were playing. Everybody had Stratocasters or Telecasters, you know, it was a Fender deal—a lot of twangy guitars, Fender amps, Fender super reverbs, and it lent itself to a country rockabilly sound with a twist of the blues in it. The Ventures were real popular when I was growing up, and everybody that played guitar had to know "Walk, Don't Run," "Pipeline," "Wipe Out." Those were staples.

Of course, everyone in our church sang. We were in the Church of Christ, so they didn't have any instruments, they thought that was kind of sinful. They just had singing, which was great, but I think the fact that they didn't want anybody to play instruments was another reason I wanted to play an instrument, you know.

I got a guitar first, I guess, when I was around ten, a little Kingston acoustic—I still have it—and started bashing out chords and listening to the radio and playing along to the TV and playing to records, and I basically taught myself. It just came natural and easy for me. After I learned how to play some chords and some progressions of stuff, I wanted to play piano, too, for some reason, and my parents told me that they would rent a piano and if I learned how to play it, that they would buy it. So I started practicing every day on the piano. I was listening to a lot of Jerry Lee Lewis and boogie-woogie piano players, and my mother was into Frankie Carle and all these lounge-lizard piano players. I was listening to her stuff and listening to mine, and I just taught myself how to play the piano. I never had any lessons or nobody ever showed me anything, really.

Some older fellows at our church, they had a little band and they would jam in their shed out behind the house. I was just a teenager, but they let me sit in and I learned a lot of great songs from those guys. They were playing Freddie King tunes, and

Kenny Bill Stinson on the deck of the Wharf Master's House

Lonnie Mack, and the Ventures, and the Bar-kays—a lot of that good Memphis soul music, and mixing it up with blues and country. Then, my girlfriend's stepdad played in a country band, and we'd go stand behind the nightclub with the door open; we could look in and watch the band play, so that really corrupted me, too, you know. I thought, "Wow, that's something I got to do."

After a while, I decided that my favorite kind of musician/player was somebody who played all the solos, sang all night, and wrote his own songs. I don't know where I got that, probably from Bob Dylan or something, but that's what I think you should be if you're going to do this. Especially for me, singing other folks' songs just doesn't give me the feeling I get when I sing something I've written myself. I get a better feeling, and I come off the stage thinking that I really did something, you know, that I really told a story about my life or something that I've been going through. It just makes me feel more honest to sing my own songs, and anybody who writes and sings and plays, that's the guy I always look at and go, "Wow, I want to be like that guy."

So basically, now, I play all over northern Louisiana, and down in the southern part of the state as well. I have a band, or I can work by myself like I am today. I play guitar and piano, I switch it up during the evening, and sing, too. I do anything and everything that I can do to make a little money here and there. Whatever they need, man, I'll be there.

Today, Kenny Bill is doing a low-key bar set for an audience that has come to drink and chat in the sun rather than to listen to music. Nonetheless, though most of them have never heard of him, he captures several tables with his solid guitar rhythm and the wry, bluesy humor of his vocals. People clap, and occasionally yell encouragement when he hits a line they particularly like. His set is heavy on original tunes, but also includes blues standards, Jimmy Reed's "Big Boss Man," and tips of the hat to country and rockabilly singers from Jimmy Rodgers to Hank Williams to Carl Perkins. Stinson brings a rambunctious energy to the blues, but sounds most natural when he slips into a country whine, his voice sliding up to a honky-tonk yodel at the end of his lines in a way that carries hints of Jerry Lee Lewis, who grew up across the river from Natchez, in Ferriday, and became north Louisiana's most distinctive gift to country and rock 'n' roll.

I want to tell you a story of a love gone bad
I treated her mean and brother, she got mad
Come home, come on, little baby, come home
I'm down on my knees, beggin' you please to come home

Well, I was standing at the bar around closing time
A lot of whiskey and women on my mind
Come home, come on, little baby, come home
I want you to know, I still love you so, so come home

North Louisiana and south Louisiana, it's two different worlds. I believe Alexandria is where they say the "coon-ass cutoff point" is; it's coon-ass below Alexandria, and then it's redneck from Alexandria on up. It's two entirely different cultures; it's more country music up north, and the more south you go, you get Cajun, zydeco, blues; and then, of course, New Orleans is a melting pot, it's everything there. New Orleans is the hippest city in the world as far as I'm concerned. I see every kind of music there when I go there.

There's a pretty good circuit up here, from here in Natchez all the way to Shreveport, not to mention Arkansas and Mississippi and Texas on the fringe. I play a lot of festivals and a lot of bars, and weddings and stuff with the band. People around here—you could drop a plate of forks and people will dance. That's what they live for. They work hard and they play hard, and on the weekends, man, they want to go out and have a good time, and they want a live band. They don't care what kind of music it is, just so you got a drummer. You don't get too many snobs; you see all kinds of people dancing to our music. It's neat.

North Louisiana is an area that's really been overlooked. Another thing that's great up here is the food; it's just as good as the Cajun food. I mean, I like 'taters and gravy and chicken fried steak, you know, that's a staple here. Rice and gravy and grits. I mean, it's country food, and people up there know how to cook good. This whole little area, it's kind of overlooked in a way, but I intend to change that.

Kenny Bill laughs at his presumption, but at heart he is serious. He believes in what he does, and believes that, if he could get some more exposure, there are plenty of people who would sit up and take notice.

My music is all about having fun in life, and all the little stuff that I go through in this area. It all builds up and then a song comes out—it might take six months or a year, but all of a sudden all these songs start coming to my mind. And it seems to be that it's all pretty true to what I'm living through. So I'm just hoping that this music that I play spreads and people enjoy it, you know. I like it myself. It's real good-feeling music—it makes me feel good, so I'm hoping it makes other people feel good, too.

◆ ◆ ◆

2

The Singing Governor Turns Ninety-Eight: JIMMIE DAVIS AND FRIENDS

Standing on the observation platform on the sixteenth floor of the Louisiana State Capitol at Baton Rouge, you can look almost straight down at a green park, a lake, and the Governor's residence. Not the residence of the current governor, but that of Governor Jimmie Davis. Davis served twice, in 1944 and 1960, and he retains the title and a mansion on the Capitol grounds. Today, though, he is not home. He is over in Shreveport, in the northwestern corner of the state, celebrating his ninety-eighth birthday with the cast of the old *Louisiana Hayride* radio show, a collection of old regulars and some newer friends like Kenny Bill Stinson, and special guest Merle Haggard.

The event is being held in Shreveport's Strand Theatre. Fifty years ago, Jimmie Davis was Governor of Louisiana and the Strand was holding the debut showing of *Louisiana,* a Hollywood bio-pic starring Jimmie Davis as Jimmie Davis. Meanwhile, his song "Bang Bang" was the number-four pop hit in the country, his third record since getting elected to hit the top five. Louisiana Lieutenant Governor Kathleen Blanco is not old enough to remember those days, but she has become a friend of the Governor's, and has turned up to pay her respects.

This event is a beautiful tribute to a man that has been more than just a governor or more than just a superstar for Louisiana—he is just one of our beloved people who touched our lives in such a special and unique way. His musical talent was shared with everyone and one of his most famous songs, "You Are My Sunshine," continues to be one of the favorite songs of people in Louisiana and all over the world. It's a simple, beautiful ballad that touched the hearts of so many people through the years. And I think you can't think of Jimmie Davis without thinking of that beautiful ballad and the joy that it expresses.

Merle Haggard is meeting the Governor for the first time this evening, and he seems pretty excited about the fact.

"You Are My Sunshine" was the first or second song that I learned to play on the fiddle. "San Antonio Rose" and "You Are My Sunshine" were the two most popular country songs of the time when I was nine years old. I've just done a tribute album of Jimmie Davis music. So I've done tributes to Jimmy Rodgers, to Bob Wills, to

Elvis Presley, and to Jimmie Davis. So that lets you know what category I place Jimmie Davis in.

All the comments are coming from other people, because the ex-governor himself is feeling tired. He recently suffered a fall while walking in his yard, and there was some question whether he would even make it to Shreveport for the celebration. In the end, he arrived this morning, but is still resting in his hotel, so other people are doing the talking for him. They all seem eager to put in a few words. Although Davis's prosegregation stance clouded his final term as governor, the country-western crowd admires him as a singer and as probably the most honest governor Louisiana has had in this century. Tillman Franks, the bass player and songwriter who has been credited as the brains behind the country stardom of multiple artists, including Johnny Horton, David Houston,

Governor Jimmy Davis (left) celebrates his birthday in an onstage duet with Merle Haggard.

and Claude King, is here as part of the Louisiana Hayride Revue, and remembers traveling with the Governor on his second run for office.

I was playing in a quartet with Johnny Horton, and we kicked off his campaign in Bunkie, Louisiana. That's where the coon-ass border is. All south of there are coon-asses, and all north of that are like Texas. Then, the last time he hit the chart was a song I helped him rewrite and I promoted for him. It's called "Where the Old Red River Flows," and it got in the top ten while he was governor.

Jimmie Davis is in the Country Music Hall of Fame, and he's in the Gospel Hall of Fame, too. He did all of it. When he first started singing he could yodel like Jimmy Rodgers but he quit yodeling way back there. And years and years ago he did old blues songs. He had a black guy playing the guitar with him way before anybody else did that, and he blended it together. He just sang so much a variety of music.

The first time he went out to run for governor, he wasn't going to sing, but the people just demanded it. So he would talk about the politics a little and he would sing in all them towns. And the Cajun people in south Louisiana liked him much as they did in north Louisiana and he was elected governor twice. And he made a good governor. He left lots of money in the pot down there when he left. More money, I guess, than was ever left in the treasury by any other governor.

Maggie Warwick, another *Hayride* star, chips in another story about that first campaign.

One of his opponents one time was going to use some of his early music—that was this sort of acoustic blues and had the black influence, and they were going to try to use it against him. They were playing one of his records, I think it was "Red Nightgown Blues," and they were going to try to shame him, you know. So they were on the same platform doing this debate and they started playing this record and the people stopped listening to his opponent and got up and started dancing. The people just loved it, you know. So then Jimmie Davis got up and started singing "You Are My Sunshine," and of course won the election easily. He was just a real special fellow to Louisiana, and to all these Southern states, and his music, I think, will live on and on. He has been recording and performing for eight decades, and I don't know anybody else that's done that, and at ninety-eight years old he's still loving the business, still loving to be out on the road.

The evening's program starts out with the Louisiana Hayride Revue. Maggie sings "It Wasn't God that Made Honky-Tonk Angels," and Tillman's quartet sings "Keep on the Sunny Side." Maggie leads the whole cast on the gospel standard "I'll Fly Away," they play the show's closing theme, and it is time for Merle Haggard. Merle's set is loose and swinging, mixing classic hits with a couple of Cajun numbers led by the band's fiddler, doubling on accordion and vocals. Then, it is time for Governor Davis to make his appearance.

First, of course, come the speeches, from Kathleen Blanco and other dignitaries. Then the curtain rises to reveal the governor himself, seated on an armchair at center stage. He looks frail, and speaks very slowly, but his sense of humor is intact.

I'd like to thank Merle Haggard for coming here and entertaining you. That's his business. Now, my business is seeing the doctor. Two days ago, I told him I was gonna come up here.

He says, "For what?"

I said, "They're going to honor me."

He says, "They're not gonna honor you, they're gonna bury you."

The crowd laughs and applauds, and the Governor goes into a long, winding joke. Then, it is time for him to sing. He gestures to his guitarist, and they confer a bit about the key. Then the band strikes a chord and Jimmie Davis, for what must be the several-thousandth time, starts to sing "You Are My Sunshine."

The other night, dear, as I lay sleeping
I dreamed I held you in my arms
When I awoke, dear, I was mistaken
And I hung my head and cried

Shaky as his voice is when he speaks, the minute he starts to sing he is another man. The notes are sure and full, the time solid. As he reaches the end of the verse, Haggard strides on from the side of the stage and bends over the microphone at his side. Cheek-to-cheek, Haggard and the Governor harmonize on the most famous chorus in American music.

You are my sunshine, my only sunshine
You make me happy when skies are gray
You'll never know, dear, how much I love you
Please don't take my sunshine away

◆◆◆

3
The Cajun Hank Williams: D. L. MENARD

As one pulls up in D. L. Menard's front yard, on a quiet road in the heart of the bayou country, the man himself is working in the yard. There is nothing about him that would suggest that he is one of the most popular performers in Cajun music. Dressed like an oil rig worker, with a blue feed cap on his head, he could pass for just another local guy, raised on a farm and now picking up his cash from the drilling company down the road. He sidles up to the car, a big smile on his face, and begins talking immediately. His speech is wild and untrammeled, a mix of aphorisms, stories, and old-fashioned hospitality, all couched in a quirky Cajun French accent.

D. L. leads visitors into his front room, which is adorned with photos of himself, his bands, his children, and Hank Williams, who is also represented in a large, framed painting, and on through to the kitchen. This is where the family normally congregates, and Menard's wife, Louella, hoists herself up out of a rocking chair to make coffee. Their daughter Becky is sitting in another chair, and several kids are peeping out of corners at the strangers. The Menard's seven children are grown and gone, but now the house is regularly full of the seventeen grandchildren and a new great-grandchild.

Once everyone is settled in chairs, and coffee has been poured, D. L. starts to tell his story.

When I heard my first Cajun band, I was tickled to death. I was sixteen and a half years old, but I had never heard a live Cajun band before because I couldn't get in the dance hall, I was too young. But I had two uncles that had some Cajun groups, and one night they had a practice session. I went to the practice, and in those days they didn't have no drums, they just had two guitars; one would play choke rhythm and the other one would play open rhythm. And while they was tuning the guitars and making some chords on the guitar, boy, I just fell in love with that guitar.

So, after the practice session, I asked one of the fellas if he was going to teach me how to play, and he say yeah. So I get home, I started looking at a Montgomery Ward catalog. My daddy tells me, "What you doing?"

I said, "I want to buy me a guitar."

"Oh, lord," he said, "You're going to spend that money? It's just burning you in

D. L. Menard playing in his backyard.
Leo Abshire joins in on fiddle.

Terry Huvel, fiddle and steel guitar; Leo Abshire, fiddle; D. L. Menard.
(bottom photo:)
A country dance in the Menards' backyard.

your pocket, you got to get rid of it." He said, "You know you're not going to do nothing with that."

"Yeah," I said, "I'm going to do something with that. I asked somebody to teach me."

My guitar cost me $11, with postage paid and everything. Well, in those times, I knew my chords and that guitar wasn't good enough for me. So what happened, I took a Sears-Roebuck catalog, and I ordered the $24.95 model guitar. They had one for $45, a beautiful guitar, but I didn't have enough money. So I ordered the $24.95 one, $24.95 for the guitar and the case. When it came in at the post office, I go get it, I opened the case, and they had made a mistake: They had put the $45 one in the case. So I hurried up—to me, the postmaster would have known, you know—and closed it and I ran home. We used to live in town in those days. And six months after, I played my first band job.

The reason why they hired me, they found out I was able to sing Hank Williams songs. Our Cajun music had kind of died down over here for a while, and country and western had took over. A Cajun band that couldn't play a country song would not be working; they'd be home on Saturday night. And especially a Hank Williams song, because he was the most popular one at that particular time, and his songs was so simple and natural that they fitted perfect in our Cajun music.

So they hired me to sing those Hank Williams songs. One of the guitar players had quit, and I started out in the band at seventeen years old. That was in 1949. And I sang country and western songs for three years before I started singing Cajun songs. What happened then was that one night we had a practice session, and Louella, my wife, asked me to sing a Cajun song called "Big Texas."

They all said, "Aw, he can't sing in French, he just can sing in English." 'Cause I had never done it, you know. So they didn't think I could do it. But I sang it, and that's how I started out singing Cajun songs. It's kind of funny, because French was my first language. I learned my English in school—I couldn't tell you "good morning" when I started in school.

As the day goes on, people start dropping by. Rather than arranging a dance-hall gig, D. L. has decided to cook up an outdoor meal and hold a concert in his backyard, and has invited neighbors and relatives over to be the audience. A local deputy sheriff minds a big pot of crawfish étouffé, and Louella and Becky pull together the rest of what it takes to feed the hungry throng. Meanwhile, D. L.'s sidemen are plugging in their instruments. It is a full Cajun band in the style of his first outfit, with not only accordion and fiddle but also a steel guitar to give it some country flavor. A couple of special guests have been added: Christine Balfa, daughter of the legendary fiddler Dewey Balfa and a fine singer and bandleader in her own right, and Robert Jardell, a singer and accordionist who grew up under the tutelage of the great accordionist Nathan Abshire. After the requisite tuning, and some tinkering with the superannuated sound system, the band strikes up the first tune.

It is a sprightly two-step, with D. L. holding down the rhythm on his guitar and singing in his distinctive nasal twang. The lyric is in French, except for an English tag line:

Tu traines les chemins presque tous les soirs
(You walk the streets almost every night)
Toute la journée, t'es après dormir
(All day, you're always sleeping)
Quand le monde se lève, toi, t'es après te coucher
(When people are getting up, you're just going to bed)
Écoute-moi bien, porte attention, moi, je veux te parler.
(Listen to me well, pay attention, I want to talk to you)
Si moi, je serais toi, je changerais ma vie.
(If I were you, I would change my life)
J'essayerais de vivre quand le soleil se lève
(I would try to live while the sun was up)
Là t'es après vivre après le soleil couché
(Now you're living after sundown)
Comme on dit en anglais, "Listen to me when I talk to you."
(As one says in English, "Listen to me when I talk to you.")

A few older couples dance a shuffling two-step that looks like the country cousin of a jitterbug. Others sit in lawn chairs, chuckling at the lyrics and the scolding tone D. L. assumes as he sings the tag line. It is one of his newer songs, in a long line of compositions that have made him the most popular Cajun songwriter of the modern era.

The first time I had wrote a song, I didn't even know I had wrote a song. Mr. Badeaux, the leader of the group, the accordion player, had a waltz, but he didn't have no words for it. He had a melody, and we played that melody and I would start humming along, and I put some words together just so I would have something to sing about. I didn't have no idea that I had wrote a song. I just put them together like that. Come to find out it was a good melody and it was a good story.

One of my uncles, he had a little money, and he tells us one time, he said, "Our band sounds good, I'd like to cut a record just to see how it sounds."

Well, Mr. Badeaux had a two-step he wanted to record, and I said, "What are you going to put on that other side?"

He say, "We're going to put your song."

I argued three weeks with him that I did not want to put that song on a record; I didn't think it was good enough. But they got on me enough that I finally gave in, and it sold fairly well. And, oh, it's a terrific feeling when you first record! I had never heard a recording in the studio, and after we heard the first tape, I said, "You mean to tell me it's going to sound like that on that record?"

He said "Yeah."

"Well," I said, "Let's hurry and finish it." Wow, I was tickled to death.

Then, the next record was "The Back Door," and that made a hit and it's still a hit. We recorded that song in 1962, and it's still popular today.

"The Back Door," or "La Porte d'en Arrière" would become the most popular Cajun song after "Jolie Blonde," a standard in the repertoire of every Cajun band. It was written to the tune of Hank Williams's "Honky Tonk Blues," and inspired by a conversation D. L. had with Williams when the country star came to town in 1951. Williams had by then become the biggest name in country music, and was particularly popular in Louisiana due to his years of broadcasting on Shreveport's *Louisiana Hayride.*

I went to see him, and I stayed with him from nine till, well, I left the dance hall at fifteen to one. He played from nine to one, and I stayed in front of that bandstand almost all the time, and I studied that man from head to toe. I had a chance to meet him, and I talked with him for about ten minutes. He told me a lot of things, but I was nineteen years old, so more or less half of what he told me went inside this ear and out the other side. Then, later on, when I started traveling, I started to find out what he meant.

We started talking, and I noticed that we had a crowd surrounding us and they was watching us. They'd turn to me, and they'd turn to him; I'd ask him a question, he'd answer it. He told me, he said, "The music that you play, you've got to play it from the heart."

I said "What you mean? How do you do that?"

Then he named me a song. He said, "Is that a sad song?"

"Oh Lord," I said, "Yes it is. It is a sad song."

He said, "How would you feel if it happened to you?"

"Oh, Lord," I said.

"Well," he said, "that's exactly it. When you sing a song, any song you sing onstage, pretend it's happening to you. Put in your heart that it's happening to you." He

said, "When you cut a record, that really has got to come out on that record. That's what I mean by singing from the heart."

"Oh," I said, "But Hank, it's French music; it's not hardly some music you put on a record."

He said, "It's yours, huh? It's your music?"

"Well," I said, "yeah, that's what I grew up with."

He said, "Then it's good music." He said, "No matter what kind of music you play, if it's your music, it's good."

And he said, "When you start a song, you got to have a story. A song that don't have a story don't go too far. You start with a story, you got to have the story in the middle, and you got to end it."

Another thing Hank Williams told me, he said, "The best story you can put in back of a song is everyday life. People take it for granted, they don't notice what they're doing during the day." He said, "You put that in a song, it's going to catch the ear."

That's how I wrote "The Back Door." It's just everyday life. Every once in a while I'd hear or see that people would get drunk and was too ashamed to go in the front door, that they'd come in through the back door so that nobody could see them. That's a natural, everyday story. People never pay no mind to the everyday procedures, but that's what makes the best songs. It's just like water: You wash your hands or face and take your shower, you don't think nothing of it. But let that water run dry. Where you going to take a shower? See if you don't notice it right away. So it's just like that; it's an ordinary story that's been happening all along, and I put it together and it so happened I was fortunate enough to put it right.

After a couple of songs from Christine and Robert, it is time for D. L. to sing his trademark number, as he has at every concert for the last thirty-five-plus years.

Moi et la belle, on avait été au bal
(Me and my girl, we had gone to the dance)
On a passé dans tous les honky-tonks
(We went to all the honky-tonks)
S'en a revenu le lendemain matin
(Got home the next morning)
Le jour était après se casser
(Day was already breaking)
J'ai passé dedans la porte d'en arrière
(I went in through the back door)

Leo Abshire, fiddle. (inset) Two stars of the younger generation: Robert Jardell, accordion; Christine Balfa, guitar.

I wrote that song at a service station. I was pumping gas and fixing flat tires, greasing cars, washing cars. I had a little pad in my pocket, but I couldn't write it all the way through because I was disturbed a lot, I was busy. But I knew what I was going to write, I knew the story, so every once in a while when I had a little break I'd catch my little pad and write a few words. Then a car would come in with some guys, I had to put my little pad in my pocket and go pump some gas again. To tell you the truth, the time it would of took me to tell the story and write it without stopping, it would have took about a half an hour. Once I had the story, I knew exactly what to do, and it's more or less Hank Williams that told me how to do it. And that's one of the reasons why I like to sing his songs. That song is a standard now, and I only wish I could write another one like it, "Front Door," or "Side Door," or something.

D. L.'s voice recalls Williams's clear country phrasing, though he has more of a nasal twang, and his lyric reflects both Williams's advice and his own keen sense of humor and natural gift for observing the world around him.

J'ai eu un tas d'amis tant que j'avais de l'argent
(I had a bunch of friends as long as I had money)
Asteur j'ai plus d'argent, ils voulont plus me voir
(Now that I'm out of money, they don't want to see me any more)
J'ai été dans le village, et moi je m'ai mis dans le tracas
(I was in town and I got into a brawl)
La loi m'a ramassé, moi je suis parti dans la prison
(The law picked me up, and I am off to prison)
On va passer dedans la porte en arrière
(I'll be going in through the back door)

D. L. worked the gas-station job while his children were growing up, playing music on weekends to bring in a little extra money. Then, when the music began to catch on and he wanted to tour more widely, he developed a new profession. He learned how to make old-fashioned wooden chairs, and built a factory next to his house. All the furniture in the kitchen is his handiwork, and it has the solid, long-lasting look of classic country craftsmanship.

When I have to leave, I just lock the shop, go play my music; when I come back, I start working right away, my job's waiting for me. I don't stay on the road constantly, but it's always good to go to the festival, go to the concert, and then come back home. It comes a time in the shop, you're working all the time, when you're ready to leave to go play music, and you stay away for a while. Then, when you come back home, you're ready to go back to work. It changes. Always working and always working, it gets to where if you work too much, you get a headache. You have to have something else besides the work to put your mind at ease.

So it feels good in my life, being that I'm working for myself and I can leave any time I want to. My boss can't fire me. I wouldn't let him—hah!—being that I'm the boss! So everything works well, the music and the shop works well together. Oh, yeah, I don't have no complaints.

D. L. exudes good cheer, offstage and on. He is always more than just a songwriter and singer; he is an entertainer, keeping the crowd amused with wry comments. Asked for a particular tune, he apologizes, and says he cannot remember the words. "I've got a real good memory," he says, "But it's short." On another occasion, talking about the strange people he has met, he says, "They say it takes all kinds to make a world, but it's not true. Some of them are just there!"

Despite the clowning around, though, D. L. is among the most soulful singers in modern Cajun music, with a raw, bluesy twang that is all his own. This afternoon, he does a beautiful version of Williams's "My Son Calls Another Man Daddy," and another song of his own, "It's Just the Angels that Are Crying." A lonesome Cajun waltz, it shows the sincere sentimentality that is the flip side of his folksy humor.

T'as perdu un bon ami. Il est mort après dormir.
(You've lost a good friend. He died in his sleep.)
Merci bon Dieu, il a pas souffert avec tout sa maladie.
(Thank God, he didn't suffer in his sickness.)
A tout moment, il se lamentait. Il disait il sentait pas bien.
(Now and then he'd complain. He'd say he didn't feel good.)
N'importe quoi le bon Dieu fait, c'est fait tout le temps pour une raison.
(Whatever the good Lord does, it is always done for a reason.)
T'es en train de sortir de ta maison. Après aujourd'hui tu vas plus le voir.
(You're leaving the house. After today, you'll never see him again.)
Aujourd'hui c'est l'enterrement. Ça a commencé à brumasser.
(Today is the burial. It has begun to drizzle.)
C'est pas la peine que tu te tracasses. Tu vas pas te faire tremper.
(It's not worthwhile for you to worry. You won't get wet.)
C'est pas de la pluie qu'après tomber. C'est juste les anges qu'après pleurer
(It's not rain that's falling. It's just the angels that are crying)

That's music from the heart, that's for sure, and it's always been that way. That's how our ancestors sang it. There are some people that gotta sing some songs, you'd swear they're crying. Their music is happy, and the lyric is more or less sad. It's the two combined. But you can't tell unless you understand the lyric. There's a lot of people that don't even know what the song means, because they can't speak Cajun French, you know. Our Cajun French, it falls in between Canada and France. From generation through generation, our language changed. Now there's a lot of English mixed into the Cajun language, because there's a lot of items that from generation through generation they forgot how the item was called, and they put an English word.

While D. L. has been talking, Louella has busied herself around the kitchen, but at this point she speaks up.

Among ourselves, when we were growing up, it was not right to speak French at school, so we learned English. For a long time we were ashamed of our language, because we were punished if we talked French in school or on the school ground. My kids learned French because his [D. L.'s] daddy couldn't speak a word in English, so they had to learn it in order to talk to their grandpa. My youngest one was born after he passed away, and he can talk a little and he understands everything, but he won't talk French. He's afraid of saying something wrong.

All of my kids were musical, but when Becky was young, the kids at school would laugh at her music. They'd pass here when they were practicing and holler, "Chanka-chank!" They really laughed at my kids when they went to school. Then, when D. L. started making a name for himself, oh, it wasn't that "chanka-chank" anymore. Now they talk about how they used to remember coming over here when they had practice and listening to them. Becky hates it, because

Taking a break. (top) A deputy sheriff dishes out the *étouffée.* (bottom) Christine Balfa mends a broken string.

she says, "Mama, they used to laugh at us at school and now that Daddy made a name for himself, they say they always came and listened to the music, and they never did." And it's true. But my kids always loved French music. It was just like D. L.—Cajun music was always cool to them.

D. L.: *I have a lot of respect for Cajun music, because it's part of our culture. The only place you can find that particular type of culture and that particular music is in the Cajun country, southwestern Louisiana. Now there's a lot of other different people that plays Cajun music, some outsiders, people from all over the world, and I tell you what, I'm really proud of that. It's not the actual stuff, but they do it the best way they can, and it makes me feel good to see that somebody thinks enough about our music to be wanting to play it.*

Louella: *You know, the reason why the Cajun music is so popular now is because they started having what they call* fais do-do, *street dances. The kids weren't allowed to go in the dance hall, but when they started having street dances, the kids were involved in it, and they started seeing that this is a good music to play. And now we have more young people trying to learn the music than we had a few years back.*

D. L.: *They started calling the street dance the* fais do-do, *because it was a special night, especially at the Fourth of July. But the real* fais do-do *was when the Cajun music first started.* Fais do-do *["go to sleep"]meant that the people could go to the house dance and bring their children; they didn't have to have a baby-sitter. At the* fais do-do, *they had a special room where the kids was able to go to sleep. They'd put them to bed and then they'd go back and dance. That was a* fais do-do.

But like Louella is saying, at the new fais do-do the kids was exposed to the music, and they also started playing Cajun music in the restaurants, they started making folk festivals around the area. At one point, our music was dying out. Nobody was picking it up, because they'd only hear it on records. They had no idea how the people would respond to the musician, how the musician would respond to the crowd. When they started having the fais do-do and the restaurant music, music at folk festivals, they seen how the people react to the musicians, how the people loved what the musicians were doing onstage. That started making the kids want to play, to be like the musician onstage.

And now it's also beginning to help our language. Up till about twenty to twenty-five years ago, our language was not a written language, but now it is. The Cajun French is a different language than Canada and France and Belgium. It's our own language. And the music the kids want to play, if they want to sing a song, some of them just memorize the words, but some of them are learning the language in order to be able to sing the songs. So the music is helping our language and our culture.

Among older musicians, there is some controversy about the younger generation of players. Young Cajuns are no more immune to the world around them than any other young Americans. Even Christine Balfa, daughter of the man who led the Cajun revival, was tempted by other sounds.

I grew up hearing Cajun music all my life. But, you know, like most teenagers, you kind of get sidetracked, you want to hear whatever the popular music is. But it didn't take me long to realize that we had something very special here.

Now, young artists like Christine and Steve Riley are keeping the classic sound alive while trying to establish their own approaches. Others are more radical, following in the wake of Zachary Richard, who became a sort of Cajun rock star by fusing the older music with rock, jazz, and a substantial infusion of Afro-Louisianan zydeco. This new wave—Wayne Toups is the most familiar example—displays a loud, raunchy style, sometimes called "zyde-cajun," that bears only the most tenuous relationship to the backyard sound of D. L.'s band. Robert Jardell, a staunch traditionalist, is outspoken in his criticism of those who would rock the old Cajun sound. As he stands around with the other musicians after the party, he talks of his pride in being able to play with artists like "Mr. D. L." and Christine Balfa, who exemplify the true Cajun tradition.

We do traditional Cajun music. We don't get up there and jump around and do long-haired music, you know. This thing today of "zydecajuns," there's no such thing as zydecajun. Either you play Cajun music or you don't. You can't be both sides of the fence. And I find these two people here are as traditional as you can get, you know.

D. L., though old enough to be Robert's father, has a different view of the matter. He loves the old style, but remembers the days when he was on the cutting edge of a country-Cajun fusion. For him, preserving the culture does not mean blocking out new ideas.

What these new people are trying to do with the music, more or less, is they want to progress it. It's like country and western, progressive country; it's a different beat, and I tell you what: For me, it don't bother me at all. They play the music like they feel. The young people are not going to be the same way as the old people. They got to more or less develop a style of their own because they're young. They haven't been fifty years ago like we have, they're just starting now, and that's why they're playing it that way.

But like Robert said, we're not going to change, because this kind of music is us. I don't have no problem with somebody that want to play differently, but for us, we're going to stay with our same style. Because we're too far gone to change, and we love what we're doing. And it's fun music. I always say, if you can't have fun with the music it's time to hang it up. Because you can't play this kind of music mad.

◆ ◆ ◆

D. L. Menard

4
Zydeco Cowboy: GENO DELAFOSE

Well, down in Louisiana on a Saturday night
Everybody gathers round and they go to town
They do the French rockin' boogie
They do the French rockin' boogie
They do the French rockin' boogie and they rock till broad daylight

It is Friday night at Slim's Y-Ki-Ki, on Highway 10 outside Opelousas. The lights are dim, the music is loud, and the dance floor is crowded. On stage, Geno Delafose is pushing and pulling the bellows of his accordion and singing the rocking lyric. His band is kicking the rhythm like an old-time soul outfit,the rub-board player twisting and shaking as he runs two spoons across the corrugated metal sheet covering his chest. Geno is dressed in a white cowboy shirt and a white hat. His big smile shows his enjoyment as he looks around the room.

I've been playing at Slim's since I started with my dad, John Delafose and the Eunice Playboys, when I was eight years old. That was eighteen years ago, and the club's been here a long time before that. Seen a lot of dances here. Yeah, yeah, yeah. Slim's Y-Ki-Ki.

I started out playing the washboard. The way I got my role in the band is my brother, John Jr., stopped playing, he joined the service, so my dad needed another member and there I was. I started out on the washboard, and then I started playing the drums a little bit. I have my oldest brother that played also, he played the drums, and then, after I started playing the drums real good, about a year later our bass player passed away and then my brother started playing bass and then my regular job was to play the drums. That put us back to four people again, and that's how my little cousin, Jermaine, started playing with us. He started playing the rub-board and we showed him to play the drums, and then whenever I would play accordion he'd play the drums and we just all kind of switched around.

I started playing the accordion at thirteen. Dad would just leave his accordion out and I decided to pick it up one day and when I done that I played a song and I said, "Well, if I can play one song, I can play two," and just kept on and on. It was a small, single-note accordion, a nine-button Cajun diatonic. My dad showed me a couple

Geno Delafose, playing a zydeco dance at Slim's Y-Ki-Ki.

of licks and all kind of things, and it worked out really good. He was very proud, very happy that I learned.

And I was excited. After that, I'd open a lot of shows for him on the road.

Then, once I got older and my daddy got sick and stuff, I used to go out and play the dances for him. I kept the business going, and it's been a lot of fun.

On the bandstand, Geno switches to a little diatonic accordion, the kind the first Cajun players were using at the turn of the century. The band goes into a lighter groove, with the repetitive, Cajun-Creole lilt, and Geno starts to sing an old song of his father's.

Ma 'tite fille est gone
(My little girl is gone)
Ma 'tite fille est gone
(My little girl is gone)
Elle a passé dans la porte
(She has gone out the door)
Dans la porte d'en arrière
(Out the back door)

Bye-bye, jolie
(Bye-bye, pretty)
Bye-bye, jolie
(Bye-bye, pretty)
C'est pas la peine brailler
(There's no use crying)
Ma 'tite fille est gone
(My little girl is gone)

My dad played a pretty traditional style. He done a couple of blues things and stuff like that, but he's pretty much a traditional style and that's where I got my start from, just seeing how he'd read the crowd and the style of music he played, and that's what I adapted to.

I'm a lot more old-fashion than all of the other zydeco bands that's coming out now. I like to do more the old traditional style of music, like some stuff from Bois-Sec Ardoin and Canray Fontenot and older players like that. And I do some older Cajun songs, you know, stuff from Amédé Ardoin and all those guys. You don't see that too much with the new zydeco bands that are coming out. They're a little bit more funky, doing more the Beau Joque groove and the Keith Frank groove and things like that.

These days, people tend to divide Cajun and zydeco music as if black and white French Louisianans came from totally different traditions, but Geno's oldest songs hark back to another era, when the black accordionist Amédé Ardoin and the white fiddler Dennis McGhee were the hottest instrumental duo in rural southern Louisiana. Ardoin had a more syncopated rhythmic style than most of the white players, and a bluesy inflection to his voice, but both were widely imitated and his sound is at the roots of both Cajun and zydeco as it exists today. The later divergences in the styles are at least as much a reflection of differing influences from the outside world as of different roots.

Really, they're cousins. I don't really know what makes a zydeco tune a zydeco tune or a Cajun tune a Cajun tune, because I can take a zydeco song and play it with a Cajun band and it will sound like a Cajun song, or take a Cajun song and play it with a zydeco band and it's basically a zydeco song. Basically, they're the same songs, just the difference is zydeco is a little bit bluesier, kind of funky, and a bit more up-tempo. I guess you could say zydeco is a little bit more like blues and Cajun music is a little bit more like country, because they have the steel guitars in Cajun music and they have the fiddle, whereas in zydeco you've got a lot of bass, a lot of lead guitar solos, and they don't use the fiddle anymore.

You know, the zydeco, a long time ago it was called "la-la" music or "chanka-chank." It's what people played after a long, hard week of work; they'd get together and play. What Clifton [Chenier] done is he played that music, but he jacked it up some. He added a little blues to it and he played the piano accordion so he was more versatile. He really helped commercialize it a whole bunch, and he took it out there, and it was really good.

When I first got started playing with Daddy, French music and zydeco and all that stuff wasn't cool. Young people didn't listen to it. But that's changing now, and, you know, it surprised me. I see a lot of my classmates now, they would laugh at me 'cause I wear cowboy boots and a cowboy hat and everything, and now a couple of them came to the dance a while back and they were wearing cowboy boots and cowboy hats.

Geno laughs. The recent zydeco boom has indeed produced a crop of black drugstore cowboys, folks who pull on boots and hats to go to the dances and impress the girls. Geno was there a long time ago, though, and he was not wearing the clothing just for his stage act. The afternoon after his gig at Slim's, he is back at home outside Eunice, taking care of his horses and cows. The address is on Delafose Road, the place where he was born and raised.

Overleaf: A dancer takes a break.

I've lived here all my life except two years of it. I moved into town with my

Budweiser

AMERICANA II

mom, and then on my twenty-first birthday I moved back here, and I've been here ever since. And I really don't want to go anywhere. The whole family was brought up here. Actually, right before I was born our house used to be right on the side of the big tree right there. Then, when I came along, Dad bought half of the house that I have now and added on, and then the whole family moved in there and that's where we grew up. I've seen some places that would be nice to move to, but there's no place like home—you can't beat it. It's just so down-home over here, and people are pretty laid back, and all my friends are around here.

Geno walks over to his stable, just a few dozen yards from the house. He has six horses now, and starts to brush one down and saddle it as he talks. Through the open door, one can see a field where a few cows graze.

When I'm back home, I have to get right to work, riding the horses and hauling hay and keeping up the lawn. It's kind of my hobby, raising horses and cows. I always wanted to rodeo but just haven't had the time, and it's a little bit too dangerous, you know. Now I can't afford to mess up a finger. I always wished my high school would have had a rodeo team, but they didn't. If they would have, I don't know if I'd be playing music, 'cause I really, really like to ride. But I never did compete or anything, though I did train racehorses for a little while.

Now I just ride pleasure horses. Sometimes the family comes over and we'll get together and ride, but really out of all of us kids I'm the only one that likes to fool around with horses and all that stuff. That's always been in me, always. It's just a hobby—I've got some that used to race, but they don't race anymore and I can't get into the racing field. If I would, I'd want to be there all the time, training my own horses, 'cause I enjoy that. Since I can't train and everything, I just make them some saddlehorses. Get more use out of them like that.

I enjoy the horse business, but I think I'm a lot more successful with my music, because I have a chance to stumble in my music and come back up again. With horses, you fall and you're pretty much out of luck. It's hard, because racehorses take a lot of money to upkeep and everything. If you're not winning, it's hard to get up and down the road. And music has been taking care of me so far, so I think I'm going to stick with that.

But it goes hand in hand: I guess I'm just an old country boy doing some old music. Right now, everything is looking good for me, I've been going to a lot of new places, and I hope to be kind of a guardian of the older, Creole style. 'Cause there's not many bands are doing that, and I don't want people to forget where this music comes from and how it was played a long time ago.

We're losing a lot of that right now with the new bands that's coming out. Here in Louisiana, except for New Orleans, people don't really care for the older style of music too much. They've moved to the hip-hop, funky zydeco, that style is what's really going on. Slowly but surely, the older generation is dying off, and the younger crowd, they don't know anything about the old music and they don't give a damn about it.

For myself, I can get funky and do all that other stuff, and I enjoy that too, but if everybody does that, then the older style is gone. So I want to preserve that old-time French singing and just basic straight dance music. I'm not changing my style to adapt to the people here in Louisiana. Sooner or later they'll get tired of that hip-hop, funky style—not that it's bad, but after a while it gets just a little too repetitious and I think my music has got a bigger variety than what's popular in Louisiana right now.

The youngsters need to get a grip on the old style, 'cause if they don't then when the older musicians are gone the music is going to go with them. For instance, I see a lot of these younger zydeco musicians, they start playing and they do a fine job playing, but they can't speak a word of French. They don't really know what they're saying, they just sing it the way they hear it. But if you're going to do some traditional stuff, you need to know your French, at least enough to know what you're singing about.

We, the young generation, are the glue that keeps the culture going, and if we don't continue playing the music then it's gonna be lost. And I like the older music. It comes from the heart.

It tells true stories. It's not something somebody's just playing a beat to, and just shouting out a word here, shouting a word there that doesn't even make any sense. There are stories behind these songs. And that's why I like this music. It's real.

Geno has finished saddling the horse, and it is getting time for the film crew to knock off, as the light is fading fast. There is only one more shot to get: Geno mounts the horse, guides him out to the dirt road running on beyond the house, and rides off into the sunset.

◆◆◆

ACCORDIONS LARGE & *Small*

Going down the river, along with the variety of music, one comes across a variety of accordions. All have reeds at either end, and force air through those reeds by pushing and pulling a bellows, but other than that they may have little in common. The Swedish players in Minnesota play either two-row diatonic instruments or piano accordions. The Dutchman bands feature a fancy sort of "German-style" concertina. Mexican bands normally use a three-row diatonic, while the Cajuns use the older, one-row instrument.

The instruments differ in size, shape, sound, and versatility. The piano accordion and the Dutchman concertina, though they look completely different, are similar in that both are chromatic—they can play in any key, and get all the "accidental" notes needed to play complex melodies and harmonies. The concertina, however, has buttons rather than piano keys, and each button gives two different notes, one if the player is pushing the bellows together, and the other if the player is pulling. The arrangement of the notes means that playing in some keys is much easier than in others, and many players have more than one concertina to facilitate key changes. (As for the difference between accordions and concertinas, a concertina has buttons set flat on both ends, which are pressed in towards the bellows, while an accordion has at least the right-hand keys or buttons set at an angle to the end of the instrument.)

The Cajun and Mexican accordions, by contrast, are diatonic, which means that they can only get a limited set of notes. The one-row style normally has a single row of ten buttons on the right-hand end, tuned like the holes of a ten-hole harmonica. Each button gives a different note depending on whether one pushes or pulls the bellows, and the Louisiana players can play a one-row in two keys, the "straight" key the instrument was designed for (for examples C) and a bluesier "cross"key (like G). The two- and three-row instruments are simply expansions of the one-row with, for example, G and C or G, C and F rows lying parallel to each other, allowing some key changes and more melodic variation.

When Clifton Chenier popularized the fusion of blues, r&b, and Louisiana French music that came to be known as zydeco, he used the piano accordion rather than the traditional button instruments, and players like Buckwheat Zydeco and Rockin' Sidney followed his lead, but the instrument has since tended to fall out of favor. Geno Delafose is the only major player in Louisiana who regularly uses both button and piano accordions.

I use three different types, because certain songs sound better on certain accordions. The small, single-note accordion and the triple-note accordion basically are the same, diatonic, but with the single-note you get more of the old-style, "chanka-chank" sound. With the triple note you can get a little bit bluesier. There's certain licks you can play, and it just totally sounds different.

And you can play in different keys, whatever fits your voice—certain songs sound better in certain keys. You can still play Cajun songs on a triple-note, but they sound different. It's like driving a Cadillac and a Pinto, you know. You can do so much in the Pinto, it'll get you where you need to go, but it won't give you the luxury of a Cadillac. They're both cars, regardless, but they're different.

Then with the piano accordion you can get a lot bluesier, and you can really do anything, but you can't get a "chanka-chank" sound out of it, because it's chromatic. The piano accordion is not used very much anymore in Louisiana, people don't care too much for it, but once you go out on the road people enjoy it.

Some of the older generation like it, too; they remember Clifton and they know what it's all about. But the new, younger generation, all the music is played on the small diatonic accordion.

On a piano you can play a lot of minor chords and sevenths and stuff like that, and you can play in any key, 'cause it's just like a piano. If you want to blues it up a little bit, you know, cross your keys and stuff like that, you can play some minor chords on the triple-note, but only in certain keys—depending on what key triple-note you have—so that's the main reason you would play the piano.

But I have fun with all of them, and I use them to get across different things to different people. I just kind of read the crowd, notice what they like and what they want, and then I choose what I want to play.

Geno with two sizes and styles of accordion: (above) one-row diatonic; (left) piano.

Baby

LOUISIANA

David and Roselyn, belting it out on Royal St. Roselyn plays the kalimba, or African thumb piano. Preceding pages: Trombone Shorty's brass band plays for tips in Jackson Square.

5
The Streets of the French Quarter: DAVID AND ROSELYN

The sun is shining, hot and bright, and the streets of the French Quarter are full of tourists. Around Jackson Square, the portrait artists and caricaturists are soliciting the custom of the passing throng, competing with tarot card and palm readers. A lone trumpeter is playing outside the Café du Monde, hoping that some of the coffee drinkers will toss him tips. Across the street, two kids are tapdancing on the sidewalk, a sheet of cardboard in front of them for whatever coins may come their way. On the square itself, a full brass band is playing, Trombone Shorty and his collection of embryonic jazz horn players, none of them out of their teens. Off to one side, trying to make himself heard over the other noise, is Peter Bennett, a tall, white-bearded gentleman playing a table full of tuned musical glasses.

Walking up into the heart of the Quarter, passersby are accosted by a teenage shoe-shine hustler. "You want a shine?" The tourists shake their heads and try to walk on. "Hey, I bet I can tell you where you got them shoes," the teenager yells. A tourist pauses, puzzled. "I bet I can tell you where you got your shoes," the teenager repeats. "If I'm wrong, I'll pay you ten dollars; if I'm right, you pay me ten dollars and I'll give you a first-rate shine in the bargain." The tourist can't resist. "OK, where did I get them?" "I'll tell you where you got them. You got them on your feet, on Bourbon Street, New Orleans, Louisiana, USA."

On Royal Street, which is shut off to automobile traffic during the day, there is a skiffle band playing, a slide guitarist and singer accompanied by harmonica, washboard, and washtub bass. The next block has a classical duo, violin and cello, earning appreciative nods from older passersby. Then a wild scream cuts through the normal street sounds. From a block away, one can hear Roselyn Lionhart's voice, soaring through the air and bouncing off the buildings. She is singing about Marie Laveau, the legendary voodoo queen of New Orleans.

She lives in a swamp in a hollow log
With a one-eyed snake and a three-legged dog

She got a bent, boney body and long, stringy hair,
And if she ever see y'all messing round there
She'd go eeeee-yeeeeah! Another man done gone

Roselyn throws back her head and howls, then frowns ominously. As she sings, she thumps out a bass rhythm line on a Caribbean rumba box, a variant of the ancient African mbira, or thumb piano, consisting of a wooden box with tuned metal tongues that she plucks with both hands. A striking, dark black woman, with long, beaded braids, Roselyn is an arresting presence, and the tourists stop and stare, fascinated. Next to her is her husband, David Leonard, a tall man with a tall hat, long white hair and a beard and mustache, looking like a cross between a gentle Wild Bill Hickock and an anarchist Uncle Sam. His guitar fills in the holes under Roselyn's vocals, and he smiles every time she cuts loose with another one of those screams.

Roselyn finishes the song and laughs a big laugh. Then she picks up a mandolin, and David leads off a blues song, singing and playing expert harmonica. The concert will last all afternoon, and maybe into the evening if it is the end of the month and bills are coming due. For over twenty years, David and Roselyn have been fixtures of the French Quarter, playing a quirky mix of blues, folk, pop, r&b, and jazz numbers.

In the winter, it's cold; in the summer, it's hot. And the cops bother us. It's a drag. But other than that, it's a lot of fun out here.

Roselyn puts on her best complaining face, then collapses laughing.

David: *Ahh, it's a lot of fun. It's very rewarding. And we get to work in a smokeless environment, which is better for the vocal chords.*

Roselyn: *Unless somebody happens to be standing upwind with a big cigar.*

David: *That has happened. And we get to play for little kids who come up and look at us with wonder in their eyes.*

Roselyn: *And dance.*

David: *And dance. Can hardly stand, and they're dancing. That's fun. And old people will come up who like it too.*

Roselyn: *We're probably one of the best all-round family entertainments in New Orleans, and it's free. Like, half a dozen members of the family can throw us one dollar and they feel real good about it, too. If they had to take everybody in someplace to hear music, it will cost them a minimum of five dollars apiece, you know, so I like it better if they throw us a five, especially if there's six of them standing around. But hey, we take what we can get.*

She laughs again. David is trying to be diplomatic and give a good interview, but Roselyn is irrepressible, offstage as well as on. She is bawdy, funny, cranky, and confrontational.

I find that people like me to talk to them. They're interested in knowing what's happening with us. Our biggest crowd yesterday was when I got mad at David and I just started singing, "I'm gonna hit you on the head with my mandolin, because I'm mad at you and all you do is sit there and grin." You know, he was doodling around. I don't even remember what I was mad at him about! But I just started singing like that, and I wound up writing this new song, and the audience loved it. We just kept getting bigger and bigger crowds because, you know, I was seen as sort of so mad; like I was really going to hit him in the head with my mandolin. Of course, there's no way I'm going to hit him with my mandolin. My shoe, maybe. My mandolin, no.

David and Roselyn first met in San Antonio in 1959. Both were with Air Force bands, David playing trumpet and Roselyn singing, and they met in rehearsals for a cross-country talent show. They have a wonderful wedding picture, Roselyn in a lovely, fluffy white gown and David in his dress uniform with a neat little Ronald Colman mustache. They have been coming to New Orleans regularly since 1975, and for years alternated the warm months here with winters playing a pitch on the boardwalk in Venice, California, before moving here full-time a few years ago.

David: *Music brought us here. My parents are Connecticut Yankees, and I was born in Virginia and raised in southern California. Roselyn's family comes from Georgia and northern Louisiana, and we came down here originally in 1963, on a voter registration project with the Congress of Racial Equality.*

Roselyn: *But we didn't get to see much of New Orleans.*

David: *No. Came here once for r&r and went back out in the field, and came down—*

Roselyn: *We were up in New Roads and Hammond, registering voters and hearing the blues and having a good time, and dodging the cops. Then we sort of avoided the South for a few years, because we were illegal down here until* Love v. State of Virginia *in 1969, but after that we figured, well, we can go back down South. So in seventy-five we came back to New Orleans and we started coming back and forth from California, and then we began to spend more and more time here. We had Autumn and Stormy, the two youngest kids, in school out in California, and they were getting racist stuff thrown at them, and I felt that if they were going to have to deal with that, they should learn how to deal with it down here where there were a lot of other interracial kids and they could see how it worked.*

Roselyn hits a final note on the Caribbean rumba box.

We always loved it down here, because New Orleans is the heart and soul of music, as far as we're concerned. It has all kinds of music: You have the Indian rhythms and the African rhythms; you have the French folk music and the Appalachian folk music; you have the Creole classical string ensembles and the German marching bands. And you have jazz, which is sort of a combination of all those things, and blues, and spirituals, and it's just like everything bubbles up—like the swamps just keep giving more life to the music.

I still say that jazz was invented by the mockingbirds. If you've ever listened to a mockingbird, the variations on a theme, you know that's where jazz came from.

Today, the kids are almost grown up—Stormy, the youngest, is about to graduate high school—and David and Roselyn have a nice house downriver from the Quarter, but for years they lived out of an old van parked in a lot across Rampart Street and brought the kids out with them on their street pitches.

David: *Actually, see, we had the kids when we were playing clubs. So we'd get a baby-sitter, go play the club, come home from the club at three in the morning, take the baby-sitter home, and the kids woke up at six or seven in the morning, and you can't get a baby-sitter then. So we played the streets, and we'd take the kids out with us. We used to bring our little girl out here when she was a baby, and we'd play until she turned blue, then we'd go inside and warm up and we'd come back out again. She survived. She's at Yale now, so she's okay.*

Now David and Roselyn are both laughing.

David: *But, yeah, we've done good. We raised the kids, and we have a house, and we make enough money to do that. But we work hard. Some people just come out and do this so they can buy some pizza and beer and they're happy. No, we can't do that. We have aims, goals, desires, needs, wants. We're very middle class.*

He laughs, but Roselyn is not letting him get away with that remark, joke or not.

Roselyn: *David's very middle class. I'm upper class.*

David: *Ai yi yi!*

Roselyn: *My consciousness is that in the first place I find nine-to-five boring, and I resented being a secretary, in that I did all the work and my boss got all the money. And I never, ever had a boss that I thought was as smart as I was. I've done all sorts of jobs. I've worked as a legal secretary, I worked as a waitress, I've driven taxis, edited newspapers. Whatever came my way, I managed to do and had a great time doing it. For a while. But anytime anything interesting came up with music, it was, "Excuse me, I need to take a vacation from this." I find that if I do a boring job for any length of time, I start getting bored and depressed and unhappy, and I will sit at my desk or at my computer and I'm writing poetry, or I'm writing a treatise on what's wrong with this job, or else I'm organizing the secretaries into a union. I did all of that.*

On the streets, even, I've gotten involved in organizing the street performers to fight the city council, to stop them from coming up with dumb rules and regulations like, "No music can be heard further than fifty feet." You know, like this conversation, and I'm talking in a conversational tone, you can hear me further than fifty feet. So if I'm clearly audible in fifty feet, I'm in violation of this law. So come on, give us a break.

The street performers here have to keep working to keep the streets free, because freedom is always being squeezed by those interests [businesses, city officials, yuppies] that are more concerned about propriety or quiet than they are about letting the streets happen, you know? I mean, imagine people who move a half a block off Bourbon Street and then complain about the noise. Or people who move into the apartments on either side of Jackson Square and complain about the brass bands. The brass bands have been there since before the apartment buildings were! So where do they get off at that? But you know, we don't worry about that to much. We just make the music, have fun.

A crowd of tourists are passing, and David and Roselyn have to stop chatting and make some more money. With a thump of the rhumba box, they are into the old LaBelle hit, "Lady Marmalade."

Hey sister, go sister, soul sister, go sister
I met Marmalade down in old New Orleans
Struttin' her stuff on the street
She says, "Hey, hello Joe, you want to give it a go?"
Getcha, getcha ya-ya, ya ya ya ya
Getcha, getcha ya-ya-yeah!
Mocha chocolata ya-ya
Creole Lady Marmalade
"Voulez-vous coucher avec moi, ce soir?
Voulez-vous coucher avec moi?"

David and Roselyn, shout, croon and growl, teasing every nuance of raw, exuberant sexuality out of the lyric. David sails into a harmonica break. A passing drunk, caught up in the spirit of the moment, starts an impromptu dance. A couple of the tourists look nervous, but most smile, tapping their feet and soaking up the spirit of the New Orleans streets. It is a scene that could hardly happen anywhere else, at least not at this level of wild fun. Though, if you suggest to Roselyn that they are wild at all, she suddenly will get demure.

I don't think you can characterize us as wild. I think that we're exciting and interesting and a lot of fun, but wild?

She seems maybe half serious, but in seconds both she and David are laughing. OK, maybe if this wasn't New Orleans they might seem a little wild.

Roselyn: *This is not really an American town. It's a Caribbean town, so it's much more African and Indian than it is American. Thank God.*

David: *And you know, what's wild varies with who's in town. If we're playing for a bunch of young gynecologists, we can have a lot of fun. But if the convention that's in town is the hardware store owners of the Midwest, then we're really different.*

Roselyn: *We reflect our audience a lot. If we've got people out there who are partying and having a good time, then it gets, you know, partying and having a good time. If we have people out there going, "What's that?" then we sort of get a little less exuberant.*

David: *And we switch back and forth. Like we might do a "My Baby Rocks Me with a Steady Roll," and then the next song might be "Just a Closer Walk with Thee."*

Roselyn: **Gambit** *magazine called us "a one-band jazz festival," which I think is a great way to name us because we do folk, we do gospel, we do blues, we do jazz, we do African rhythms. We throw in all the kinds of things that we like, that are part of* *our soul. We do a little bit of country, a little bit of this, a little bit of that. Put it all together and have a good time.*

David: *It can get a little hard sometimes. There's so many people wanting to play the streets now, we've got to come out at six in the morning sometimes to secure our spot. So we end up being out here for eleven or twelve hours, during which time we might get to play for six or seven of those hours. So that cuts into the fun of it all. But I stay and sit in the car and break in harmonicas or read a book or do a crossword or something to pass the time. But that's another thing about working the streets: if you don't feel like going out and you don't go out, the only penalty you get is you don't make any money for that day, you know.*

Roselyn: *You can't get fired. You can always go back out tomorrow. Of course, you don't get paid sick leave or paid holidays or any of that stuff. So there are penalties, too. How you feel about it depends on the day. Some days you feel like you're invisible. Other days you can't do a song without having a crowd. And you just never know what's going to happen. I mean, a week ago Sunday, we had a crowd all day long. Today we had, what, one crowd? What can I say? You can't tell. It depends on who's in town and whether or not they like your kind of music as opposed to the music a block away. It's like anything else, you just put in the time and you get the rewards. If you don't put in the time, nothing's going to happen. But we get to control our own lives. Stormy, our youngest, graduates in June, and then maybe we'll rent out our house and head to Southeast Asia or something. Who knows?*

As always, there is more laughter. Then, as we head off, David and Roselyn break into a final song, a classic from Fats Domino. Roselyn's mandolin tinkles out the melody and her foot keeps time on a tambourine, while David's guitar strums solid rhythm and their voices blend in comfortable harmony.

I'm walking to New Orleans
I'm walking to New Orleans
I'm gonna need two pair of shoes, when I get through walking these blues
I'm walking to New Orleans

I've got no time for talking
I've got to keep on walking
New Orleans is my home, and that's the reason I'm goin'
I'm walking to New Orleans

◆◆◆

6
The Soul Queen of New Orleans: IRMA THOMAS

I got fired for singing on the job twice. The first time, I was a dishwasher at a place called the Cooper Kitchen, at fifty cents an hour. I was keeping myself company on the seven—eleven shift, and my boss didn't like the music, so he said if I did it again he would fire me. I thought he was out of earshot, and I started singing again and he came in and he fired me.

The next time I got fired, I was a waitress at a club that's not too far from where I am now, on Broad Street, called the Pimlico Club. I was supposed to be waiting tables, and I decided to sit in with the band and sing, and people started asking for the singing waitress, and my boss didn't like that either. So he said the next time I got onstage to sing when I was supposed to be waiting tables, he would fire me. Well, I thought he wasn't there one night and I got onstage and I was singing, and in the middle of one song he walked in and fired me.

So I guess I was destined to be in this business.

Irma Thomas throws back her head and laughs. She is sitting at the bar in the Lion's Den, a club that she owns with her husband on a quiet side street a few blocks from the French Quarter. As always, at least when in public, she looks immaculate, every hair in place, and it is hard to believe that she had her first hit almost forty years ago, in 1959. "Don't Mess With My Man," on the local Ron record label, served notice that there was a tough new voice in town.

As the evening wears on, fans begin to fill the Lion's Den's back room, and at nine o'clock Irma takes the stage, fronting her crack soul band. She starts with "Proud Mary," but soon is into her own hits, and the hometown crowd greets each with enthusiastic applause. Irma brings the pace down for a couple of recent ballads, then kicks into high gear. The band lays down a funky, New Orleans beat, her eyes flash, and the years drop away as she sings with a fierce humor that no singer has ever bettered.

You can have my husband, but please don't mess with my man
You can have my husband, but please don't mess with my man
I'm telling all you women, I want you all to understand
The money my husband made was for red beans and rice

Irma Thomas, queen of the Lion's Den

My man keeps me in steaks, now ain't that nice?
You can have my husband, but please don't mess with my man
You can have my husband, but please don't mess with my man
I'm telling all you women, want you all to understand

In 1959, Irma's record was considered shocking, especially considering that the singer was only seventeen years old.

That's a very bold statement. In fact, it was so bold at the time I recorded it that they snatched it off a lot of the stations; they would not play it. So it became an underground record—everybody had to have it because you couldn't get it on the radio. So that helped to promote that song. And I kind of knew what I was talking about, even though I was only seventeen. Oh, yeah. I had been married for quite a few years at the time I was seventeen. I had three kids, so I wasn't actually a prude, you know. I had to grow up quick, fast, and in a hurry. And I did. And I had a lot of experiences that I wouldn't wish on anybody, but by the same token I've grown from that—you live what you live and experience what you experience, and hopefully you learn from it.

The way that song happened was that, after I got fired from singing, Tommy Ridgely, who had the band at the club, he brought me to audition. Actually, I didn't go the first time he told me to go, because I thought he was, you know, one of these guys that's giving you a line of bull. So he literally came to my house, got me, and took me to the company to audition for them, and while I was there, Dorothy Labostrie, who had written some hits for other people, she had this song and she sung it for me. I think it was either Tommy or Eddie Bo, one of those, played the piano and taught me the song, and I went into the studio that week and the next couple weeks I had a record out.

It worked in my favor that at that time, in the late fifties, New Orleans was an explosive city when it came to recording; they had several record companies stationed here. Although I had auditioned for several of them, and they all turned me down. Their bad luck.

When I recorded "Don't Mess with My Man," it really took off, though I didn't know it was as big as it was until some years later. If I'd known, I would have learned to ask for more money. Anyway, then I switched over to the Minit label and recorded "It's Raining," and "Ruler of My Heart." Allen Toussaint was the producer and, believe it or not, he used to tailor-make songs for all the artists he produced—he literally wrote those songs for me. He'd teach them to us before we went into the studio, because we used to do split sessions. I might go in the studio and do "It's Raining" and "Ruler of My Heart" and one other song, and then some other artist might be in on that same three-hour recording session and do another three songs.

Allen would play piano, and we would rehearse a lot in his living room before we'd get to the studio, so the only persons who had to rehearse in the studio were the musicians. He had everything written out, so all they had to do was go over it and find out how he wanted it structured, and go for it. There were no overdubs in those days.

Those records really caught on—in fact, locally they kind of exploded. "It's Raining" stayed on the local charts for, like, not a few weeks, but months, and it's still my most popularly requested song. Then I started playing around some of the schools, and sometimes it was like they weren't quite ready for Irma, but it worked out. I used to travel a lot, doing college towns. For instance, the University of Alabama had twenty-seven fraternities; I played twenty-six of them. That was during the era when you had the Hot Nuts and Tina Turner and all these people on campus for "rush week," you know.

During that time, I didn't do a lot of work really in New Orleans. When I started in the business, black entertainers had to travel. We were on the chitlin' circuit, driving from gig to gig, because we were not allowed to travel these other ways, unless you were going to be miserable in the back of the bus. So you either carried your own equipment in your car or you had your own bus or your own station wagon. You'd get to the job, and most of the time we would show up at these places and we couldn't even refresh ourselves, we'd have to, like, put on our show clothes, go on, and just pray nobody got too close to us when we were out there.

But I was having the time of my life, and I didn't find it a drudgery. Here I am, this young parent, making more money than she's ever made in her life, even though she may spend ten or twelve hours on the highway doing it. But it's better than punching somebody's clock, and I knew I could pay my bills when I got back home. So what was there to complain about? I was having a ball!

I mean here I am, a kid, dropped out of school young, never had any great education in terms of going to school, learning about a lot of the places that I traveled to. And then, in later years—no one could have told me that one day I would be going to England, or to Japan, or to Italy, or to France. These are things you just don't fathom when you're that young, especially when I was coming up, and especially being a black child. No. To go and have these experiences, and be able to tell my kids about them from an experienced point of view and not from some picture. I mean, God, I'm blessed. What am I going to complain about? I didn't make a whole lot of money, but I had fun, you know. And these are experiences you just can't talk to someone and make them understand what you're saying and where you're coming from.

Irma remains consistently upbeat, but when she sings it is easy to hear the years of experience that have gone into her music. She is one of the great soul vocalists, and her biggest hits were aching ballads that have little of the bright, good-time sound that people often associate with New Orleans r&b. Her biggest hit, in fact, was recorded out in Los Angeles, and she remembers that the only Louisiana player on the session was the drummer, Earl Palmer.

Hurricane Camille kind of gave me a little nudge. It wiped out a lot of the work I had along the coastal area of Mississippi, there wasn't a lot of work anywhere until maybe a year or so later when people recovered. So I just took that opportunity to move; I thought I'd seek my adventurous career someplace else.

The move was propitious. Her first West Coast recording, "Wish Someone Would Care," cracked the pop Top 40 in 1964. Unlike her other hits, it was written by Irma herself, out of the pain she was feeling at the breakup of her first marriage. Today, it remains a centerpiece of her stage show, and the audience nods in recognition and shouts encouragement as she goes into the first line.

Sitting home alone, thinking about my past
Wondering how I made it, and how long it's gonna last
Successes count a lot for them, and failure's always there
Time, time waits for no one
And I wish, how I wish someone would care

Some folks think you're happy, when you wear your smile
What about your tribulations and all, all of your trials?
Smiles, smiles hide lots of things:
The good, the bad, the hurt, all of this goes too
And I wish, I wish, how I wish someone would care

I've had my nights when I've had total recall about some incidents, and it comes out in my songs. I've worked with the guys that I work with so long that they can almost tell when I'm going to have one of those nights, depending on the selection of songs I choose and how I sing them that night. It has a little edge on them that they can tell, "Oh, well, it's one of those nights, fellas." And I'm sure it's obvious to my audience, because I'm not good at hiding my feelings. So when I'm a little peeved, it comes across that way; something may get sung with a little bit more gusto than it got sung the night before. It all comes out.

◆

Irma rode the soul wave, but without ever getting a record label that could provide consistent support. The records themselves were strong, from "Ruler of My Heart," which gave Otis Redding his first national hit when he remade it as "Pain in My Heart," to "Time Is on My Side," covered by the Rolling Stones ("That was what they called the 'British Invasion,' and I got invaded," Irma says wrily), but the companies could never follow up and keep Irma's name in front of the public. After a fling with Chicago's Chess label, she ended up living in Los Angeles, working a day job.

I was a car-parts salesperson at Montgomery Ward's—which made me appreciate being a singer more. But, you know, I had fun doing that, too. At that time, when men would walk into the department, here's a lady gonna sell them a spark plug? No, not today. The fun part was that I was the department manager; they would go to this other guy, who would come back and say, "Irma..." and I would say, "No, he doesn't want me to wait on him, you find him what he wants." That was the fun part.

Other parts were less fun, but by 1974 Irma was back in New Orleans and on the way to building a new career. The annual Jazz and Heritage Festival, which would grow into the biggest regularly held music festival in the United States, focused new attention on the city's musical heritage, not only the classic jazz players but also the great r&b artists of the fifties and sixties. Of all these singers, Irma was the strongest, most consistent live performer, and she soon was working regularly around town and beginning to tour out as well. In 1975, she married Emile Jackson, and he helped her form a permanent band and took over management of her business affairs. Eventually, they opened the Lion's Den to handle the overflow of fans who came to see her during Jazzfest, though Irma is as likely to be found singing in Boston or Italy as in the small New Orleans bar.

I play in Japan and England; I played Perretta, Italy, this past July, and I was surprised at how many people had been to New Orleans, to the jazz festival. They knew a hell of a lot about Irma that I didn't expect. I mean, they speak Italian—you'll say something in English and they'll tell you they don't speak English—but you get on that stage and sing all these songs and they know every last one of them. I was totally in awe of that.

I think that a lot of my longevity in this business I would attribute to the fact that I always tried to please my audience, and so they kept wanting me to come back. I enjoy what I do, I enjoy singing. It's not difficult. I don't have to have a shot or a drink to go onstage. The adrenaline comes from just seeing an audience who want to hear what I'm going to do. And when you enjoy what you do, it's not hard to keep the freshness in a song.

I'm not your typical entertainer, I don't believe. I do things that most entertainers wouldn't dare do, in terms of rapport with an audience. If I don't remember the words to a song, I will literally stand there and read the words. I don't know of very many entertainers with that kind of guts, to do that, because they want to give this impression that they remember all this stuff, and they'll hide their pages on the floor or stick them on the back of an amp. I don't go that route. I just say, "Look, I don't remember this, let me read it for you," and then read it. And I think that, by having that kind of rapport with my audience and not feeding them a line of crap, I've maintained some stability in this business, because they know what they see is what they're going to get, you know. I don't try to hide anything from them.

I'm still working regularly and making records. Especially after I got the Grammy nomination, I was sent a lot of good material. But the fact is that I have not been getting any Top 40 hits in the last thirty-some years. I've recorded some very good music, but, whatever the market is demanding, it's just not quite what they're after. You know, I'm no longer eighteen years old. Every now and then there comes a song that should appeal to any age group, but, by the same token, eighteen-year-olds and younger are looking for the scantily clad females on videos, and my scantily clad days are long since gone. Not that I couldn't get the body in shape and do it, but I don't want to. I would rather do what I do best, and that's sing good ballads and good r&b music. And I do enough popular music of today mixed in with my own music that I keep a pretty well-balanced audience.

I'm enjoying myself, and I don't have any plans to retire. There's too much I still want to do. I'd like to go to Brazil, I'd like to go to Australia; even though it's a long flight, I still would like to go, and I'm scared to death of flying, but I fly. You know? These are experiences that are, to some people, just dreamed of—they have no way of going to these places. I have that opportunity. I don't have to pay for it, somebody else is paying for it; so why not, you know, why not?

As long as I'm physically able and still having fun, I'm going to keep singing. I may have to slow down, because age tends to do that to you, but not yet. Why should I? I'm having too much fun. I have to be the kid that I didn't have a chance to be when I was having kids. Now I'm that kid. Does that make sense to you?

I'm an optimist—what else is there in life? I can take a bad situation and turn it into something good. Because it's experience; if I don't find out about it, how would I know? Okay? I mean, there are nights when I'm not as up as I'd like to be, because physically I'm tired. But once I hit that stage, for some reason the tiredness I felt getting to the job seems to disappear—of course, when I stop, it says, "I'm back."

Irma laughs again. She has seen a lot of ups and downs, but her face is unwrinkled, her eyes shine, and it is easy to believe her when she says that she has faced them all with humor and optimism. Indeed, were it not for the fact that too many fans think it is a Rolling Stones number, she might adopt her 1965 hit as a theme song.

For a long time I wouldn't sing that at all. It wasn't until Bonnie Raitt and I did a New Year's Eve show together, when she enticed me—that's the song she wanted to do with me, and she said that we should take it as our torch song, because time has been on our side. So I put it back into my repertoire and some nights, if I get around to it, I'll do it.

Tonight it is a special request, and she fits it in near the end of the set. The older audience members act as if they were hearing it for the first time: They nod, clap, and shout encouragement as Irma struts and growls her classic challenge.

Ti-iime is on my side, yes it is
Time is on my side, yes it is
You're searching for good times, but just wait and see
One of these days, baby,
You'll come running back to me
'Cause time, time, time, is on my side...

After the performance, Irma is back behind the bar, making sure the place is in shape for the next day's business. Friends come over to say hello, and she greets them with the same open enthusiasm she shows onstage. She laughs and commiserates with the older fans, moaning about how exhausted she is and joking about getting into her comfortable shoes. Maybe it is all part of the job, but the warmth feels real, and it is obvious why these people, some of whom have been following her career for four decades, keep coming back. As a band member points out, she has never stopped being an "everyday person," someone the hometown folks can relate to as an old family friend.

Of course, she is also a professional, and as she dismisses the film crew she grimaces in a theatrical display of relief.

I don't watch soap operas, because it's a joke. Nobody walks around in Armani suits all day long, and Versace dresses, going through this period in their life. Oh, please. Please! No, the minute that camera's off, I'll get off the makeup, take off the hair, and have fun being Irma.

◆ ◆ ◆

7
New Orleans Keyboard Wizard: HENRY BUTLER

Henry Butler is improvising variations on "Basin Street Blues," sitting at a grand piano in the second-floor cabaret of Funky Butt hall. He starts off simply, his left hand thumping out stride accompaniment while his right plays the familiar melody. As chorus builds on chorus, he becomes more experimental, using the song as a skeleton for a whole new creation. His right hand dances across the keys, tracing a lightning filigree of notes somewhat reminiscent of the master of New Orleans baroque, James Booker, but with a unique rhythmic approach, a cascade of surprising syncopations, startling stutters, and bangs. His performance melds the old-time jazz sound with classical, soul, and funk, all processed through his own sensibility. As he plays, Henry seems completely caught up in the music, as if listening in fascination to his imagination working. Then, with a final flood of notes, he swings to a gentle stop, turns toward the camera and smiles.

I learned "Basin Street Blues" in the mid seventies, when I realized that I was going to take this gig that was catering to tourists, mostly. It was a fun gig, actually, and "Basin Street" is one of the classics here in New Orleans, and most pianists play it in the stride style, which I do too. But that gig was when I first started taking a tune like that and just playing the hell out of it, really playing it like I wanted it to be played, as opposed to playing it just as a cocktail pianist or as background music.

Musicians who have an innate sense of harmony, and an innate sense of rhythm, as well as maybe a little bit of study, you can sort of merge anything and make it work musically. Once you have good fundamentals, you can start writing your own book, and I think that's kind of the important thing. I'm often compared to other players like James Booker—or Art Tatum or Phineas Newborn on the jazz side of the fence—and I don't know about that, frankly. I've listened to all of them and I like them for who they were, but I also like Henry Butler for who he is. I think Henry Butler has something unique to offer, just like all those others. When I listen to people like Bach, or like Booker, or like Thelonius Monk, they really didn't abide by anybody's rules but their own. We try to teach what they did in schools, but we also should be teaching how people can develop their own sense of creativity and express that, using the influences of Bach or Monk or James Booker—or Henry Butler, for that matter.

Henry Butler, onstage in Armstrong Park

Henry, who looks to be in his early forties but gives his age variously as twenty-one or somewhere over seventy, is the reigning prince in a royal line of New Orleans keyboard players that reaches back at least to Jelly Roll Morton. Like Morton in his day, he refuses to be typed, ranging with equal ease through jazz, r&b, or funk and on into the classical repertory.

I was born here in New Orleans, but I went to school up in Baton Rouge, Louisiana, at the Louisiana State School for the Blind, for all of my precollege years. I started playing music there when I was in third grade. I was actually volunteered to take piano lessons—it's sort of like the army: When you were volunteered there, it meant that you were drafted.

I evidently had a loud voice, and I made the mistake of singing over everybody else, so that meant that I had to start taking piano lessons. But I got to the point where I really kind of liked it. I started taking drum lessons the next year in addition, and about three years later I started taking lessons on lower brass instruments, mainly baritone horn and valve trombone. I got to the point on drums where I had learned all the basic rudiments and I was the reserve snare drummer in the school concert band. Then, in college, I actually minored in piano and majored in voice. Got my degrees in voice, the first one from Southern University in Baton Rouge and the next one from Michigan State. I've also studied with voice teachers in other places, including Franco Correlli and some of those well-known classical types.

The classical background fits well with Henry's rather professorial demeanor as he sits at the piano, talking about his life and music, but is likely to surprise anyone who has only seen him on stage. Yesterday, he was across the street from the Funky Butt, playing an outdoor concert in Armstrong Park (hallowed by tradition as the site of Congo Square, where slave dances were held in antebellum times), pounding out a funk beat and wailing the lyric of Professor Longhair's "Tipitina," the quirkiest, wildest hit from the all-time defining genius of New Orleans r&b piano, and letting loose with a wailing, utterly uninhibited yodel that would have done credit to 'Fess himself. Henry is well aware of the apparent contradiction between his formal training and the informal, rocking street sound he has since mastered.

Oh yeah. Well, I always had a good ear and when I first started—this is a thousand years ago—I remember picking out the melodies for pop tunes that were being played all the time on the radio. And I never lost that. Even when the teachers discouraged me from using my ears, I just sort of went underground with it. I remember sitting in the practice rooms at the School for the Blind, and every time I smelt this perfume of my piano teacher I would run out, because I knew she was coming to get me because I was playing the beginnings of rock 'n' roll and blues in the practice rooms when I should have been playing music by Haydn or something like that, whatever I was supposed to be working on.

Later on, as they realized they weren't going to stop me, the teachers started to give me arranging projects so that I could hone my skills. My first official arranging project was when I was in the sixth grade and I had to arrange two pieces for two trombones and myself at the piano. Then I was given the school band as a project to arrange for dances, and it just went on and on until I was sort of drafted to be in my teacher's pop band when I was in the eleventh grade.

From then on, I always had sort of a dual musical life: I was preparing things as a classical musician in voice and I was preparing other things as a pianist to make money. And frankly, I really enjoyed having both roles. I met totally different people working in both sectors of that musical circle. More intellectual types when I was doing classical things, and more real, down-to-earth types as I was doing other things.

Since I was in Baton Rouge, I wasn't really hanging out that much with the New Orleans musicians, but I did know them, I was visiting, and I sort of studied through the recorded medium. I also knew of the various Indian tribes, and I was sort of intrigued with that. Unconsciously, I was kind of studying all of that stuff: Mardi Gras and the whole concept surrounding Mardi Gras was kind of important to me, because every time I was home around that time of year I'd go out to the parades and hang out. So I got a chance to hear the Wild Magnolias and all the different Indian groups up close.

For a lot of New Orleans music, I sort of came in the back door; I came to it first intellectually, and then became a participant. But it's definitely a part of my heritage, and it's a part of a lot of what I do right now. The roots part of my presentation features that kind of thing, Professor Longhair and many of the composers of New Orleans.

But even if I'm playing under the banner of, say, jazz, or playing under the banner of blues, or r&b, or New Orleans r&b, I take every chance I get to merge some other elements into it. In my opinion, all of music is one infinite circle, and each idiom or each ethnicity produces only parts of that circle. I always feel that I'm the sum total of all of my experiences. I didn't realize that everything had such a different label until I moved to Los Angeles in 1980 and I found that the pop musicians were over here in one place and jazz musicians were somewhere over there and country musicians were somewhere else and the rock 'n' roll musicians might have been somewhere else again.

It really took me a while to adjust to that, and I think that happens to a lot of Louisiana musicians who leave Louisiana and go to the big metropolitan areas.

I certainly understand why the labeling happens—I mean, they've got to have a way to package those things, and so, I guess in a narrow way it makes sense. But as much as I love blues or r&b or jazz, or some of these other labels, I love other styles just as much. I love Appalachian music; I have a pretty comprehensive collection of Bill Monroe that I use and study just as much as I study some of the stuff from the Stax years. You know, I just take whatever I can use, for my own gratification. And yes, I think I

Listeners relax in the heat of the afternoon.

probably could have been a little better known had I not chosen to be so eclectic, but in my opinion, musically, that's a great problem to have. And I think, in the years to come, people will come to appreciate that about me.

Butler's versatility is certainly one of the most striking things about him. Onstage at Armstrong Park, he started off on acoustic piano, playing old standards like "Margie," then switched to electric keyboard and brought out a rhythm section to deliver his own funky "Dixie Walker," segueing into a Longhair tribute. Then he introduced Eddie Bo, one of the great New Orleans r&b singers, to sing and play piano on a couple of numbers, before taking the show out with a jazz-funk version of "When the Saints Go Marching In" that reworked the standard to the point that, except for the words, it was completely unrecognizable.

Today, he is giving a history of New Orleans piano. He starts out with a general discussion of Caribbean music, and how the mambo beat was adapted by New Orleans players, from Longhair to the Hawketts (a high school combo led by Art Neville, later of the Meters and Neville Brothers).

I'm getting off track a little bit, but the good thing about music, generally speaking, and rhythm and texture and melody and the different aspects of music, specifically, is if you shift or change any one thing, especially rhythmically, you're automatically in a different culture. So New Orleans has benefited by shifting, just a tiny bit, some of those Caribbean rhythms, and that's why right now people associate certain rhythms with only New Orleans.

Moving toward blues, he traces Longhair's sound back to the barrelhouse pianist Champion Jack Dupree, then gets onto Ray Charles, Little Richard, and their New Orleans connections. Then he is onto the classical influence, citing players as diverse as James Booker, Scott Joplin, and Jelly Roll Morton, and explaining how each adapted European harmonies and melodic approaches to his own music. Every point is illustrated with a demonstration on the piano, a section of the "Maple Leaf Rag," an early Morton composition, or a mambo beat as adapted by each of several players.

Morton, in particular, is cited as a fundamental figure.

Jelly Roll, to me, represents not only one of the first great, if not the very first great, composer in jazz, but the first vehicle for fusing all kinds of styles in the U.S. He is a prime example of a guy who understood and was also able to articulate the things that he was doing. I'm not sure about all of his schooling, but he certainly understood the European forms and used them, just as Scott Joplin did. Joplin used them in ragtime, and Jelly Roll sort of broke the mold in a way because he took Scott Joplin's "Maple Leaf" and started improvising on it and played it in a stride style. Now a lot of what Jelly Roll did was in the stride style, but he also played using the bamboula, or some of the Spanish influences. Let's see—

Henry reaches out musingly, and begins to play a few scattered notes which coalesce into a sort of Morton pastiche.

I'm focusing on the rhythm right now. Da-de-da-da-de-da-da. That's a very important rhythm to New Orleans music. It wasn't just important in his time; people like the Neville Brothers use that same rhythm today, but they use it in more of an up-beat, faster tempo. That rhythm has been with New Orleans at least since the turn of the century when Jelly Roll used it, then the Meters grabbed it and then the Neville Brothers got it and that's been sort of the foundation of modern New Orleans music.

Though all New Orleans musicians tend to be aware of their music's past, at least to a greater extent than most American popular players, Butler is particularly immersed in the history. Along with years as a concert artist and studio player, he recently spent some time teaching in the jazz studies program at Eastern Illinois University. The professorial role suits him, and he takes obvious pleasure in instructing his interviewers on the finer points of New Orleans music studies. He adds, though, that after a while he had to come back home.

I was in Charleston, Illinois, which is a town of about 20,000 inhabitants. I liked the teaching, but I decided that I had to realize that I was a big-city boy or that I was going to be doomed in this small town for the rest of my life, where the only serious music I was going to hear was Henry Butler practicing or doing a concert. I was getting burned out—of course now I'm fired up and I'm ready to teach again, but I was just a little tired of being in that locale, and I was glad to come back to New Orleans, just to kind of simplify things and to perform and write again. Mainly to write using more of the New Orleans flavors. I like the rawness of the music here, the raw flavors. You know, I've had a lot of schooling and spent a lot of time in theory classes, and I wanted to be around the raw stuff so that I could take it and polish it the way I want to polish it. So I've been doing some of that, and it's been kind of nice. I'm writing right now for eight or nine pieces, like a nonet-type group and a lot of the stuff is based on New Orleans flavors, so it's nice to be here to hear it in person. It's nice to just capture it, and we'll see where that leads me to, two or three years down the road.

At least at this time in my life, this is a good place for me to be. And you know, a lot of musicians like to be here, because it's so easy to live, and then there's a fairly good regional airport here, so it's not hard to get to other cities. People like, say, Nicholas Payton, they can play almost any kind of job they want to do in New Orleans and it won't hurt their career, their national visibility. I kind of feel like that myself. I can take rootsy kinds of gigs here and it won't bother whatever I decided to do in New York or wherever.

This scene is a lot more insular than people realize, which can be fun for some musicians. What happens here doesn't necessarily get out. Like if you do something in

Los Angeles, you might have somebody from the Times *there or from* Variety *or one of those papers to write about it, and it may wind up being adverse to your career if you're doing the wrong thing—that is, the wrong thing in accordance with those people who label you and who package, and who are concerned about what you do nationally. Those same kinds of gigs here, you know, they could be written up in local magazines, but they don't get out to the national audience. That can be both good and not so good, because a lot of the stuff that really ought to be reported doesn't get reported. But it does give you a kind of freedom.*

New Orleans has always had a problem in terms of being able to have a good strong economic base, and for taking care of its musicians. But, especially if you're pretty good, New Orleanians always have supported their own. I mean, New Orleans is a poor city, but poor cities many times do put money up for entertainment. The fans, the audience, they'll come out to see a Henry Butler or a Snooks Eaglin or, say, the Meters.

That allows all of these musicians to practice and to play, and it gives them more incentive for playing the kinds of things that they play. I mean, this whole revival of the brass bands in the nineties wouldn't have happened if New Orleanians didn't have the kind of pride in their music and the appreciation for their music that they have. That doesn't mean that all these brass bands are that great, but I'll tell you, many of these bands that I heard last September when I first got back here are twice as good today because they've had the chance to practice and they've had the chance to play and work on their craft.

One thing I've learned about many New Orleans musicians—not all of them—if they don't have the incentive to practice they don't always do it. So, it's good that they have an audience here, and places where they can play. And the nation, at some point in time, will benefit by some of these musicians staying in New Orleans. Because eventually, just like it has in the past, it filters into the whole national musical circle. Eventually, whatever is happening in New Orleans now will filter into the mainstream, and I think that's good for the overall musical consciousness of this country.

The Mississippi: River of Song crew shooting an interview with Henry Butler. In the background (from left to right), sound recordist John Paulson, cinematographer Foster Wiley, writer Elijah Wald, and second cameraman Brett Wiley.

◆ ◆ ◆

SECOND LINE PIANO: EDDIE BO and the NEW ORLEANS BEAT

It is a typical afternoon, and Edwin "Eddie Bo" Bocage is holding court in the bar of Margaritaville, across the street from the French Market. A small, bearded man in a colored fez, Bo is a roots piano master who won his place in music history back in the 1950s. His seminal records included "I'm Wise," which became a hit for Little Richard as "Slippin' and Slidin'"; "Check Mr. Popeye,"which was on its way to hit status until Bo was sued for using the cartoon character without permission and forced to change the theme to "Check Your Bucket"; and the wonderfully bizarre "Hard Times (Every Dog's Got a Day)."

Other players of his generation are in semiretirement, but Bo is still an entertainer in his prime, keeping the good times rolling at Margaritaville four afternoons a week and picking up other gigs as they come along. When he gets excited, and the music is cooking like it should, he will sometimes rise from the piano bench and do a little impromptu dance, swinging his hips, shaking his head, and conducting the rhythm section with his whole jerking, animated body.

Bo never got that breakthrough hit that would have made him a national star, but he has arrived at a kind of security rare in New Orleans. He looks around the full bar and his eyes twinkle as he breaks into what has become something of a theme song:

If I ever get a dollar
I'm gonna squeeze it until it holler
Hard times, hard times got me now
But old Confucius say:
"Every dog got a day"

My mother was a pianist, and I've been hearing the music since I was in her womb. She played all of the Professor Longhair-type things; that was back in what we call the "gospel bird" days, when the chicken was sold on Saturdays and there was nothing but a piano in the house. When the pianist had to play with both hands, had to formulate something of a drive, you know, with a good left hand, and they had to kick that drum beat at the bottom of them upright pianos—that was all we had. We knew everywhere Professor Longhair played, 'cause there was a hole in the bottom of the piano where his foot would kick for the bass drum. So we'd look and see if 'Fess been here.

Professor Longhair was a partner of my dad, and I was around him a lot. Him and Tuts Washington, Alan Toussaint, and, oh God, there were so many pianists around at that time. I mean, in New Orleans, piano players, you can get them on almost any corner. Now, Professor took the triads and added some more fingering to them, and made it known, and we've got to give him credit for doing that. But that style of playing had been played for years. It started way back before he was born, and it's a tradition of the pianists here.

There's that mysticism, that little extra beat that you can always tell comes from New Orleans. It's an extra beat inside the beat that we can't seem to explain to people. For instance, in Cleveland right now they're studying the way that beat is produced, playing it in slow motion and trying to figure out what I'm doing with the fingers, and it's not that easy. You have to have grown up listening to it and you have to have it inside you, the feeling of that second and third beat that's inside the beat.

We call it a stutter step, that extra step that the second liners do, and we incorporate that from [when we are] children. You know what a second line is? You understand, the first line, that's the parade itself. The second line are the people that's walking up and down on the side of the parade. People will tell you all kinds of things, but I'm telling you the way it really is. The umbrellas they carry mean the sun's hot or it's raining, but the parade goes on. Like at a funeral, we go and we bring them in mourning to the grave, then we come back happy, all right? And that's when the second line really starts. You'll see stutter steps and extra steps and steps you've never seen.

I had a friend here the other day, he's from up in around Washington, and it was his first time seeing a second-line parade. And he was so amazed he bought every second line record he could find to see if he could learn to do this. I said, "Man, any kid on the street can teach you how to do it. 'Cause it's just a natural thing for the kids to have that second line beat." And when you hear it, then you know it, 'cause there's only one set of people that's able to bring that forth, to incorporate that extra little thing that's going on in there. There's just an aura about New Orleans, and a feel. Mister, you can tell New Orleans anywhere you go.

◆◆◆

Eddie Bo joins Henry Butler onstage at the park.

Hanging out on
the sidewalk, across
the street from
Joe's Cozy Corner

8
Hip-Hop Brass Band Revolutionaries: SOUL REBELS

Night has fallen on the Sixth Ward, out across Rampart Street, back of the French Quarter. This is not tourist territory. The Sixth, or Treme (pronounced "Tremay"), is in what Louis "Satchmo" Armstrong called "Back o' Town," the poor, black section of New Orleans that has produced many of the town's hardest-blowing jazzmen. Tonight, the streetlights glint off the horns of a group of young men as they march along, trailing a second line of dancers. The music is a strange mix; Stevie Wonder's "Living for the City" blares out, followed by something that sounds like the pure rhythmic essence of the old New Orleans marching-band style of the turn of the century. Then, the horns stop for a moment, and the crowd joins the musicians in singing the group's war chant:

Soul Rebels, Soul, Soul Rebels
Soul Rebels, Soul, Soul Rebels

The horns take up a new, wild melody, and the Soul Rebels swing into their theme song:

Walking 'round in the Sixth Ward
Everybody's asking who we are
Soul Rebels in the place to be
Let your mind be free! Oh yeah!
Free your mind with education
Help to build a better nation
Stop killing for recreation
Let your mind be free!

The parade winds through the streets, circling back to Joe's Cozy Corner, where the Rebels are playing tonight. The club is already packed with fans, overflowing out onto the street, where they hang out, drinking beers and chatting in the warmth of the evening. The musicians set up at the back of the room, a front line of horns backed by bass drum, snare drum, and a thumping, swinging tuba, and go back into "Let Your Mind Be Free." In the small room, the sound is incredible, an onslaught of brass that shakes the walls and wounds the eardrums. Byron Bernard takes the first solo on his tenor sax, then Mervin Campbell lowers his trumpet, steps up to the mike, and sings a soulful chorus:

Brother to brother, how long will we live in simplicity
Lift up our minds to world peace
Open our hearts for unity
Let our minds be free

The horns come in, then snare drummer LuMar LeBlanc starts to rap, using a headset microphone. The sound mix is not perfect, and the words are incomprehensible, but the spirit comes through. To someone not from this area, the musical blend is bizarre, but it is the sound of the Treme today, a fusion of hip-hop beats and local tradition that blares from car radios and fills halls with acrobatic dancers.

LuMar: *Hip-hop is from the streets. It's a mentality of taking what you do naturally, not what you have to, so to say, learn. It's like walking: you just come out of your house, you pick up on language, you pick up on different movements, different things, and you just do it and bring it to the screen. That's what hip-hop is about. And that's what brass band is about. So we sort of parallel between the two. At this point, the hip-hop is more worldly accepted—you see it on TV every day. Kids in Japan know about hip-hop. Kids in Japan may not know about brass band. But hopefully we can teach them about brass band through the vessel of hip-hop.*

Earlier, in the afternoon, LuMar, Mervin, and Byron sat on the front steps of a nearby house and talked about their band. Even in an interview, the three function as a team, supporting each other's opinions and finishing each other's sentences. They have known each other since high school. Mervin and Byron got together first, through their shared interest in New Orleans jazz.

Byron: *Mervin, myself, and LuMar—we all attended St. Augustine High School, we had the "Marching 100," the best high school band here in the South, maybe in the world. Anyway, I saw Mervin one day at St. Augustine and he said, "Man, I'm out to start a jazz band, man. You just in time. You still play your horn?"*

I said, "Well, I can." And from that point on Mervin and I got together and then we would call this one, call that one, start the band up.

They started out by following one of New Orleans' great old marching bands.

We was first the Young Olympia Brass Band, from the Olympia Brass Band. That was like a two-year stint, and then we talked to a couple of guys in the band and we realized we needed to come up with our own identity; it was good to be under Olympia, but when we get out there into the world and maybe start making a success for ourself, we need to have our own name. So that's when Cyril Neville of the Neville Brothers came into play. We did a couple of rehearsals with Cyril, and he said, "Man, I got a good name for y'all." He said, "Y'all ought to call yourself the Soul Rebels." And everybody was like, "Hey, that works." We'd thought of all kind of names, you know, but that one is the one that we adopted and we've had since.

Soul represents the music that we play, and it tells where it comes from when we play it; when you hear it, you can feel it's from the soul. And Rebels, you know, people always use rebel as negative, but we use rebel as a positive vibe. We're rebelling for and not against. For the people, all people, regardless of race, color, and creed. So you put that together, Soul Rebels, and that's it.

The Soul Rebels are part of a movement that has been growing in New Orleans since the early seventies. That was when Danny Barker, banjo and guitar player for everyone from New Orleans revival bands to Cab Calloway's swing orchestra, started the Fairview Baptist Church Band to introduce young people to the classic brass band tradition. That grew into the Dirty Dozen Brass Band, which mixed Charlie Parker, r&b, and modern jazz harmonies in with the old-time marching band rhythms. Inspired by the Dozen, a new generation began picking up horns and putting their own spin on the music.

Mervin: *I'd pretty much say this is like holy ground. You know, like from Satch, from all the other people that was here before us. This is the only city that kids walk around with horns, without cases, and be blowing on the corner all the time and trying to get something happening. I never seen that nowhere else.*

LuMar: *The kids here, from very young, when they go to school they want to learn how to play music. Whereas in other parts of the world they might want to do sports. You know, sports is in now because sports is so proliferated on television, everybody want to be Michael Jordan or whoever, but down here people really do love music. It's definitely a mentality that's been passed down from generations and generations. I do think it's sacred in the sense that it's special.*

Some place like New York is such a mecca for entertainment and industry; you can catch just about anything in New York and if it's happening in New York it's damn near going to be happening in the world. But here in New Orleans, it's kind of like a hidden heritage. I mean, unfortunately, because of the poverty, because of the way we're living together, we don't experience a whole lot sometimes outside of what's happening here and that's kind of kept the culture, as far as the musical thing, going on for so many years.

The Soul Rebels at the Cozy Corner: (top) Mervin Campbell, trumpet, and Byron Bernard, tenor sax, at center. (bottom) Drummer and rapper LuMar LeBlanc (left) talking with the guys.

Byron: *We first started in the tradition, and even right now we can set up and do a traditional set just as good as anybody in the city right now. But our main focus when we got together was to hit the mainstream. That's why we try to reach all avenues; we want to do it all, reggae, hip-hop—*

LuMar: *You know, the reggae, from a rhythm player's standpoint, it parallels with the New Orleans music. You got the consistent pulse, you got the deep rhythm, that deep back-beat, then you got the cymbal hitting. So it parallels. But we work all kind of songs in. We might take a song like the "Macarena"—I never heard a brass band play that before. We done put Lionel Ritchie in there. We done put "Footprints," by Wayne Shorter. We done put—what's this classical dude? Beethoven. You know, we mix it all in. It's nothing that we can't mix in with the music. But we just want to make it real for the world, you know.*

Byron: *A lot of people didn't like the fact that we didn't too much stick to the tradition, but we want to be the first brass band to not only get to the Grammy awards but to receive a Grammy. To go mainstream and to turn on VH1, BET, MTV, and see the Soul Rebels. If we were afraid to take that step and to be aggressive, and kept worrying about what other people say, we wouldn't even have gotten this far.*

LuMar: *Everything has to evolve, man, it can't just stay dormant. And that's what we're trying to do, make this thing evolve. We caught all kind of hell and criticism from our own peers who just didn't want to give us the credit for what we were doing. People tried to break us down and destroy us, but we're still here. The nucleus is still here, and when you got that nucleus you can put all kind of seeds in and it'll grow all kinds of flowers. So we're still going on, to others' dismay. They wish we would fall right now, but we ain't going to fall. We're too real for that.*

Byron: *There's going to always be people like that, and that makes it more interesting. That makes the drive more desirable, makes it more worth it, because it's like, "Hey, we want to show you."*

The crowd at Joe's is a packed, sweaty mass of true believers. There is no room to dance, but feet tap, hands wave, and people shout back at the band. The set is heavy on rhythm, with snatches of everything from funk hits to TV theme songs. Like the rap DJs, Soul Rebels are into sampling, but they have to play the riffs themselves rather than borrowing them off other people's recordings, and it is fascinating to hear how they weave the disparate strands together into bubbling, cooking combinations.

The horns lock into another favorite number, "Asiatic Funk." The first few moments are wild, loud jamming, then LuMar's voice comes from the back, rapping in easy counterpoint to the horn riffs.

Everybody, where you at?
My boy rebel beat, you know he's got my back
We're up in the house with this smooth, cold rhythm
Listening hard, because you know we got to get 'em
If it ain't pitched right, I don't want to see it
You know damn well I won't be able to feel it
Wrapped in jazz, with a twist of funk
Just come on back and give me a big old hunk...
Brothers got to rise in their minds
Before we find ourselves out of time
Soul Rebel this and Soul Rebel that
It's about time that we give back
A message of love to the one from above...
Listen tonight, with the sticks in my hand
Trying to get the beat that is grand
I need it all the time, like a vine of wine
I'm talking about knowledge that is refined
Asiatic Funk is on the line
With a busy signal keeping the time...

The group comes in, singing in a loose chorus:

Ain't nothing but an Asiatic Funk
Ain't nothing but an Asiatic Funk

Byron: *In the majority of brass bands, they develop a concept of whatever is going on right now and figure, "We have to be like that." I'm not saying we're down on that, but we just dare to be different. We going to do whatever it takes for us to get to where we want to be, in the mainstream, you know.*

LuMar: *We tried to incorporate all of these—how could I say it—more commercial elements, to basically make more money and to get more popular. Because we see people who don't really know about music out there—I'm not going to name anybody, but they're making millions of dollars off of just selling a mentality and just selling an idea, while here in New Orleans these cats really know about music but are not getting the credit for being the couriers of music. And people are noticing what we're doing. We've done did things with Tribe Called Quest, Lollapalooza, Gap Band, uh—*

Byron: *Bootsie Collins.*

Mervin: *Neville Brothers.*

LuMar: *Counting Crows, all them kind of people.*

Byron: *Robert Plant.*

LuMar: *Robert Plant done came, he sung with us, shipped us to New York. So we know what we're doing is good, because not just the traditional consumer that pulls from brass bands pulls in on us. We got people from all other avenues trying to pull Soul Rebels. Just somebody got to have the guts, you know, to come in and say, "I'm'a take y'all and put y'all on the world scene," you know. Somebody who got the backing and money.*

While they wait for opportunity to knock, the Rebels are keeping their music going, and working day jobs to pay the rent. They would prefer to be doing music full time, but in the interim they are proud of the successes group members are having in the daytime world.

Byron: *That's another thing I like about our group. We have college graduates in our group, and a potential college graduate that's going to school. I mean, other groups, they just tend to want to do this, but I think once you get in the educational system you must go to a certain level in order to succeed. Most groups—and I'm not downplaying anyone, but just being real, you know—most of them drop out of school and they use music to kill idle time. Then, as the growing process goes on, they use music as a way of life. Which is good. We want to do this as a means of life, but the system doesn't allow that right now.*

But LuMar, for example, he's working on his masters right now.

LuMar: *Yeah, I have a degree in social work. I work as a psychiatric technician, that's what they call me, and I'm working on my masters. And this man [Byron] works with computers.*

Byron: *I work at the high school. I don't want to be there but that's what I have to do. I've been there like sixteen years. And I do Uncle Sam, I'm in the reserves, and I'm coaching the kids in the playground. I'm just doing what I have to do to survive but it's, its legal and it's real, you know.*

LuMar: *And Merv, he work at a record store.*

Byron: *Whatever he do, you'll catch him around music.*

Mervin: *Just got to survive.*

LuMar: *It's hard to make it just on a musical level. I mean you have to live—*

if you want to live at a certain level, then you will just rely on music, but if you want other things out of life, then you have to subsidize. But we want to get this to the point where we making the money like Puff Daddy or Dr. Dre. We want to make that kind of loot, so we could give back to the people here—and bring our adversaries up too. We don't play to hate. We'll bring them up too if we make it; we ain't going to keep nobody down. That's what Soul Rebels is about, man.

Mervin: *Our dream—we'd love to be traveling, seeing the world, you know, having big bucks, brand new cars like, "Hey, what you want, that Range Rover?"*

LuMar: *I want the Range Rover.*

Mervin: *And I want a 735IL BMW.*

LuMar: *I'll trade in the Porsche. . . .*

Mervin: *We all want the finest, and I feel that we should be rewarded with that, because we're passing nothing but love on when we're onstage. We ain't going to have no hatred and all this nonsense. People leave our show with something inside that they can go home with, you know, and that's our goal. We always put the Lord in it and keep it in there—because that's what it was built upon, love with the most high God.*

Byron: *We don't use the vulgarity, you know. A lot of hip-hop these days, they're talking about gangster this and shooting that, and dope, and undermining our female sisters. You don't hear that from us. The only thing you're going to see that's real hardcore with us is the way we dress and, other than that, what comes out of our horns, our mouths, is totally different. It's about peace and love.*

LuMar: *And it's just a matter of time before we make it, because we know what we got is gold. Somebody is going to step forward with the sword of righteousness and put us on the map. Because the industry, in my opinion, has exhausted all of its avenues as far as creative, artistic representation of music. Rap has already been there with the turntables, with the DJ. Classical has always been in its spot.*

Byron: *Country western has been there, jazz, rock. This is the only thing—*

LuMar:*—that hasn't been tapped into yet. And when it hits it's going to be so precious, because you can't get it anywhere else but here in New Orleans. And then, after that, you may start to see kids across the nation want to do brass band, you know, the way we do it. Because this music is so funky and so raw and it's so real.*

◆◆◆

Uncle Lionel Batiste, the grand old man of Treme brass music, comes by to hear the Rebels play.

In the Tradition
THE TREME BRASS BAND

The Treme Brass Band, onstage at Armstrong Park.
Page 329 (top) Uncle Lionel Batiste, Uncle Benny Jones, and Jeffrey Hills. (bottom) Hills on tuba

It's a sunny day in Louis Armstrong Park, the reputed site of Congo Square, and a small brass-band festival is taking place. There are old bands, young bands, trad bands, and funk bands. The afternoon's stars are the Treme Brass Band, among the most respected outfits in New Orleans. Treme brings together the grand old man of street bass drummers, Uncle Lionel Batiste, with the young trumpeter James Andrews, and group leader Benny Jones, a veteran of the ground-breaking Dirty Dozen Brass Band who now dedicates himself to preserving the classic, old-time sound of the New Orleans parade bands.

James: ***In the brass band revival that's going on now, the most of the bands is playing the funk style of stuff, with the old-style rhythms and the new horn stuff that's happening. Then we got the Treme Brass Band that's keeping the tradition going, playing old hymns and stuff. Everybody in New Orleans grew up with the brass band thing and the second-line thing, so them songs is installed in your head. We do the funky stuff, too, but it's like the traditional stuff is the foundation. That's there forever. Everybody can come to that pot and just dip in, like it's a gumbo pot. You can dig in and get what you need, and take it your way and make it however you want.***

Benny: ***That pot of gumbo, you can go to everybody's house and not everybody going to cook gumbo the same. You go to some people to have gumbo, they got chicken wings in gumbo. Some people have hot sauces and shrimp and crab, and some people might have chicken feet to make gumbo. Depend on what flavor you put to it. That's just the way music is. Everybody's got a groove you put to it. That's what music is about.***

If everybody adds their own meat and spice, the stock of the metaphorical gumbo is rhythm, and the rhythm comes from here in Congo Square, and the Treme neighborhood.

James: ***It's something that goes back a long time ago. Congo Square is right here, and the people came from Africa, the slaves off the slave ship, this is where they came to gather every weekend, exchange different***

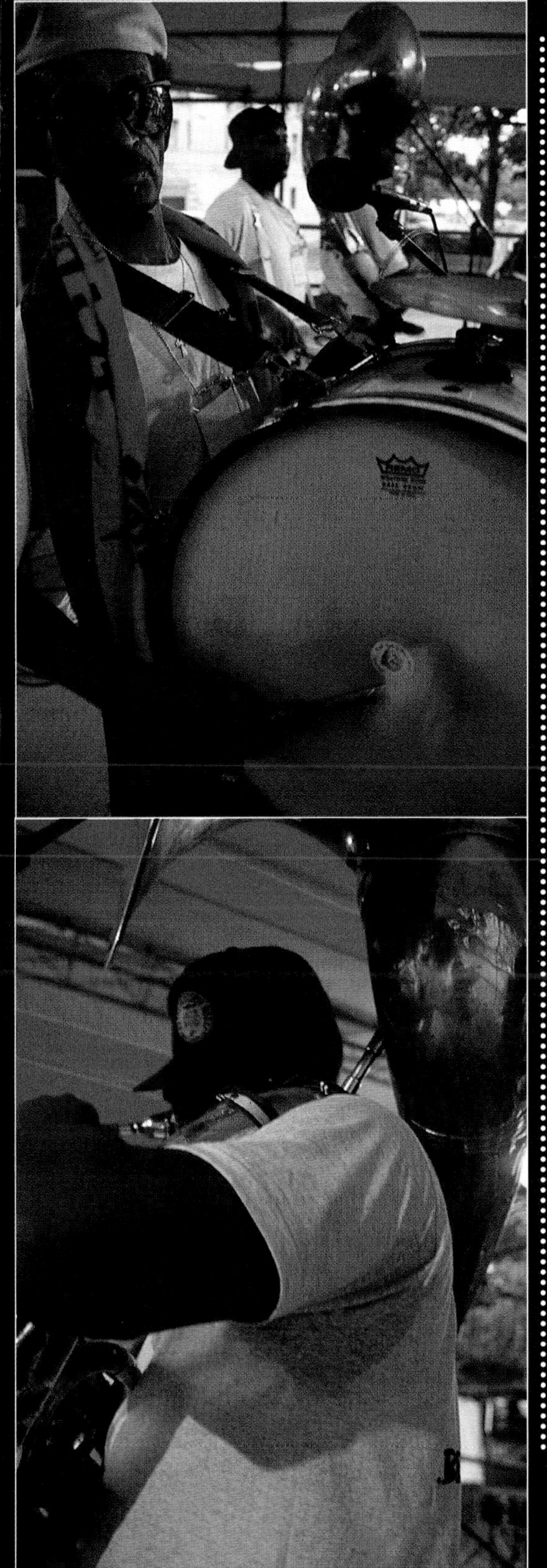

points of the culture and just be together. So from that, I guess, the beat sprung off into the neighborhood.

The Treme musicians is known for that beat. That's what makes this music pop. We call it the "big four." That beat is from the Treme area, and they've got a lot of brass bands popping up now, but the difference between the people from the Treme and the people from elsewhere is that this is our culture, this is made for us. This is something we inherited, passed down from our other people to us now.

Uncle Lionel: *Once you got that groove, the spirit of New Orleans jazz is going to rub off. If you hear it, you watch yourself: You might clap your hand, get up and you do whatever step that you can do. You may not be in time with the music but you enjoying yourself. That's the spirit of the tradition in New Orleans.*

Benny: *You can walk in the Treme area any day of the week, you find kids with horns and drums, practicing to be part of a brass band. Because they go around, they see it every day, they hear it, and they want to be a part of that. That's what happened to me in my life. My father was a drummer, had a brother who was a drummer, and during my time as a young kid in a school class, about two or three days a week you all would get the jazz funeral passing by through the neighborhood. I would say one day, "I want to be a part of that, I want to be a musician like these guys." And I just followed my father into the old brass band thing and I wound up being a part of that today.*

James: *That's what makes the Treme neighborhood so different, is that everybody is almost like family and cousins and just it's like the whole neighborhood is their relative, and the people in the Treme area respect musicians so much. As a youngster coming up, I get so much from Ben and Unc; they're playing the traditional-style music, and they're teaching me a lot. It's kind of sentimental to me. We learn the old songs together, we play all over the world together and, you know, it's just a big inspiration.*

9
Spaniards in the Swamps: IRVAN AND ALLEN PEREZ

Man, that's something you have to experience—when you're out there shrimping, and you look out over the water, the horizon, and watch that sun come up out of the water. When it's getting to its last moments, it looks like it's taking the water with it, because the glow is in the water, and I mean it's beautiful. It takes exactly one minute, one minute for it to leave the water. And if they got a boat off in the distance and it happens to pass in front that sun, it's the prettiest sight you ever want to see. They have these big boats out there, double riggings, and they got these riggings out, and sometimes he's crossing across the sun, and sometimes he's coming facing you, and he's got these rigs out, you know, pulling two nets, and the sun rises right off his stern. It's a beautiful sight, that boat embedded in that rising sun. Ain't nothing like it. It stays in your memory forever.

Allen Perez is talking quietly, and he gazes out over the water as he speaks. Irvan and Allen Perez are sitting in Allen's fishing boat, in a channel off Delacroix Island. They are cousins, Irvan in his seventies and Allen ten years younger, and they grew up in these waterways. Traveling with them by boat through the region is an amazing experience. To an outsider, every channel looks the same, and there are virtually no landmarks. In every direction, all you can see is an endless, flat expanse of reeds, surrounding your little patch of open water. As you travel along, the reeds seem to part, revealing the next bit of open channel, and every so often there is another channel coming in at the side, or a place where the water opens out into something like a lake. It is like a vast maze, hundreds of miles square, covering the area where the Mississippi breaks up into swamps extending out to the Gulf of Mexico.

To the Perezes, it is all familiar territory.

Irvan: *We don't have no problem getting around here. We were born and raised in this given area. We used to find our way in the fog, dark—it could be dark as midnight, and we never had any problem. We knew where we were going. You get to know your way just like you do in the city, like the streets in your hometown, that's the way it was for us. You get to know everything. You get to know parts that, to you they look all alike, and to us it's not. We'll be able to tell where we're at by seeing whatever— the shore, the points.*

Irvan Perez singing a *decima;*
(inset) a shrimp boat

When we used to trap for a living, you'd get there before daylight and start. Say you had 300 traps, you'd run 100, 150 and then you stop, and you almost stopped every day at the same place to go ahead and eat your lunch. And believe it or not, the shore birds, especially the marsh birds, they get to where they know this given area and they'll be waiting for you. And you'd crumb your bread in your pirogue, or wherever you're sitting down, and they'll eat. They'll be sitting on your boots. They'll be trying to pick at your sandwich if you didn't watch it.

The Perezes are Isleños, Spanish-speaking people who settled in Louisiana some two hundred years ago, when the area was under Spanish rule. The Isleños, or islanders, were settlers from the Canary Islands, and eventually made their home in the islands and swamps at the mouth of the Mississippi. Until the oil boom of the 1940s, they lived an isolated existence, fishing, hunting, and trapping muskrats. There were no roads, and few outsiders penetrated their area.

Irvan: *It was all Spanish—you could stay there three days and you never heard any English words. After the War of 1812, they had about thirty families who moved into the lower part of the parish, and they spoke very little English, and when they did they'd tangle it up so bad you couldn't hardly understand it. But they did speak Spanish, and whatever happened in the community, they would make up songs about it,* decimas. *This was all done in a capella, and in memory only. Our history wasn't written down. You could follow it by the* decima, *but that's about the only way.*

A decima *is supposedly a ten-stanza song. It originated in Spain, and was brought over to the Canary Islands, and from the Canary Islands was brought by our people to this part of the country. But our people didn't necessarily follow the ten-stanza rule—they call it a* decima, *but they put whatever they felt like; if it was fifteen stanzas, so what, that was nothing.*

Allen: *It's about whatever happened or somebody's mishap, you know. If something happened to you and they found out about it, you can be sure that a song would be composed that night. They'd be singing about you the next day.*

Irvan: *That was the newspaper for the community, and on Saturday nights, well, they sang. They could start poking fun at people, and it could start at three in the afternoon and it may wind up six tomorrow morning. Sometimes, if somebody didn't really like what they were singing about him, he could get head to head, and they would sing* decimas *back and forth.*

We had an Aunt Jessalita, which was my daddy's aunt, and she had a photostatic mind from the word go—she knew everybody, when they were born, what time, if it was raining—and they'd come from all over the parish and ask her. Her and a son-in-law didn't get along, so she would go ahead and compose a decima *about him, and he would turn around and answer her with another one. I can remember, she was singing about how no-good he was, and he answered her, "If you was a serpent, your bite wouldn't be that bad," but he was singing it in the* decima.

You had to put up with whatever they sang about you. If a man made a mistake—he went in the water and he did something foolish and he got in trouble—come Saturday night, somebody would have a decima. *If a woman went and did something that she had no business doing, run around or something, they made a* decima. *They may not mention the name, but in a small community they knew who it was. You sang it on Saturday nights or they sang it during the weddings, and all they could do was grin and bear it.*

Most of the decimas *were composed while you're trapping; you're by yourself, you're walking the marshes. Whatever you start thinking about, you start singing about it. And before you know it, you put a few lines together till you got your ten stanzas, and that's that, you had your* decima.

Allen: *There's one particular one that my father sang that takes me back to in the early thirties, when we used to do some muskrat trapping. When you trap muskrats you got to have cold weather. If you get hot weather, you're going to have high water and mosquitos.*

They had mortgages to pay on these properties; first of the year, you had to pay your note. You'd get a notice from the bank. So this particular winter, it was a bad one, it was hot, with mosquitos, and a high tide, and when my father came home from moving his trap line, my sister approached him with a letter he had got from the bank saying that he had to pay the note in full. So my father composed a decima *of mosquitos and high water.*

Allen begins to sing. His voice is thin and gentle, with a slight quaver. In the background, there is the sound of the water, and sometimes a boat engine throbbing off in the distance.

Esto si que es un trabajo, y esto si que es un fatiga
(This really is hard work, this really is a burden)
Lo que pasa un pobre trampero para mantenar su familia
(What happens to a poor trapper to maintain his family)
Esto si que es un fatiga
(This really is a misery)

Encontre el trampero esta, el mosque y el agua alta
(Against this trapper are mosquitos and high water)

Irvan Perez getting ready to go fishing.

Y para acabar completa, la banca le manda carta
(And to finish him completely, the bank sent him a letter)
Esto si que es un fatiga
(This really is a misery)

Cuando yo llegue de la trampa, a mi me dice Cecilia
(When I came from the traps, Cecilia told me)
"Padre, tu tiene una carta que te mandan de la villa"
("Father, you have a letter which they have sent you from town")
Y yo, como no se leer, en sus manos se la di
(And I, since I don't know how to read, I put it in her hands)
Esta carta de la villa, dime lo que deci
(This letter from town, tell me what it says)
Eso si que es un fatiga
(This really is a misery)

Ella se detuvo un poco en decirme lo que habia
(She hesitated a little to tell me what it was)
Yo vi a la vista par ella, y las lagrimas se le veia
(I looked into her eyes, and the years were streaming down)
Esto si que es un fatiga . . .
(This really is a misery)

The song goes on to tell of the bank's foreclosure, and the father's hope that, if the trapping does not work, they can go to fishing carp, or that their cousins who own a store may help tide them over the bad times until the weather improves. It is a sad song, with the weight of a poor man grasping at hope in the face of disaster, but Allen has a smile on his face as he sings.

It's a pleasure to sing, and it's a pleasure to know that you're carrying on your ancestry, you know, your way of life. The older people, they had their sad moments and their ups and downs, just like we all do, but they lived a happier life than what you live today, because they took life for what it was worth—no more, no less. If it went up, it went up; if it went down, it went down. Tomorrow we pick up the pieces and keep it going, and if they had any kind of dispute, they'd settle it right then and there, shake hands, and tomorrow they'd be just like if it never happened. Those people were serious when they had to be serious and they were joyful when they had to be joyful, and nothing ever bothered them too much. If something drastic happened, they sang about it.

My father, when we got on the boat in the morning, the minute the boat is started, he'd get behind the helm and he sang all the way going, all the while he was out there, and all the way home—it didn't matter what happened. They had days that I would question myself, "What does this man got to sing about?" Everything went wrong, it was a disaster. But he sang, and he used to always tell me, he says, "Nothing ain't never too bad; there's always better days to come. Life is not always flying high, like you don't have a worry in the world, it's not that way. Life is tough. You're going to have your good days, and you're going to have your bad days, and always remember that."

My father had a very sharp mind. He never went to school a day in his life, and he spoke five different languages: Spanish, English, French, Portuguese, and Greek, which I didn't know until I took him down to the plant one time and I had a friend over there was a Greek, and I see him over there, he's talking to him. I wonder what the old man's talking to, and I went over there. I didn't know a thing they were saying, but they were going at it. We got in the car to come home and I said, "Daddy, I didn't know you knew how to spoke Greek."

He says, "There's a lot of things you don't know about me."

I said, "Oh, pardon me."

Allen makes a face, the picture of aggrieved innocence, and Irvan smiles at his performance.

Irvan: *A lot of the older people had photostatic minds.*

Allen: *They had their minds sharp; they could remember things. We'd get into something, and maybe a week or so later we done forgot about it, but you can rest assured, they never forgot about it. And out of that, they'd come out with a* decima.

Irvan: *Everybody composed their own, more or less, and they sang their own. And then, around Christmas or New Year's, they'd go from house to house...*

Allen: *My daddy played the accordion...*

Irvan: *The old man played the guitar...*

Allen: *And whatever song was suitable for that house, they'd sing. I remember one occasion, they were going from house to house singing and our next-door neighbor he was French, so my daddy played the "Marseillaise," the French national anthem, you know. And then they got next door, to my uncle, and he had a bunch of kids, and your daddy said, "Well, what do you think we should play over here, Pa?" He said, "There's only one song we can play over here," he says, " 'Cry, Baby, Cry.' "*

They were always poking in fun, and nobody would get angry.

Irvan: *I remember the first time I got drunk. My grandfather was a pretty good age—of course he was older than my daddy and what have you—and for a month before Christmas, the men would start storing their liquor in his back porch, and they would have stacks and stacks of liquor, and my grandma and mom and them would bake pies, and Christmas Day or the day before Christmas, they'd start singing the* decimas *and composing and doing whatever they felt like, and drinking wine. They loved their wine.*

My first drunk was on wine. I was about ten years old, and the old man, my daddy, said "Come on, boy, we're going to tour the island"—in Spanish—I say "Yes, sir," and I was tickled pink to be accepted, you know. They were going from house to house, singing decimas, *and every place you stop, they'd give you a shot of wine. And after they had a few wines, well, they started, "Go ahead, son, take one, it ain't going to hurt you, take a little bit of this."*

Well, I done my singing and I got home, but, boy, when I lay in that bed I seen everything rotating. I say, "Oh-oh, there's something wrong here somewhere." I got out of bed, and Mama jumped my daddy, told him, "You ought to be ashamed of yourself, getting the baby drunk like that." I just thought, "Thank God they ain't fussing at me." You know, I could have kept saying no.

Irvan and Allen are laughing, enjoying the memories of old times.

Irvan: *They had songs about everything. There were songs pertaining to whatever the people did for a living: you got the "Crab Fisherman Song," you got the "Trappers Song." You got the ones pertaining to welfare, W.P.A., you got some pertaining to when they had horse and buggies, they got some pertaining to oxen, plantations.*

Then they had some that they brought over from Spain, from the Canary Islands to here. Those songs remain with us, too. When we went to the Canary Islands, the first time was in seventy-six. We didn't even know that this had originated in the Canary Islands. We knew that it had to come from somewheres, but we didn't know exactly where. But when we got there, we sang "La Orilla de un Palmar," *which is "The Edge of the Palm Trees," and this old lady come to us with tears in her eyes. She say, "That's the same song my grandmother used to sing to us."*

I say, "Well, listen to this here." That brought tears to my eyes, because I didn't even realize, didn't have an inkling. That song talks of a child that was born on an island—they got seven inhabited islands in the Canary Islands—and this one child that was born had no mother, no father, she was an orphan, and they asked her, "How did you live?" She said, "I go and come as the wave of the sea." And it goes like this:

A la orilla de un palmár, 'cuentré a una joven bella
(At the edge of a palm grove I met a beautiful young woman)
Sus boquitas de coral, sus ojitos son dos estrellas
(Her lips were coral, her eyes were two stars)
A pasar le pregunté, quien vivía con ella

(In passing I asked her who lived with her)
Y me contestó llorando, "Solo vivo en el palmar
(And she replied, crying, "I live alone in the palm grove)

Soy huerfanita, no tengo padre ni madre
(I am an orphan, I have neither father nor mother)
Ni un amiguito que me venga consolar
(Nor a little friend who comes to console me)
Solita vivo, en este mundo penando
(I live all alone in this world, suffering)
Solo voy y vengo como las olas del mar"
(I just go and come like the waves of the sea")

I went back to the Canaries with Carol, my oldest daughter. We had a girl from there that stayed with us for thirty-one days here in Louisiana, and she in turn looked up our family back there. She had about a hundred people, and she said "We're going to have a family reunion." So we did, and the first thing they told us, the old man, Don Juan, he said, "Nobody, and I mean nobody, eats till everybody sings."

I had no problem, I'll sing. I was hungry anyway. But I told my daughter, I said, "Carol, I don't know how you're going to make out, I ain't never heard you sing in my life." And I was the one raised her.

She said, "Don't worry, Daddy, when my turn comes, I'll sing." And when her turn come, she sings "The Star-Spangled Banner."

I said "That's nice, you come all the way here to sing 'The Star-Spangled Banner.' "

Of course, they clapped and laughed and joked about that.

The sun has set, and it is time to finish up the interview, but Irvan and Allen are still trading memories. The life they knew in their youth is fast disappearing, and it is pleasant for them to sit for a while and remember. Today, few of the young people speak Spanish, and no one is out roaming the swamps in search of muskrat pelts. The old ways of life began to disappear with the oil boom, and have been further eroded by a changing population and the ravages of civilization. Recent projects have diverted the river water into the swamps, altering the salinity of the water, and Irvan says that the channels are now getting clogged with grass and most of the fish have disappeared.

Irvan: *In the old days, we were working for ourselves, and when you do that you appreciate Mother Nature. We worked with Mother Nature, we didn't work against it. If we trapped, we left the mother rat alone. We got away from the nest. Always set your traps so you don't catch the young'uns.*

Allen: *You never destroy what you're going to make your living off of. That's what's happening today. People want to run over everything and catch as much as they can, and pursue it twenty-four hours a day, and anything that you pursue twenty-four hours a day, it's going to run out. Sooner or later it's gone, it's history, and that's happened to species that no longer exist because they wasn't properly taken care of.*

Irvan: *Our people, they did not fish when the trout was spawning. As soon as they seen the trouts getting ready to spawn, they'd say, "Let's get off of here, that's our future." Nobody would fish then. And when I say nobody, they meant nobody. Hunting was the same way.*

Allen: *Yeah, my daddy got me a gun when I was eleven years old, and it was just for hunting. That time you could hunt commercially, and he used to tell me, he says, "Watch what you do." He said, "Don't never disrespect any elder while you're out there, I don't want to hear nothing about that. And when it comes twelve o'clock in the day"—when that whistle sounds over at the plantation, which you could hear for miles—he said, "No more shooting. The birds have got to come in, to bathe and feed and rest overnight." He says, "No evening hunting at all."*

And if you was out there and you shot a shot, and they heard it, they went and looked for you. You better believe it, they'd hunt you down, and they'd take your gun away from you. I don't care who you was. They'd continue feeding your family, but they said, "This is our way of life and you're not gonna destroy it."

It was a different way of life, you know. My daddy was always telling me—he wasn't a real religious man, but he always told me this: "Son," he says, "That old man up there, they call him God, he can't please every so-and-so running around in circles, so don't you try." He said, "One wants rain and the other one don't want rain; this one wants cold, the other one don't want cold. He can't please them all, so don't you try. You go through life, take your life as it comes to you. Don't try to play God; it can't be done."

That's the way he looked at life, and that's the way he was. Whatever came, came, and if it didn't come, well, maybe tomorrow. Or the next day. Like I tell you in Spanish, "Si no hoy, pues sea mañana; si no pasado, cuando le de la gana." *"If it's not today, maybe tomorrow; if not tomorrow, maybe when He feels like it." That's what my daddy said, and that's the way it is. You can't put it any plainer than that.*

◆

"The Crab Fisherman Song"

Irvan: *This is a song that became very popular pertaining to fishing crabs in the month of February. I recall when my father wrote it—that was in the '30s. If you had a hurricane, and the rats were driven out of your land, then you had no choice but to go ahead and fish crabs or something. The month of February is the worst month, because the crabs will bury if it's cold, and they don't bite.*

Back then, the price of crabs was twenty-five cents a basket. You had your baskets, and you used moss for covers and you used what we called cohölla, *which is nothing but palmettos, and you made four ties to keep the crab from getting out of your basket. The song talks about an individual that goes ashore to cut the grass, and a swarm of bees get on him, and he hasn't made enough money to even get a haircut, so his hair is long and it gets tangled up in the branches and he can't get out. It's comical, really, and finally it tells you, when a poor man dies, a fisherman, don't bother mourning, 'cause he's gone to a better world.*

Yo me arrimé a la costa, buscándome el abriguito.
(I went up close to shore, looking for a little shelter)
Sentí una voz que decía, "Aquí estoy yo helado"
(I heard a voice that said "Here I am freezing")
Era un pobre jaibero, pescando en el mes de Febrero
(It was a poor crab fisherman, fishing in the month of February)

El salió calando, derecho pa' el otro lado
(He was putting out his line straight for the other side)
Y se encontró otro jaibero, que estaba médio helado
(And met another crab fisher, who was half frozen)
Entonces dice el jaibero, "Maldita sea el mes de Febrero"
(Then the crab fisher said, "Cursed be the month of February")

Lo concho a la costa donde estaba el batimiento
(He was pushed up to the shore where the waves were beating)
Entonces dice el jaibero, "Maldita sea tanto viento"
(Then the crab fisher said, "Cursed be so much wind")
Era un pobre jaibero, pescando en el mes de Febrero
(It was a poor crab fisherman, fishing in the month of February)

"De una lata a la otra" di un pobre jaibero
("From one pole to the next,"* said the poor crab fisherman)
Se fue a tierra corta paja, y le cayó un abipero
(He went ashore to cut hay, and a beehive fell on him)
Entonces dice el jaibero, "Maldita sea el mes de Febrero"
(Then the crab fisher said, "Cursed be the month of February")

Tenia pelo largo, y se enredó en los mangles
(He had long hair, and caught himself in the mangrove bushes)
No podia salir a recoger su palangre
(He couldn't get out to run his crab line)
Era un pobre jaibero, pescando en el mes de Febrero
(It was a poor crab fisherman, fishing in the month of February)

Parece que tenía rabia se echar de cuatro patas
(He looked like he had rabies, he went on all fours)
Y el compañero que a visto eso, le cayó atras con la lata
(And his companion who saw this, went after him with a pole)
Era un pobre jaibero, pescando en el mes de Febrero
(It was a poor crab fisherman, fishing in the month of February)

Cuando se muera un jaibero, que nadie le ponga luto
(When a crab fisherman dies, let no one wear mourning for him)
Porque se va a descansar, ese pobrecito difunto
(Because he is going to have some rest, this poor dead man)
Era un pobre jaibero, pescando en el mes de Febrero
(It was a poor crab fisherman, fishing in the month of February)

* "From one trouble to the next," "Out of the frying pan into the fire."

Discography

Tracks from most of the artists included in the River of Song project appear on the companion two-CD set, *The Mississippi: River of Song,* Smithsonian Folkways 40086. 1998

Babes in Toyland

Spanking Machine, Restlesss: 89183, 1989
To Mother, Twin Tone Records: 89208-2. Twin Tone Records, Minneapolis, 1991
The Peel Sessions, Dutch East India Trading: 8413-2. Rockville Center, 1992
Fontanelle, Reprise: 26998, 1992
Nemesisters, Reprise Records: 9 45868-2. 1995

Bass, Fontella

Rescued, The Best of Fontella Bass (early recordings), Chess: CHD-9335. MCA Records, Universal City, 1992
From the Root to the Source (with Martha and David Peaston), Soul Note (import): 121006. 1980
Promises, A Family Portrait of Faith with Martha Bass and David Peaston, SELAH Records: 7506. 1990
Everlasting Arms, Silver Spring: SS 210. 1991
No Ways Tired, Nonesuch: 9 79357-2. 1995
Now That I Found a Good Thing, Jewel: 5060. 1996

Bo, Eddie

Check Mr. Popeye, Rounder: 2077. Rounder Records, Cambridge, 1988
Eddie Bo and Friends, BO-SOUND: BO-2295. 1995, available through: Eddie Bo Productions, P.O. Box 50997, New Orleans, LA 70150-0997
Included on **Keys to the Crescent City,** Rounder 208
For similar music, refer to Professor Longhair and Huey "Piano" Smith

Bottle Rockets

Bottle Rockets, East Side Digital Records: 80772. 1993
The Brooklyn Side, originally released on East Side Digital Records in 1994, rereleased by Tag Recordings: 92601-2. 1995
24 Hours a Day, Atlantic: 83015-2. 1997

Boundless Love

There are no recordings of the Boundless Love Quartet, but country gospel style fuses traditional Southern white religious singing, as heard on Southern Journey Volume 4: Brethren, We Meet Again, Rounder 1704, with the upbeat, jazzy style pioneered by the Golden Gate Quartet, who can be heard on Swing Down, Chariot, Columbia/Legacy

CK 47131. This fusion was popularized in the 1950s by the Mississippi-born Blackwood Brothers, who can be heard on:

The Blackwoods, Chordant Music Group: 44905. 1997

Gospel Classic Series, RCA: 67624. 1998

Brown, Greg

Songs of Innocence and Experience, Red House Records: RHR 14. 1986

One Big Town, Red House Records: RHR 28. 1989

Down in There, Red House Records: RHR 35. 1990

Iowa Waltz, Red House Records: RHR 1. 1992

In the Dark with You, Red House Records: RHR 8. 1992

One More Goodnight Kiss, Red House Records: RHR 23. 1992

Dream Cafe, Red House Records: RHR 47. 1992

44 & 66, Red House Records: 02. 1992

Bathtub Blues, Red House Records: RHR 42. 1993

The Poet Game, Red House Records: 68. 1994

The Live One, Red House Records: 78. 1995

Further In, Red House Records: 88. 1996

Slant 6 Mind, Red House Records: 98. 1997

Burgess, Sonny

Old Time Rock 'n' Roll, Flying Fish: 445. 1987

We Wanna Boogie, Rounder: SS36. Rounder Records, Cambridge, 1990

Tennesse Border, Hightone: 8039. 1992

Sonny Burgess, Rounder: 3144. Rounder Records, Cambridge, 1996

For similar music, refer to Sun Records rockabilly anthologies, Carl Perkins, Elvis Presley Sun sessions

Butler, Henry

For All Seasons, Atlantic Jazz 82856- 2. 1996

Blue After Sunset, Black Top Records: 1144. 1998

David and Roselyn

Gospel from the Streets of New Orleans, SONO: 1033. 1993

Gumbo Ya Ya, SONO: 1041. 1996, available through Sounds of New Orleans, 5584 Canal Blvd., New Orleans, LA 70124, tel: 504.484.7222

Dirty Old Men, Ordnung & Hartman Records. Berlin, 1997, contact David and Roselyn, P.O. Box 70813, New Orleans, LA 70172

Davis, Governor Jimmie

You Are My Sunshine, Bear Family (import): 16216. 1998

Nobody's Darling But Mine, Bear Family (import): 15943. 1998

Delafose, Geno

French Rockin' Boggie, Rounder: 2131. Rounder Records, Cambridge, 1994

That's What I'm Talking About, Rounder: 2141. Rounder Records, Cambridge, 1996

For similar music, refer to John Delafose, Clifton Chenier, and Boozoo Chavis

Hartford, John

Mark Twang, Flying Fish: 020. 1976
Nobody Knows What You Do, Flying Fish: 028. 1980
Catalogue, Flying Fish: 259. 1981
Gum Tree Canoe, Flying Fish: 289. 1984
Me Oh My, How the Time Does Fly—A John Hartford Anthology, Flying Fish: 440. 1987
Down on the River, Flying Fish: 514. 1989
Morning Bugle, Rounder: 0356. Rounder Records, Cambridge, 1995
Aereo-Plain, Rounder: 0366. Rounder Records, Cambridge, 1997
Wild Hog in the Red Brush, Rounder: 0392. Rounder Records, 1996

Hartwich, Karl and the Country Dutchmen

Is Everybody Happy, Karl and the Country Dutchmen. 1991, available through Karl and the Country Dutchmen, 733 Fountain Street, Fountain City, WI 54629
Included on **Deep Polka: Dance Music from the Midwest,** Smithsonian/Folkways: 40088. 1998

Helm, Levon, The Band

Stage Fright, Capitol/EMI: 93593. 1970
The Best of the Band, Capitol/EMI: 46070. 1976
The Last Waltz, Warner Bros. Records: 3146. 1978
Jericho, Pyramid Records: 71564. 1993
Across the Great Divide [Box], Capitol/EMI Records: 89565. 1994
Live at Watkins Glen, Capitol/EMI: 31742. 1995
High on the Hog, Pyramid Records: 72404. 1996

Johnson, Jack or The Jelly Roll Kings

The Jelly Roll Kings, Jelly Roll Kings, Earwig: 4901. 1978
The Oil Man, Earwig: 4910. 1986
Daddy When Is Mama Comin' Home?, Earwig: 4916. 1989
The Jelly Roll Kings, Rockin' the Juke Joint Down, Earwig: 4901. 1993
We Got to Stop This Killin', MC Records: MC-0033. 1996
The Jelly Roll Kings, Off Yonder Wall, Fat Possum: 80310, 1997
Live in Chicago, Earwig: 4939. 1997
All the Way Back, MC Records: MC-0035. 1998

Koerner, "Spider" John

Blues Rags & Hollers, Koerner, Ray and Glover. Originally released in 1963 by Audiophile Records, rereleased as Red House Records: 76.
Running, Jumping, Standing Still with Willie Murphy, originally released in 1969 by Elektra Records, rereleased as Red House Records: 63. 1994
Nobody Knows the Trouble I've Been, Red House Records: 12. 1986
Legends of Folk with Phillips & J. Elliot, Red House Records: 31. 1990
Folk Song America, Smithsonian: RD 046-3. 1991
Raised By Humans, Red House Records: 84. 1992
Star Geezer, Red House Records: 84. 1996
One Foot in the Groove, Koerner, Ray and Glover, Tim/Kerr Records: 137. 1996

La Otra Mitad

There are no recordings of La Otra Mitad, but there are thousands of available CDs in the norteño style. Arhoolie Records has released many historical albums of the tradition, including **Chulas Fronteras & Del Mero Corazon** (Arhoolie 425), **Tejano Roots** (Arhoolie 341), and **15 Tex-Mex Conjunto Classics** (Arhoolie 104). The most popular group in the style is Los Tigres del Norte, who have dozens of albums on the Fonovisa label.

Lewis Family

Dreamin', HL Records: 0796-01. 1996

You Can't Ask Too Much of My God, 1997, contact: Bob Lewis, 106 Young Street, Doniphan, MO 63935

For similar music, refer to Bill Monroe, Lester Flatt and Earl Scruggs, and the Stanley Brothers

Little Milton

The Essential Chess Recordings (early recordings), MCA Chess 9350

Playing for Keeps, Malaco: 7419. Malaco, Mississippi, 1984

I Will Survive, Malaco: 7427. Malaco, Mississippi, 1985

Annie Mae's Cafe, Malaco: 7435. Malaco, Mississippi, 1986

Movin' to the Country, Malaco: 7445. Malaco, Mississippi, 1987

Back to Back, Malaco: 7448. Malaco, Mississippi, 1988

Too Much Pain, Malaco: 7453. Malaco, Mississippi, 1990

Reality, Malaco: 7462. Malaco, Mississippi, 1991

Strugglin' Lady, Malaco: 7465. Malaco, Mississippi, 1992

I'm a Gambler, Malaco: 7473. Malaco, Mississippi, 1994

Greatest Hits, Malaco: 7477. Malaco, Mississippi, 1995

Cheatin' Habit, Malaco: 7483. Malaco, Mississippi, 1996

For Real, Malaco: 7494. Malaco, Mississippi, 1998

Lockwood, Jr., Robert

Hanging On (with Johny Shines), Rounder: 2023. Rounder Records, Cambridge, 1980

What's the Score, Blues Interactions: 2701. 1990

Steady Rollin' Man, Delmark: DS-630. 1993

Contrasts, Trix: 3307. 1993

Plays Robert and Robert, Evidence: 26020-2, 1993

Plays Robert Johnson, Brainbow Prod. RLJ 62789—cassette reissue of Black & Blue 33.740

Does 12, Trix: 3317. 1996

I Got to Find Me a Woman, Verve: 314 537 448. 1996

Swings in Tokyo Live at the Park Tower Blues Festival '95, Blues Interactions: PCD 4927. 1996

King Biscuit Blues, Blue Sun: BSCD 2000. 1996

The Baddest New Guitar, P-Vine: Special PCD-2134.

Blues Live in Japan, Advent: 2807.

For further listening, refer to Robert Johnson

Lopez, Manny

There are no records of Manny Lopez's group. The roots of his music are in the work of Dixieland revivalists like Eddie Condon and Lu Watters, or Kid Ory's and Bunk Johnson's bands. Bix Beiderbeck's work has been reissued in many forms. His greatest small-band recordings are those done with Frankie Trumbauer.

Lor, Wang Chong

For Hmong music, refer to **The Music of the Hmong People of Laos**, Arhoolie 446. 1995

Memphis Horns

The Memphis Horns are best known not for their own recordings, but for their work on thousands of Memphis soul recordings as studio players in the 1960s and early 1970s. These included virtually all the records of Otis Redding, Sam & Dave, Rufus and Carla Thomas, some of Wilson Pickett's greatest work, and more other artists than can be counted. Their solo albums include:

Flame Out, Lucky Seven: 9201. Rounder Records, Cambridge, 1992

The Memphis Horns, Telarc Records: 83344. 1995

Wishing You a Merry Christmas, Icehouse Records: 50630. 1997

Menard, D. L.

D. L. Menard and the Louisiana Aces, Rounder: 6003. Rounder Records, Cambridge, 1974

Cajun Saturday Night, Rounder: 0198. Rounder Records, Cambridge, 1984

No Matter Where You At, There You Are, Rounder: 6021. Rounder Records, 1988

En Bas du Chêne Vert (album with Dewey Balfa and Marc Savoy) Arhoolie: 312. 1989

Cajun Memories, Swallow: 6125. Swallow, Ville Platte, LA, 1995

Le Trio Cadien (album with Eddie LeJeune and Ken Smith) Rounder: 6049. Rounder Records, Cambridge, 1992

Mississippi Mass Choir

"Live" in Jackson, Mississippi, Malaco: 6003. Malaco, Mississippi, 1989

God Gets the Glory, Malaco: 6008. Malaco, Mississippi, 1991

It Remains to Be Seen, Malaco: 6013. Malaco, Mississippi, 1993

Greatest Hits, Malaco: 6021. Malaco, Mississippi, 1995

I'll See You in the Rapture, Malaco: 6022. Malaco, Mississippi, 1996

Ojibwe (Chippewa Nation)

Objibway Music from Minnesota, A Century of Song for Voice and Drum, Minnesota Historical Society: 339-8. 1989, tel. 651.296.6126

Peebles, Ann

Straight from the Heart, The Right Stuff: 66711. 1971

I Can't Stand the Rain, The Right Stuff: 66712. 1974

Lookin' for a Lovin', Hi Records: 105. 1990

Full Time Love, Bullseye Blues: 9515. Rounder Records, Cambridge, 1992

Tellin' It/If This Is Heaven, Hi Records: 138. 1993

The Flip Side, Hi Records: 144. 1993

This Is/The Handwriting on the Wall, Hi Records: 139. 1993

U.S. R&B Hits '69–'79, Hi Records: 13. 1995

Fill This World with Love, Bullseye Blues: 9564. Rounder Records, Cambridge, 1996
The Best of the Hi Record Years, The Right Stuff: 52659. 1996

Perez, Irvan

Spanish Decimas from St. Bernard Parish, Louisiana Folklife Center: C-088. 1988
Louisiana Folklife Center, P.O. Box 3663 NSU, Natchitoches, LA 71497, tel: 318. 357. 4332

Redmond, Eugene

Eugene Redmond has no recordings, but there are several volumes of his poetry available:
Sentry of the Four Golden Pillars. Black River Writers Press, East St. Louis, 1970.
River of Bones and Flesh and Blood. Black River Writers Press, East St. Louis, 1971.
In a Time of Rain and Desire. Black River Writers Press, East St. Louis, 1973
Songs from an Afro/Phone: New Poems. Black River Writers Press, East St. Louis, 1973
Drumvoices: The Mission of Afro-American Poetry: A Critical History. Doubleday, Garden City, 1976.
The Eye in the Ceiling: Selected Poems. New York: Harlem River Press, 1991.

Rhyme Games

For similar music, refer to the following:
Children's Songs for the Playground, Smithsonian Folkways: 45013. 1989
This-a-Way, That-a-Way, Ella Jenkins, Smithsonian Folkways: 45002. 1989
African Songs and Rhythms for Children—Recorded and Annotated by Dr. W. K. Amoaku, Smithsonian Folkways: 45011. 1990
American Game and Activity Songs for Children, Pete Seeger, Smithsonian Folkways: 45025. 1990

Sain, Oliver

The Best of Oliver Sain, NASH: 4218.
St. Louis Breakdown—The Best of Oliver Sain, Excello. 1997

Skål Club Spelmanslag

Live at the Lake, 1993
In the Woods, 1995, self-distributed by Paul Wilson, 3016 Nokay Lake Road, NE, Brainerd, MN 56401

Soul Asylum

Say What You Will, Clarence... (Karl sold the Truck), Twin/Tone: 8439. 1984
While You Were Out, Twin/Tone: 8691. 1986
Time's Incinerator, Twin/Tone: 8677. 1986
Made to Be Broken, Twin/Tone: 8666. 1986
Hang Time, A & M: 215 197. 1988
Clam Dip & Other Delights, Twin/Tone: 88144. 1988
And the Horse They Rode in On, A & M: 215 318. 1990
Grave Dancers Union, Columbia: 48898. Sony Music Entertainment, 1992
Let Your Dim Light Shine, Columbia: 57616. Sony Music Entertainment, 1995
Candy from a Stranger, Columbia: 67618. 1998

Soul Rebels

Let Your Mind Be Free, Mardi Gras Records: 1020. 1995

For similar music, refer to: Rebirth Jazz Band, and an anthology, **Kickin' Some Brass,** Shanachie Records 6028

Sounds of Blackness

The Evolution of Gospel, Perspective Records: 1000. 1991

Night Before Christmas—A Musical Fantasy, Perspective Records: 9000. 1992

Africa to America: The Journey of the Drum, Perspective Records: 31454 90062. 1994

Time for Healing, Perspective Records: 31454 9029 2. 1997

Stinson, Kenny Bill

For similar music, refer to Tony Joe White

Thomas, Irma

Sweet Soul Queen of New Orleans, The Irma Thomas Collection (early recordings), Razor and Tie Music: 2097. 1996

The New Rules, Rounder: 2046. Rounder Records, Cambridge, 1986

The Way I Feel, Rounder: 2058. Rounder Records, Cambridge, 1988

Soul Queen of New Orleans, Mardi Gras Records: 5014. 1989

Ruler of Hearts, Charly: 195. 1989

Something Good: The Muscle Shoals Chess Sessions, Chess: 93004. 1990

Simply the Best: Live!, Rounder: 2110. Rounder Records, Cambridge, 1991

Safe with Me/Live at the Kingfish, Paula Records: 1004. 1992

True Believer, Rounder: 2117. Rounder Records, Cambridge, 1992

Walk Around Heaven: New Orleans Soul Gospel & Sacred, Rounder: 2128. Rounder Records, Cambridge, 1994

The Story of My Life, Rounder: 2149. Rounder Records, Cambridge, 1997

Thomas, Rufus

Walking the Dog, originally released by Stax Records in 1963, rereleased by Rhino Records: 82254. 1991

Live! originally released by Stax Records in 1971, rereleased by Stax: 88019. 1994

Crown Prince of Dance, originally released by Stax Records in 1973, rereleased by Stax: 88026. 1995

Chronicle: Their Greatest Stax Hits, Stax: 4124. 1979

That Woman Is Poison, Alligator Records: 4769. 1988

Can't Get Away from This Dog, Stax: 8569. 1992

Did You Hear Me, Stax (import): 050. 1993

Rufus Thomas, Hollywood, DNA-Rounder: 179. 1994

The Best of Rufus Thomas, Do the Funky Somethin', Rhino Records: R2 72410. 1996

Funky Chicken, Stax: 88036, 1997

Rufus Live!, Ecko Records: 1013. 1998

Treme Brass Band

Gimme My Money Back, Arhoolie: 417. 1995

For similar music, refer to Dirty Dozen Brass Band

◆◆◆

Lyrics Credits

Babes in Toyland **"Drivin' "** and **"Sweet '69"** by Babes in Toyland © Copyright 1995 Zomba Enterprises Inc./No Dukey Music Publishing ASCAP. All rights reserved. Used by permission.

John Koerner **"Everybody's Going for the Money"** Words and music by John Koerner © Copyright 1991 by John Koerner. All rights reserved. Used by permission.

Sounds of Blackness **"The Drum (Africa to America)"** Words and music by James Harris III, Terry Lewis, Gary Hines & Joseph Young © Copyright 1994 EMI April Music Inc., Flyte Tyme Tunes Inc., and New Perspective Publishing. All rights controlled and administered by EMI April Music Inc. All rights reserved. International copyright secured. Used by permission.
"Hold On" Traditional, arranged by Gary Hines, © Copyright 1994 EMI April Music Inc. and New Perspective Publishing, Inc. All rights controlled and administered by EMI April Music Inc. All rights reserved. International copyright secured. Used by permission. **"Spirit"** Words and music by Billy Steele, Levi Seacer, Jr., and Craig Mack © Copyright 1997 EMI April Music Inc. and New Perspective Publishing, Inc./Michael Anthony Music and For Ya Ear Music. All rights for New Perspective Publishing controlled and administered by EMI April Music Inc. All rights reserved. International copyright secured. Used by permission.

Greg Brown **"Canned Goods"** and **"Flat Stuff"** by Greg Brown © Copyright 1982, Hacklebarney Music. All rights reserved. Used by permission. **"Whatever It Was"** by Greg Brown © Copyright 1997, Hacklebarney Music. All rights reserved. Used by permission. **"Who Woulda Thunk It"** by Greg Brown © Copyright 1985, Hacklebarney Music. All rights reserved. Used by permission.

John Hartford **"Miss Ferris"** Words and music by John Hartford © Copyright 1977 John Hartford Music. All rights reserved. Used by permission. **"Gentle on My Mind"** by John Hartford. © Copyright 1967 & 1968 by Ensign Music Corporation. All rights reserved. Used by permission.

Western Illinois Bluegrass Days **"I'll Fly Away"** by Albert E. Brumley. © Copyright 1932 in **"Wonderful Message"** by Hartford Music Co. Renewed 1960 by Albert E. Brumley & Sons/SESAC (admin. by ICG). All rights reserved. Used by permission.

Eugene Redmond **"Milestone: The Birth of an Ancestor"** and **"River of Bones and Flesh and Blood"** by Eugene Redmond. © Copyright 1991 by Eugene Redmond. All rights reserved. Used by permission.

Oliver Sain **"Stop Breakin' Down"** Written by John Lee "Sonny Boy" Williamson © Copyright Wabash Music Company and Hill and Range Songs. All rights reserved. Used by permission.

Fontella Bass **"I Am So Grateful"** Words and music by Gloria E. Griffin © Copyright 1963, Leric Music (admin. by Copyright Management, Inc.). All rights reserved. Used by permission.

"Rescue Me" by Carl Smith and Raynard Miner © Copyright 1965, Chevis Publishing Corporation (BMI). All rights reserved. Used by permission. **"I Don't Feel Noways Tired"** Words and music by Curtis Burrell. © Copyright 1980, Savgos Music. Used by permission.

The Bottle Rockets **"Thousand Dollar Car"** and **"Get Down River"** Written by Brian Henneman. © Copyright 1997 Seven Shades Music, Koog Town Music, Ray Farm Music, Shakey Bean Music (BMI)/Administered by Bug Music. All rights reserved. Used by permission. **"Idiot's Revenge"** Written by Brian Henneman and Scott Taylor. © Copyright 1997 Seven Shades Music, Annie Battle Music, Koog Town Music, Ray Farm Music, Shakey Bean Music (BMI)/Administered by Bug Music. All rights reserved. Used by permission.

The Boundless Love Quartet **"I'll Walk Dem Golden Stairs"** by Culley Holt. © Copyright 1951. Renewed 1979, Ben Speer Music/SESAC (admin. by ICG). All rights reserved. Used by permission.

Sonny Burgess Lyric excerpts of **"One Night"** by David Bartholomew and Pearl King. © Copyright 1957 Travis Music, Inc. Copyright renewed and assigned to Unart Music Corporation. All rights reserved for the USA and Canada assigned to Elvis Presley Music (administered by R&H Music). International copyright secured. Reprinted by permission. All rights reserved. **"Red Headed Woman"** by Albert "Sonny" Burgess © Copyright 1956 Hi-Lo Music (admin. by Unichappell Music, Inc.). All rights reserved. Used by permission.

Rufus Thomas **"Walkin' the Dog"** Words and music by Rufus Thomas © Copyright 1963, Almo Music Corp. All rights reserved. Used by permission.

Big Jack Johnson **"Catfish Blues"** (traditional) arranged by John Jackson. © Copyright 1993 Earwig Music (BMI)/Administered by Bug Music. All rights reserved. Used by permission. **"Black Rooster"** Words and music by Big Jack Johnson. © Copyright 1996, Fiorina Music, BMI. All rights reserved. Used by permission.

Little Milton **"Nickel and a Nail"** Written by Deadric Malone and Vernon Morrison © Copyright 1971, Duchess Music Corp. (admin. by MCA Music Publishing). All rights reserved. Used by permission. **"Annie Mae's Cafe"** words and music by Larry Duane Addison and George Henry Jackson. © Copyright 1986, Malaco Music. Used by permission. **"The Blues Is Alright"** written by Milton Campbell. © Copyright 1984 by Malaco Music and Trice Music. International copyright secured. All rights reserved. Used by permission.

Kenny Bill Stinson **"Taters and Gravy and Chicken Fried Steak"** and **"Come Home"** by Kenny Bill Stinson. Used by permission.

Jimmie Davis **"You Are My Sunshine"** by Jimmie Davis and Charles Mitchell. © Copyright 1940 by Peer International Corp. Copyright renewed. International copyright secured. Used by permission.

D. L. Menard **"Listen to Me When I Talk to You"** and **"It's Not the Rain That's Falling, It's the Angels that Are Crying"** (both composed by D. L. Menard) © Copyright 1995, Flat Town Music Co. All rights reserved. Used by permission. **"The Back Door"** (composer: D. L. Menard) © Copyright 1975, Flat Town Music Co. All rights reserved. Used by permission.

Geno Delafose **"French Rockin' Boogie"** (Lee Lavergne & Shirley Bergeron). © Copyright 1961, Jon Music (BMI). All rights reserved. Used by permission.

David and Roselyn **"Marie Lavaux"** Words and music by Shel Silverstein and Baxter Taylor. © Copyright 1972 Evil Eye Music, Inc., Daytona Beach, FL. Used by permission. **"Lady Marmalade"** Words and music by Bob Crewe and Kenny Nolan © Copyright 1974 Jobete Music Co., Inc, Stone Diamond Music Corp., Tannyboy Music Co., and Kenny Nolan Publishing. All rights controlled and administered by EMI April Music Inc. and EMI Blackwood Music Inc. All rights reserved. International copyright secured. Used by permission. **"Walkin' to New Orleans"** Written by Dave Bartholomew, Antoine Domino, and Robert Guidry © Copyright 1960, Warner Bros., Inc. All rights reserved. Used by permission.

Irma Thomas **"Don't Mess with My Man"** © Copyright Makedwde Publishing Co. Used by permission. **"I Wish Someone Would Care"** (Sax Kari, Irma Thomas). © Copyright 1965 Kari Music. All rights reserved. Used by permission. **"Time Is On My Side"** Words and music by Jerry Ragovoy © Copyright 1963 (admin. by Warner Bros., Inc.). All rights reserved. Used by permission.

Eddie Bo **"Hard Times"** by E. Bocage © Copyright 1991 Eboville Music (BMI). All rights reserved. Used by permission.

Soul Rebels **"Let Your Mind Be Free"** by the Soul Rebels, © Copyright Soul Rebels Music. All rights reserved. Used by permission. **"Asiatic Funk"** by the Soul Rebels © Copyright Soul Rebels Music. All rights reserved. Used by permission.

◆◆◆

The Mississippi: River of Song *Field Production Staff*

Producer/director John Junkerman
Writer/music consultant Elijah Wald
Executive producers Paul Johnson, Mitsuo Kojima
Producer Toshio Murayama
Coordinating producers Cathleen O'Connell, Jana Odette
Coproducers Leah Mahan, Hillary Wells, Cynthia Johnson, Elizabeth Taylor-Mead, Lucia Small, Mark Siegel, Amy Young, and John Hiller
Associate producer and photographer Theo Pelletier
Camerapeople Foster Wiley, Joan Churchill, Brett Wiley
Additional camera Mike Flannery, Tamara Goldsworthy
Sound recordists John Tyler, John Paulson, Matt Sakakeeny, Mark Griswold
Multitrack recording Big Mo (Greg Hartman and Kevin Wait), Jim Medlin
Sound editing Todd Huslander, Joanna Champagne
Field producers Pete White, Doug Miller, Maia Harris, Foung Heu, Gary Burger, Jim O'Neal
Production assistants Toshi Eto, Tim Burke, Jannae Jacks
Support staff Charlotte Battles and Marie Gray (Smithsonian Productions), Vanessa O'Neill, Irena Fayngold, Tamar Kupiec (Filmmakers Collaborative)

◆◆◆

Authors' Biographies

Elijah Wald is a musician and writer, based in the Boston area. A student of Dave Van Ronk and Jean-Bosco Mwenda, he has recorded albums and tapes of American and African music. For the last fifteen years, he has had a second career as a writer, mostly about music and culture. He is the world and roots music writer for the *Boston Globe,* and his work has also appeared in various magazines. He coauthored *Exploding the Gene Myth,* a book on the dangers of modern genetic technologies, and recently completed work on a biography of the folk-blues singer Josh White. He is now working on a book about contemporary Mexican *corridos.*

John Junkerman, director and producer of *The Mississippi: River of Song,* has been making documentary films since the early eighties. He directed an earlier Smithsonian film for PBS, *Dream Window: Reflections on the Japanese Garden,* and he has spent many years in Japan, directing films on the Hiroshima murals, Japanese crafts, and Okinawan fishermen. A founding member of the Filmmakers Collaborative, John grew up in Wisconsin and lives with his family in Boston and Tokyo.

Early morning in the French Quarter, New Orleans